Agile Project Management
FOR
DUMMIES®

by Mark C. Layton

WILEY

John Wiley & Sons, Inc.

Agile Project Management For Dummies®

Published by
John Wiley & Sons, Inc.
111 River Street
Hoboken, NJ 07030-5774
www.wiley.com

WILEY

About the Author

Mark C. Layton, known globally as Mr. Agile, is an organizational strategist and PMI certification instructor with over 20 years in the project/program management field. He is the Los Angeles chair for the Agile Leadership Network and is the founder of Platinum Edge, Inc. — an organizational improvement company that supports businesses making the Waterfall-to-Agile transition.

Prior to founding Platinum Edge in 2001, Mark developed his expertise as a consulting firm executive, program management coach, and in-the-trenches project leader. Mark holds MBAs from the University of California, Los Angeles, and the National University of Singapore; a B.Sc. (*summa cum laude*) in Behavioral Science from the University of La Verne; and an A.S. in Electronic Systems from the Air Force's Air College. He is also a Distinguished Graduate of the Air Force's Leadership School, a Certified Scrum Trainer (CST), a certified Project Management Professional (PMP), and a recipient of Stanford University's advanced project management certification (SCPM).

When he isn't overseeing client engagements, Mark is a frequent speaker on extreme programming (XP), lean, scrum, and other agile solutions. Living mostly on an airplane, he splits his time between New York, Los Angeles, London, and Singapore. Additional information can be found at www.platinumedge.com.

Dedication

To Kiyoko — whose unwavering love and support make these accomplishments possible and worth pursuing.

Author's Acknowledgments

I'd like to thank the numerous people who contributed to this book and helped make it a reality. Anna and Liam Kennedy, whose creativity and optimism were the spark that started this journey; Scott Fennel, whose guidance ensured it happened; Caroline Patchen, for turning vague ideas into compelling images and remaining pleasant through my fickleness; Anna Kennedy (again) for driving the text forward; and Rachele Maurer, for your invaluable input, editing, and support. This book would not have been possible without every one of you, and I am eternally grateful. I'd also like to thank the amazing team at John Wiley & Sons — Katie Feltman, Colleen Totz Diamond, Mark Enochs, and the many, many others who contributed their expertise to making this book the smart, simple field guide I hoped it would become.

Publisher's Acknowledgments

We're proud of this book; please send us your comments at http://dummies.custhelp.com. For other comments, please contact our Customer Care Department within the U.S. at 877-762-2974, outside the U.S. at 317-572-3993, or fax 317-572-4002.

Some of the people who helped bring this book to market include the following:

Acquisitions and Editorial

Sr. Project Editor: Mark Enochs

Sr. Acquisitions Editor: Katie Feltman

Copy Editors: Virginia Sanders, Debbye Butler

Technical Editor: Rachele Maurer

Editorial Manager: Leah Michael

Editorial Assistant: Amanda Graham

Sr. Editorial Assistant: Cherie Case

Cover Photo: ©iStockphoto.com / Michal Krakowiak

Cartoons: Rich Tennant (www.the5thwave.com)

Composition Services

Project Coordinator: Nikki Gee

Layout and Graphics: Jennifer Creasey, Julie Trippetti, Laura Westhuis

Proofreader: John Greenough, Melba Hopper

Indexer: Valerie Haynes Perry

Special Help: Colleen Totz Diamond, Susan Pink, Kim Darosett

Publishing and Editorial for Technology Dummies

Richard Swadley, Vice President and Executive Group Publisher

Andy Cummings, Vice President and Publisher

Mary Bednarek, Executive Acquisitions Director

Mary C. Corder, Editorial Director

Publishing for Consumer Dummies

Kathy Nebenhaus, Vice President and Executive Publisher

Composition Services

Debbie Stailey, Director of Composition Services

Contents at a Glance

Table of Contents

Introduction

Welcome to *Agile Project Management For Dummies*. Agile project management is one of the fastest-growing management techniques in business today. Over the past decade, I have trained and coached companies big and small, all over the world, about how to successfully run agile projects. Through this work, I found that there was a need to write a digestible guide that the average person could understand and use.

In this book, I will clear up some of the myths about what agile project management is and what it is not. The information in this book will give you the confidence to know you can be successful using agile techniques.

About This Book

Agile Project Management For Dummies is meant to be more than just an introduction to agile practices and methodologies. This book defines agile project management approaches and teaches you the steps to execute agile techniques on a project. The material here goes beyond theory and is meant to be a field manual, accessible to the everyday person, giving you the tools and information you need to be successful with agile processes in the trenches of project management.

Foolish Assumptions

If you are reading this book, you might have a passing familiarity with project management. Perhaps you are a project manager, or a member of a project team, or a stakeholder on a project. Here are a few terms related to project management that you will see throughout this book:

- ✔ **Project:** Planned program of work that requires a definitive amount of time, effort, and planning to complete. Projects have goals and objectives and often have to be completed in some fixed period of time and within a certain budget.

- ✔ **Project management:** The processes used to complete a project.

- ✔ **Waterfall:** A traditional style of project management. Waterfall relies on completing work in distinct stages like requirements, design, development, testing, and deployment. In waterfall projects, you do not start one stage until you have completed the previous stage.

- ✔ **Agile project management:** A style of project management that focuses on early delivery of business value, continuous improvement of the project's product and processes, scope flexibility, team input, and delivering well-tested products that reflect customer needs.

- ✔ **Requirements:** The list of product features desired from a project.

- ✔ **Design:** The stage where an outline or plan is made for creating individual product features.

- ✔ **Development:** The stage where product features are created.

- ✔ **Testing:** The stage where the developed product features are ensured to work.

- ✔ **Integration:** The stage where individual product features are enabled to work with one another and related products.

- ✔ **Deployment:** The final stage of a project where completed product features are moved to a state where they can be used.

- ✔ **Scope:** Everything included in a project.

- ✔ **Estimate (verb):** To determine the effort, length, cost, or priority of a task, requirement, release, or even a whole project.

- ✔ **Estimate (noun):** The effort, length, or cost of a task, requirement, iteration, release, or even a whole project.

Conventions Used in This Book

If you do an online search, you will see the word *agile*; different agile roles, meetings, and documents; and various agile methodologies capitalized. I shied away from this practice for a couple of reasons.

To start, none of these items are really proper nouns. "Agile" is an adjective that describes a number of items in project management, agile projects, agile teams, agile processes, and so on, but it is not a proper noun, and except in chapter or section titles, you will not see me use it that way.

For readability, I did not capitalize agile-related roles, meetings, and documents. Such terms include agile project, product owner, scrum master, development team, user stories, product backlog, and more. You may, however, see these terms capitalized in places other than this book.

There are some exceptions. The Agile Manifesto and the Agile Principles are copyrighted material. The Agile Alliance, Scrum Alliance, and Project Management Institute are professional organizations. Certified ScrumMaster and PMI-Agile Certified Practitioner are professional titles.

How This Book Is Organized

Agile Project Management For Dummies has six parts. Each part focuses on a different aspect of agile project management, and will help you understand, use and implement agile processes.

Part I: Understanding Agile

In Part I, I introduce you to agile project management. You find out why agile approaches are becoming popular and how they are changing product development. You learn about the foundation of all agile methodologies: the Agile Manifesto and the 12 Agile Principles. You see why agile processes work better than traditional project management processes.

Part II: Being Agile

In Part II, I tell you how agile affects fundamental behaviors and thought processes around product development. You get a closer look at specific agile frameworks. You find out about the different roles on agile projects and how to create an environment and establish values conducive to success with agile project management.

Part III: Working in Agile

In Part III, I show you how to work on an agile project and what the different iterative stages are in agile projects. You find out how to define a product and how agile approaches help you refine the product as you learn more about the product. I cover the day-to-day work in the life of an agile project. You find out how to showcase working product functionality at regular intervals in the project and how to continuously improve your processes. I also go over how to release a product in an agile project.

Part IV: Managing in Agile

In Part IV, I help you understand how to manage each of the different project management areas using agile approaches. You'll know how agile processes affect project scope, procurement, time, cost, teams, communication, quality, and risk.

Part V: Ensuring Agile Success

In Part V, I tell you what you need to know to successfully transition your organization to agile project management. You find out how to build a strong agile foundation and learn specific steps for moving from a traditional project management approach to an agile approach.

Part VI: The Part of Tens

In Part VI, I show you three groups of important, useful information about agile project management. You'll see ten benefits of agile project management, ten metrics you can use to measure agile project success, and ten resources to help you along your agile journey.

Icons Used in This Book

Throughout this book, you will find a few icons. Here is what each icon means.

Tips are points to help you along your agile project management journey. Tips can save you time and help you quickly understand more about a particular topic, so when you see them, take a look!

The Remember icon is a reminder of something you may have seen in past chapters. These icons can help jog your memory when an important term or concept appears.

The Warning icon indicates that you want to watch out for a certain action or behavior. Be sure to read these to steer clear of big problems!

The Technical Stuff icon indicates information that is interesting but not essential to the text. If you see a Technical Stuff icon, you don't need to read it to understand agile project management, but the information there might just perk your attention.

The 12 Principles icon appears any time I refer to the 12 Agile Principles throughout the book. See Chapter 2 to quickly get up to speed on the Principles.

On the Web means that you can find more information on the book's website at www.dummies.com/go/agileprojectmanagementfd.

Where to Go from Here

I wrote this book so that you could read it in just about any order. Depending on your role, you may want to pay extra attention to the appropriate sections of the book. For example:

- ✔ If you are just starting to learn about project management and agile approaches, it would be a good idea to start with Chapter 1 and read the book straight through to the end.

- ✔ If you are a member of a project team and you want to know the basics of how to work on an agile project, you might start with the information in Part III — Chapters 7 through 11.

- ✔ If you are a project manager and are wondering how agile approaches affect your job, Part IV — Chapters 12 through 15 — is a great part to review.

- ✔ If you know the basics of agile project management and you are looking at bringing agile practices to your company or organization, Chapters 16 and 17 in Part V provide you with helpful information.

Occasionally, we have updates to our technology books. If this book does have technical updates, they will be posted at:

www.dummies.com/go/agileprojectmanagementfdupdates

Part I
Understanding Agile

"Where's the product roadmap for this project?"

In this part . . .

Project management has traditionally been a challenging practice, with high expectations, limited resources
and, unfortunately, low success rates. In the following
chapters, I uncover why project management needs to
modernize. I show you historical approaches to project
management and explain their flaws and weaknesses.

You find out why agile methodologies are quickly growing as
an alternative to traditional project management. I also provide an introduction to the foundation of agile project management: the Agile Manifesto and the 12 Agile Principles.
Finally, I show you the advantages that your products, project, team, customers, and organization can gain from adopting agile project management.

Chapter 1

Modernizing Project Management

In This Chapter

▶ Understanding why project management needs to change

▶ Finding out about agile project management

Agile project management is a style of project management that focuses on early delivery of business value, continuous improvement of the project's product and processes, scope flexibility, team input, and delivering well-tested products that reflect customer needs.

In this chapter, you find out why agile processes emerged as an approach to software development project management in the mid-1990s and why agile methodologies have caught the attention of project managers, customers who invest in the development of new software, and executives whose companies fund software development departments. This chapter also explains the advantages of agile methodologies over long-standing approaches to project management.

Project Management Needed Makeover

A *project* is a planned program of work that requires a definitive amount of time, effort, and planning to complete. Projects have goals and objectives and often must be completed in some fixed period of time and within a certain budget.

If you are reading this book, it's likely that you are either a project manager, or you are someone who initiates projects, works on projects, or is affected by projects in some way.

Agile approaches are a response to the need to modernize project management. To understand how agile approaches are revolutionizing projects, it helps to know a little about the history and purpose of project management and the issues that projects face today.

The origins of modern project management

Projects have been around since ancient times. From the Great Wall of China to the Mayan pyramids at Tikal, from the invention of the printing press to the invention of the Internet, people have accomplished endeavors big and small in projects.

As a formal discipline, project management as we know it has only been around since the middle of the twentieth century. Around the time of World War II, researchers around the world were making major advances in building and programming computers, mostly for the United States military. To complete those projects, they started creating formal project management processes. The first processes were based on step-by-step manufacturing models the United States military used during World War II.

People in the computing field adopted these step-based manufacturing processes because early computer-related projects relied heavily on hardware, with computers that filled up entire rooms. Software, by contrast, was a smaller part of computer projects. In the 1940s and '50s, computers might have thousands of physical vacuum tubes but fewer than 30 lines of programming code. The 1940s' manufacturing process used on these initial computers is the foundation of the project management methodology known as waterfall.

In 1970, a computer scientist named Winston Royce wrote "Managing the Development of Large Software Systems," an article for the IEEE that described the phases in the waterfall methodology. The term *waterfall* was coined later, but the phases, even if they are sometimes titled differently, are essentially the same as originally defined by Royce:

1. Requirements.
2. Design.
3. Development.
4. Integration.
5. Testing.
6. Deployment.

On waterfall projects, you move to the next phase only when the prior one is complete — hence, the name waterfall.

Pure waterfall project management — completing each step in full before moving to the next step — is actually a misinterpretation of Royce's suggestions. Royce identified that this approach was inherently risky and recommended prototyping and working within iterations to create products — suggestions that were overlooked by many organizations that adopted the waterfall methodology.

Software project success and failure

Unfortunately, the stagnation in project management approaches is catching up with the software industry. In 2009, a software statistical company called the Standish Group did a study on software project success and failure in the United States. The results of the study showed that

✔ *24% of projects failed outright.* This means that the projects were cancelled before they finished, and did not result in any product releases. These projects delivered no value whatsoever.

✔ *44% of projects were challenged.* This means that the projects finished, but they had gaps between expected and actual cost, time, quality, or a combination of these elements. The average difference between the expected and actual project results — looking at time, cost, and features not delivered — was 189%.

✔ *32% of projects succeeded.* This means the projects finished and delivered the expected product in the originally expected time and budget.

In 2009, companies and organizations in the U.S. spent $491.2 billion on application development. That means that more than $103 billion was wasted on failed projects.

Until improved approaches based on agile techniques surpassed it around 2008, the waterfall methodology was the most common project management approach in software development.

The problem with the status quo

Computer technology has, of course, changed a great deal since the last century. I have a computer in my pocket with more power, memory, and capabilities than the largest, most expensive machine that existed when people first started using waterfall methodologies — and my computer has a telephone attached.

At the same time, the people using computers have changed as well. Instead of creating behemoth machines with minimal programs for a few researchers and the military, people create hardware and software for the general public. In many countries, almost everyone uses a computer, directly or indirectly, every day. Software runs our cars; it provides our daily information and daily entertainment. Even tiny children use computers — my friends' two-year-old is almost more adept with the iPhone than her parents. The demand for newer, better software products is constant.

Somehow, during all this growth of technology, the processes were left behind. Software developers are still using project management methodologies from the 1950s, and these approaches were all derived from manufacturing processes meant for the hardware-heavy computers of the mid-twentieth century.

Today traditional projects that do succeed often suffer from one problem: *scope bloat*, the introduction of unnecessary product features in a project.

Think about the software products you use every day. For example, the word-processing program I'm typing on right now has a lot of features and tools. Even though I write on this program every day, I use only some of the features all the time. There are some elements that I use less frequently. There are quite a few tools that I have never used, and come to think of it, I don't know anyone else who has used them, either. These features that few people or no one uses are the result of scope bloat.

Scope bloat appears in all kinds of software, from complex enterprise applications, to websites that everyone uses. The chart in Figure 1-1 shows data from another Standish Group study that illustrates just how common scope bloat is. In the figure, you can see the proportion of requested features that are actually used when the software goes into production. Sixty-four percent of the features are rarely or never used.

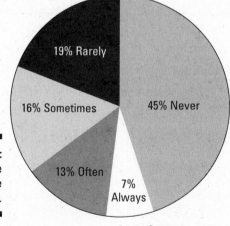

Figure 1-1: Actual use of software features.

The numbers in Figure 1-1 illustrate an enormous waste of time and money. That waste is a direct result of traditional project management processes that are unable to accommodate change. Project managers and stakeholders know that change is not welcome mid-project, and that their best chance of getting a potentially desirable feature is at the project start, so they ask for

- ✔ Everything they need
- ✔ Everything they think they may need
- ✔ Everything they want
- ✔ Everything they think they may want

The result is the bloat in features that results in the statistics in Figure 1-1.

The problems associated with using outdated management and development approaches are not trivial. These problems waste billions of dollars a year. The $103 billion lost in project failure in 2009 (see the sidebar, "Software project success and failure") could equate to millions of jobs around the world.

Over the past two decades, people working on projects have recognized the growing problems with traditional project management and have been working to create a better model: agile project management.

Introducing Agile Project Management

The seeds for agile techniques have been around for a long time. Figure 1-2 shows a quick history of agile project management, dating back to the 1930s with Walter Sherwart's Plan-Do-Study-Act (PDSA) approach to project quality.

In 1986, Hirotaka Takeuchi and Ikujiro Nonaka published an article called "New New Product Development Game in the Harvard Business Review." Takeuchi and Nonaka's article described a rapid, flexible development strategy to meet fast-paced product demands. This article first coined the term *scrum* in conjunction with product development, comparing product development to a game of rugby. Scrum eventually became one of the most popular agile project management approaches.

In 2001, a group of software and project experts got together to talk about what their successful projects had in common. This group created the *Agile Manifesto*, a statement of values for successful software development:

> **Manifesto for Agile Software Development***
>
> We are uncovering better ways of developing software by doing it and helping others do it. Through this work we have come to value:
>
> **Individuals and interactions** over processes and tools
> **Working software** over comprehensive documentation
> **Customer collaboration** over contract negotiation
> **Responding to change** over following a plan
>
> That is, while there is value in the items on the right, we value the items on the left more.

> * *Agile Manifesto Copyright© 2001: Kent Beck, Mike Beedle, Arie van Bennekum, Alistair Cockburn, Ward Cunningham, Martin Fowler, James Grenning, Jim Highsmith, Andrew Hunt, Ron Jeffries, Jon Kern, Brian Marick, Robert C. Martin, Steve Mellor, Ken Schwaber, Jeff Sutherland, Dave Thomas*
> *This declaration may be freely copied in any form, but only in its entirety through this notice.*

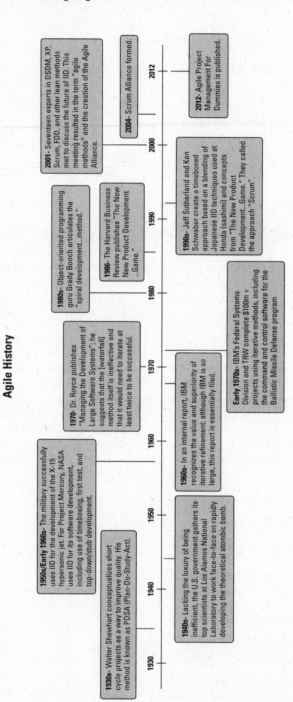

Figure 1-2:
Agile
project
management
timeline.

Agile History

1930s- Walter Shewhart conceptualizes short cycle projects as a way to improve quality. His method is known as PDSA (Plan-Do-Study-Act).

1940s- Lacking the luxury of being inefficient, the U.S. government gathers its top scientists at Los Alamos National Laboratory to work face-to-face on rapidly developing the theoretical atombic bomb.

1950s/Early 1960s- The military successfully uses IID for the development of the X-15 hypersonic jet. For Project Mercury, NASA uses IID for its software development, including use of timeboxing, first test, and top-down/stub development.

1960s- In an internal report, IBM recognizes the value and superiority of iterative refinement; although IBM is so large, this report is essentially filed.

1970- Dr. Royce publishes "Managing the Development of Large Software Systems", he suggests that the [waterfall] method itself is ineffective and that it would need to iterate at least twice to be successful.

Early 1970s- IBM's Federal Systems Division and TRW complete $100m + projects using iterative methods, including the command and control software for the Ballistic Missile Defense program

1980s- Object-oriented programming guru Grady Booch articulates the "spiral development...method."

1986- The Harvard Business Review publishes "The New New Product Development ...Game."

1990s- Jeff Sutherland and Ken Schwaber create a timeboxed approach based on a blending of Japanese IID techniques used at Honda (sashimi) and concepts from "The New Product Development...Game. They called the approach "Scrum".

2001- Seventeen experts in DSDM, XP, Scrum, FDD, and other lean methods met to discuss the future of IID. This meeting resulted in the term "agile methods" and the creation of the Agile Alliance.

2004- Scrum Alliance formed.

2012- Agile Project Management For Dummies is published.

These experts also created the *Agile Principles*, 12 practices that help support the values in the Agile Manifesto. I list the Agile Principles and describe the Agile Manifesto in more detail in Chapter 2.

Agile, in product development terms, is a description for project management methodologies that focus on people, communications, the product, and flexibility. There are many agile methodologies, including scrum, extreme programming, and lean, but they all have one thing in common: adherence to the Agile Manifesto and the Agile Principles.

How agile projects work

Agile approaches are based on an *empirical control method* — a process of making decisions based on the realities observed in the actual project. In the context of software development methodologies, an empirical approach can be very effective in both new product development and enhancement and upgrade projects. By using frequent and firsthand inspection of the work to date, you can make immediate adjustments, if necessary. Empirical control requires

- ✔ **Transparency:** Everyone involved on an agile project knows what is going on and how the project is progressing.

- ✔ **Frequent inspection:** The people who are invested in the product and process the most should regularly evaluate the product and process.

- ✔ **Adaptation:** Make adjustments quickly to minimize problems; if inspection shows that you should change, then change immediately.

To accommodate frequent inspection and adaptation, agile projects work in *iterations* (smaller segments of the overall project). On agile projects, you still have the same type of work that is involved on a traditional waterfall project: You have to create requirements and designs, you develop your product, and if necessary, you integrate your product with other products. You test the product, fix any problems, and deploy it for use. However, instead of completing these steps for all of your product features at once, you break the project into iterations, also called *sprints*.

Figure 1-3 shows the difference between a linear waterfall project and an agile project.

Mixing traditional project management methods with agile approaches is like saying, "I have a Porsche 911 Turbo. However, I'm using a wagon wheel on the front left side and right rear side. How can I make my car as fast as the other Porsches?" The answer, of course, is you can't. If you fully commit to an agile approach, you will find you have a better chance at project success.

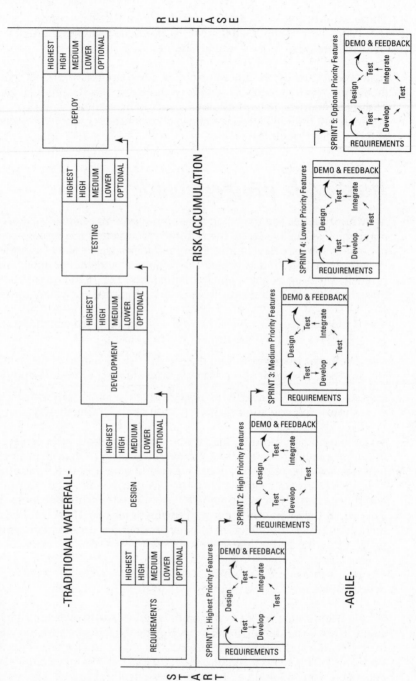

Figure 1-3:
Waterfall
versus agile
project.

Why agile projects work better

Throughout this book, you will see how agile projects work better than traditional projects. Agile project management methodologies have been able to produce more successful projects. The Standish Group, mentioned in the sidebar "Software project success and failure," also did a study of project success rates in 2009. That year, the group found that 26 percent of projects failed outright — but in 2011, that number fell by 5 percent. The decrease in failure has, in part, been attributed to wider adoption of agile approaches.

Here are some key areas where agile approaches are superior to traditional project management methods:

- ✔ **Project success rates:** In Chapter 15, you will find out how the risk of catastrophic project failure falls to almost nothing on agile projects. Agile approaches of prioritizing by business value and risk ensures early success or failure. Agile approaches to testing throughout the project help ensure that you find problems early, instead of after spending a large amount of time and money.

- ✔ **Scope creep:** In Chapters 7, 8, and 12, you see how agile approaches accommodate changes throughout a project, minimizing the idea of scope creep. On agile projects, you can add new requirements at the beginning of each sprint without disrupting development flow. By fully developing prioritized features first, you'll prevent scope creep from threatening critical functionality.

- ✔ **Inspecting and adaptation:** In Chapters 10 and 14, you find details of how regular inspecting and adaptation work on agile projects. Agile project teams can improve their processes and their products with each sprint armed with information from complete development cycles and actual product.

Throughout many of the chapters in this book, you discover how you gain control of the outcome of agile projects. Testing early and often, adjusting priorities as needed, using better communication techniques, and regularly demonstrating and releasing product functionality allow you to fine-tune your control over a wide variety of factors on agile projects.

If you're interested in the possibility of agile, then this is the perfect book for you.

Chapter 2

The Agile Manifesto and Principles

This chapter describes the basics of agile: the Agile Manifesto, with its four core values, and the 12 Agile Principles. I also expand on these basics with three additional Platinum Principles, which my corporation, Platinum Edge, crafted after years of experience supporting organizations transitioning to agile. This foundation provides software development teams with the information needed to evaluate whether the project team is following agile principles, as well as whether their actions and behaviors are consistent with agile values. When you understand these values and principles, you'll be able to ask, "Is this agile?" and be confident in your answer.

Understanding the Agile Manifesto

In the mid-1990s, the Internet was changing the world right before our eyes. The people working in the booming dot-com industry were under constant pressure to be the first to market with fast-changing technologies. Development teams worked day and night, struggling to deliver new software releases before competitors made their companies obsolete. The information technology (IT) industry was completely reinvented in a few short years.

Given the pace of change at that time, cracks inevitably appeared in conventional project management practices. Using traditional methodologies like waterfall, which is discussed in Chapter 1, didn't allow developers to be responsive enough to the market's dynamic nature and to emerging new approaches to business. Development teams started exploring alternatives to these outdated approaches to project management. In doing so, they noticed some common themes that produced better results.

In February 2001, 17 of these new methodology pioneers met in Snowbird, Utah, to share their experiences, ideas, and practices; to discuss how best to express them; and to suggest ways to improve the world of software development. They couldn't have imagined the effect their meeting would have on the future of project management. The simplicity and clarity of the manifesto they produced and the subsequent principles they developed transformed the world of information technology and continues to revolutionize project management in every industry.

Over the next several months, these leaders constructed the following:

- **The Agile Manifesto:** An intentionally streamlined expression of core development values
- **The Agile Principles:** A set of 12 guiding concepts that support agile project teams in implementing agile and staying on track
- **The Agile Alliance:** A community development organization focused on supporting individuals and organizations that are applying agile principles and practices

The group's work was destined to make the software industry more productive, more humane, and more sustainable.

The Agile Manifesto is a powerful statement, carefully crafted using fewer than 75 words:

Manifesto for Agile Software Development

We are uncovering better ways of developing software by doing it and helping others do it. Through this work we have come to value:

Individuals and interactions over processes and tools
Working software over comprehensive documentation
Customer collaboration over contract negotiation
Responding to change over following a plan

That is, while there is value in the items on the right, we value the items on the left more.

* Agile Manifesto Copyright© 2001: Kent Beck, Mike Beedle, Arie van Bennekum, Alistair Cockburn, Ward Cunningham, Martin Fowler, James Grenning, Jim Highsmith, Andrew Hunt, Ron Jeffries, Jon Kern, Brian Marick, Robert C. Martin, Steve Mellor, Ken Schwaber, Jeff Sutherland, Dave Thomas

This declaration may be freely copied in any form, but only in its entirety through this notice.

No one can deny that the Agile Manifesto is both a concise and an authoritative statement. Where traditional approaches emphasize a rigid plan, avoiding change, documenting everything, and hierarchal-based control, the Manifesto focuses on

- ✔ People
- ✔ Communications
- ✔ The product
- ✔ Flexibility

The Agile Manifesto represents a big shift in focus in how projects are conceived, conducted, and managed.

The creators of the Agile Manifesto originally focused on software development because they worked in the IT industry. However, since 2001, agile project management techniques have spread beyond software development and even outside of computer-related products. Today, people use agile approaches to create products in a variety of industries, including medicine, engineering, marketing, nonprofit work, and even building construction. If you can create a product, you can benefit from agile methods.

The Agile Manifesto and Agile Principles directly refer to software; I leave these references intact when quoting the manifesto and principles throughout the book. If you create products that are not software, try substituting your product as you read on.

Outlining the Four Values of the Agile Manifesto

The Agile Manifesto was generated from experience, not from theory. As you review the values described in the following sections, consider what they would mean if you put them into practice. How do these values support meeting time-to-market goals, dealing with change, and valuing human innovation?

Value 1: Individuals and interactions over processes and tools

When you allow each person to contribute his or her unique value to a project, the result can be powerful. When these human interactions focus on solving problems, a unified purpose can emerge. Moreover, the agreements come about through processes and tools that are much simpler than conventional ones.

A simple conversation that talks through a project issue can solve many problems in a relatively short time. Trying to emulate the power of a direct conversation with e-mail, spreadsheets, and documents can require a lot of overhead. Instead of adding clarity, these types of managed, controlled communications are often ambiguous and time-consuming and distract the development team from the work of creating a product.

Consider what it means if you value individuals and interactions highly. Table 2-1 shows some differences between valuing individuals and interactions and valuing processes and tools.

Table 2-1 Individuals and Interactions Versus Processes and Tools

	Individuals and Interactions Have High Value	Processes and Tools Have High Value
Pros	Communication is clear and effective. Communication is quick and efficient. Teamwork becomes strong as people work together. Development teams can self-organize. Development teams have more chances to innovate. Development teams can customize processes as necessary. Development team members can take personal ownership of the project. Development team members can have deeper job satisfaction.	Processes are clear and can be easy to follow. Written records of communication exist.
Cons	Development team members must have the *capacity* to be involved, responsible, and innovative. People may need to let go of ego to work well as members of a team.	People may over-rely on processes instead of finding the best ways to create good products. One process doesn't fit all teams — different people have different work styles. One process doesn't fit all projects. Communication can be ambiguous and time-consuming.

You can find a blank form like Table 2-1 on the book's companion website at www.dummies.com/go/agileprojectmanagementfd — jot down the pros and cons of each approach that apply to you and your projects.

If processes and tools are seen as the way to manage product development and everything associated with it, people and the way they approach the work must conform to the processes and tools. Conformity makes it hard to accommodate new ideas, new requirements, and new thinking. Agile approaches, however, value people over process. This emphasis on individuals and teams puts the focus on their energy, innovation, and ability to solve problems. You use processes and tools in agile project management, but they're intentionally streamlined and directly support product creation. The more robust a process or tool, the more you spend on its care and feeding and the more you defer to it. With people front and center, however, the result is a leap in productivity. An agile environment is human-centric and participatory and can be readily adapted to new ideas and innovations.

Value 2: Working software over comprehensive documentation

A development team's focus should be on producing working products. On agile projects, the only way to measure whether you are truly done with a product requirement is to produce the working product feature associated with that requirement. For software products, working software means the software meets what we call the *definition of done:* at the very least, developed, tested, integrated, and documented. After all, the working product is the reason for the project.

If you have worked on projects in the past, have you ever been in a status meeting where you reported that you were, say, 75% done with your project? What would happen if your customer told you, "We ran out of money. Can we have our 75% now?" On a traditional project, you would not have any working software to give the customer — "75% done" traditionally means you are 75% in progress and 0% done. On an agile project, however, by using the definition of done, you would have working product features for 75% of your project requirements — the highest-priority 75% of requirements.

Although agile approaches have roots in software development, you can use them for other types of products. This second agile value can easily read, "Working products over comprehensive documentation."

Tasks that distract from development must be evaluated to see whether they support or undermine the job of creating a working product. Table 2-2 shows a few examples of traditional project documents and their usefulness. Think about the documents produced on a recent project you were involved in.

Table 2-2	Identifying Documentation That's Useful	
Document	*Does the Document Support Product Development?*	*Is the Document Barely Sufficient or Gold-Plated?*
Project schedule created with expensive project management software, complete with Gantt Chart.	No. Start-to-finish schedules with detailed tasks and dates tend to provide more than what is necessary for product development. Also, many of these details change before you develop future features.	Gold-plated. Although project managers may spend a lot of time creating and updating project schedules, the truth is project team members tend to want to know only key deliverable dates. Management often wants to know only whether the project is on time, ahead of schedule, or behind.
Requirements documentation.	Yes. All projects have requirements — details about product features and needs. Development teams need to know those needs to create a product.	Possibly gold-plated. Requirements documents can easily grow to include unnecessary details. Agile approaches provide simple ways to describe product requirements.
Product technical specifications.	Yes. Documenting how you created a product can make future changes easier.	Possibly gold-plated; usually barely sufficient. Technical documentation usually includes just what it needs — development teams often don't have time for extra flourishes and are keen to minimize documentation.
Weekly status report.	No. Weekly status reports are for management purposes, but do not assist product creation.	Gold-plated. Knowing project status is helpful, but traditional status reports contain outdated information and are much more burdensome than necessary.
Detailed project communication plan.	No. While a contact list can be helpful, the details in many communication plans are useless to product development teams.	Gold-plated. Communication plans often end up being documents about documentation — an egregious example of busywork.

All projects require some documentation. On agile projects, however, documents are useful only if they're barely sufficient to serve the design, delivery, and deployment of a working product in the most direct, unceremonious way.

With agile project management, the term *barely sufficient* is a positive description, meaning that a task, document, meeting, or almost anything on a project includes only what it needs to achieve the goal. Being barely sufficient is practical and efficient. The opposite of barely sufficient is *gold-plating,* adding unnecessary frivolity — and effort — to a feature, task, document, meeting, or anything else.

When you work on an agile project, however, you concentrate on documents that are necessary to support product development. Agile approaches dramatically simplify the administrative paperwork relating to time, cost control, scope control, or reporting.

You can find a blank form like Table 2-2 at www.dummies.com/go/agile projectmanagementfd. Use that form to assess how well your documentation directly contributed to the product and whether it was barely sufficient.

I'll often stop producing a document and see who complains. Once I know the requestor of the document, I'll strive to better understand why the document is necessary. The *five whys* work great in this situation — ask "why" at least five times to get to the root reason for the document. Once you know the core reason for the document, see how you can satisfy that need with an agile artifact or streamlined process.

Agile project teams produce fewer, more streamlined documents that take less time to maintain and provide better visibility into potential issues. In the coming chapters, you find out how to create and use simple tools (such as a product backlog, a sprint backlog, and a task board) that allow project teams to understand requirements and assess status daily. With agile approaches, project teams spend more time on development and less time on documentation, resulting in a more efficient delivery of a working product.

Value 3: Customer collaboration over contract negotiation

The customer is not the enemy. Really.

Historical project management approaches usually involve customers at three key points:

- ✔ **Project start:** When the customer and the project manager — or another project team representative — negotiate contract details.

- ✔ **Any time scope changes during the project:** When the customer and the project manager negotiate changes to the contract.

- ✔ **End of a project:** When the project team delivers a completed product to the customer. If the product doesn't meet customer expectations, the project manager and the customer negotiate additional changes to the contract.

This historical focus on negotiation discourages potentially valuable customer input and can even create an adversarial relationship between customers and project teams.

You will never know less about a product than at the project start. Locking product details into a contract at the beginning of your project means you have to make decisions based on incomplete knowledge. If you have flexibility for change as you learn more about a product, you will ultimately create better products.

The agile pioneers understood that collaboration, rather than confrontation, produced better, leaner, more useful products. As a result of this understanding, agile methodologies make the customer part of the project on an ongoing basis.

Using an agile approach in practice, you'll experience a partnership between the customer and development team in which discovery, questioning, learning, and adjusting during the course of the project are routine, acceptable, and systematic.

Value 4: Responding to change over following a plan

Change is a valuable tool for creating great products. Project teams that can respond quickly to customers, product users, and the market in general are able to develop relevant, helpful products that people want to use.

Unfortunately, traditional project management approaches attempt to wrestle the change monster to the ground and pin it down so it goes out for the count. Rigorous change management procedures and budget structures that can't accommodate new product requirements make changes difficult. Traditional project teams often find themselves blindly following a plan, missing opportunities to create more valuable products.

Figure 2-1 shows the relationship between time, opportunity for change, and the cost of change on a traditional project. As time — and knowledge about your product — increases, the ability to make changes decreases, and costs more.

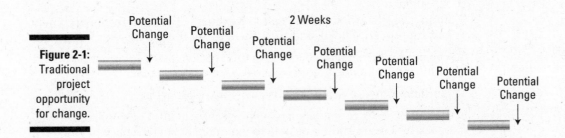

Figure 2-1:
Traditional
project
opportunity
for change.

By contrast, agile projects accommodate change systematically. In later chapters, you discover how the agile approaches to planning, working, and prioritization allow project teams to respond quickly to change. The flexibility of agile approaches actually increases project stability, because change on agile projects is predictable and manageable.

As new events unfold, the project team incorporates those realities into the ongoing work. Any new item becomes an opportunity to provide additional value instead of an obstacle to avoid, giving development teams a greater opportunity for success.

Defining the 12 Agile Principles

In the months following the publication of the Agile Manifesto, the original signatories continued to communicate. They augmented the four values of the Manifesto with 12 guiding Agile Principles to support teams making the transition to agile.

These principles, along with the Platinum Principles, explained later in the section, "Adding the Platinum Principles," can be used as a litmus test to see whether the specific practices of your project team are true to the intent of the agile movement.

Following is the text of the original 12 Principles, published in 2001 by the Agile Alliance:

1. Our highest priority is to satisfy the customer through early and continuous delivery of valuable software.

2. Welcome changing requirements, even late in development. Agile processes harness change for the customer's competitive advantage.

3. Deliver working software frequently, from a couple of weeks to a couple of months, with a preference to the shorter timescale.

4. Business people and developers must work together daily throughout the project.

5. Build projects around motivated individuals. Give them the environment and support they need, and trust them to get the job done.

6. The most efficient and effective method of conveying information to and within a development team is face-to-face conversation.

7. Working software is the primary measure of progress.

8. Agile processes promote sustainable development. The sponsors, developers, and users should be able to maintain a constant pace indefinitely.

9. Continuous attention to technical excellence and good design enhances agility.

10. Simplicity — the art of maximizing the amount of work not done — is essential.

11. The best architectures, requirements, and designs emerge from self-organizing teams.

12. At regular intervals, the team reflects on how to become more effective, then tunes and adjusts its behavior accordingly.

These Agile Principles provide practical guidance for development teams.

Another way of organizing the 12 Principles is to consider them in the following four distinct groups:

- Customer satisfaction
- Quality
- Teamwork
- Project management

The following sections discuss the principles according to these groups.

Agile principles of customer satisfaction

Agile approaches focus on customer satisfaction, which makes sense. After all, the customer is the reason for developing the product in the first place.

While all 12 Principles support the goal of satisfying customers, principles 1, 2, 3, and 4 stand out for me:

1. Our highest priority is to satisfy the customer through early and continuous delivery of valuable software.

2. Welcome changing requirements, even late in development. Agile processes harness change for the customer's competitive advantage.

3. Deliver working software frequently, from a couple of weeks to a couple of months, with a preference to the shorter timescale.

4. Business people and developers must work together daily throughout the project.

You may define the customer on a project in a number of ways:

✔ In project management terms, the customer is the person or group paying for the project.

✔ In some organizations, the customer may be a client, external to the organization.

✔ In other organizations, the customer may be a project stakeholder or stakeholders within the organization.

✔ The person who ends up using the product is also a customer. For clarity and to be consistent with the original 12 Agile Principles, in this book, I call that person *the user*.

How do you enact these principles? Simply do the following:

✔ Agile project teams include a *product owner,* a person who is responsible for ensuring translation of what the customer wants into product requirements.

✔ The product owner prioritizes product features in order of market value or risk and communicates priorities to the development team. The development team delivers the most valuable features on the list in short cycles of development, known as *iterations* or *sprints*.

✔ The product owner has deep and ongoing involvement throughout each day to clarify priorities and requirements, make decisions, provide feedback, and quickly answer the many questions that pop up during a project.

✔ Frequent delivery of working product features allows the product owner and the customer to have a full sense of how the product is developing.

✔ As the development team continues to deliver complete and demonstrable features every eight (ideally, four) weeks or less, the value of the total product grows incrementally, as do its functional capabilities.

✔ The customer accumulates value for his or her investment regularly by receiving new, ready-to-use product features throughout the project, rather than waiting until the end of what might be a long project for the first, and maybe only, delivery of releasable product features.

In Table 2-3, I have listed some customer satisfaction issues that commonly arise on projects. Use Table 2-3 and gather some examples of customer dissatisfaction that you've encountered. Do you think agile project management would make a difference? Why or why not?

You can find a blank form at `www.dummies.com/go/agileproject management fd`

Table 2-3	Customer Dissatisfaction and How Agile Might Help
Examples of Customer Dissatisfaction with Projects	**How Agile Approaches Can Increase Customer Satisfaction**
The product requirements were misunderstood by the development team.	Product owners work closely with the customer to define and refine product requirements and provide clarity to the development team. Agile project teams demonstrate and deliver working product features at regular intervals. If a product doesn't work the way the customer thinks it should work, the customer is able to provide feedback at the end of the sprint, not the end of the project.
The product wasn't delivered when customer needed it.	Working in sprints allows agile project teams to deliver high-priority product features early and often.
The customers can't request changes without additional cost and time.	Agile processes are built for change. Development teams can accommodate new requirements, requirement updates, and shifting priorities with each sprint — offsetting the cost of these changes by removing the lowest priority requirements.

Agile provides specific strategies for customer satisfaction, as follows:

- ✔ Producing, in each iteration, the highest-priority features first

- ✔ Ideally, locating the product owner and the other members of the project team in the same place

- ✔ Breaking requirements into groups of features that can be delivered in eight (ideally, four) weeks or less

- ✔ Keeping written requirements sparse, forcing more robust and effective face-to-face communication

- ✔ Getting the product owner's approval as each feature is completed

- ✔ Revisiting the feature list regularly to ensure that the most valuable requirements continue to have the highest priority

Agile principles of quality

An agile project team commits to producing quality in every product it creates — from development through documentation to test results — every day. Each project team member contributes his or her best work all the time. While all 12 Principles support the goal of quality delivery, principles 1, 3, 4, 6, 7, 8, 9, and 12 stand out for me:

1. Our highest priority is to satisfy the customer through early and continuous delivery of valuable software.

3. Deliver working software frequently, from a couple of weeks to a couple of months, with a preference to the shorter timescale.

4. Business people and developers must work together daily throughout the project.

6. The most efficient and effective method of conveying information to and within a development team is face-to-face conversation.

7. Working software is the primary measure of progress.

8. Agile processes promote sustainable development. The sponsors, developers, and users should be able to maintain a constant pace indefinitely.

9. Continuous attention to technical excellence and good design enhances agility.

12. At regular intervals, the team reflects on how to become more effective, then tunes and adjusts its behavior accordingly.

These principles, in practice on a day-to-day basis, can be described as follows:

✔ The development team members must have full ownership and be empowered to solve problems. They carry the responsibility for determining how to create the product, assigning tasks, and organizing product development.

✔ Agile software development requires agile architectures that make coding and the product modular, flexible, and extensible. The design should address today's problems and make inevitable changes as simple as possible.

✔ A set of designs on paper can never tell you that something will work. When the product quality is such that it can be demonstrated and ultimately shipped, everyone knows that the product works.

✔ As the development team completes features, the team shows the product owner the product functionality to get validation that it meets the acceptance criteria. The product owner's reviews should happen throughout the iteration, ideally the same day that development of the requirement completed.

✔ At the end of every eight (ideally, four) weeks or less, iteration, working code is demonstrated to the customer. Progress is clear and easy to measure.

✔ Testing is an integral, ongoing part of development and happens throughout the day, not at the end of the iteration.

✔ Checking that new code integrates with previous versions, is tested, and is shown to be working occurs in small increments and may even occur several times a day. This process, called *continuous integration (CI)*, helps ensure that the entire solution continues to work when new code is added to the existing code base.

✔ On software projects, examples of technical excellence include establishing coding standards, using service-oriented architecture, having automated testing, and building for future change.

Agile approaches provide the following strategies for quality management:

✔ Defining what "done" means at the beginning of the project and then using that definition as a benchmark for quality code

✔ Testing aggressively and daily through automated means

✔ Building only the features that are needed when they're needed

✔ Reviewing the code and streamlining (refactoring)

✔ Showcasing only functioning code that has been accepted by the product owner

✔ Having multiple feedback points throughout the day, iteration, and project

Agile principles of teamwork

Teamwork is critical to agile projects. Creating good products requires cooperation among all the members of the project team, including customers and stakeholders. Agile approaches support team-building and teamwork, and they emphasize trust in self-managing development teams. A skilled, motivated, unified, and empowered project team is a successful team.

While all 12 Principles support the goal of teamwork, principles 4, 5, 6, 8, 11, and 12 stand out for me as supporting team empowerment, efficiency, and excellence:

4. Business people and developers must work together daily throughout the project.

5. Build projects around motivated individuals. Give them the environment and support they need, and trust them to get the job done.

6. The most efficient and effective method of conveying information to and within a development team is face-to-face conversation.

8. Agile processes promote sustainable development. The sponsors, developers, and users should be able to maintain a constant pace indefinitely.

11. The best architectures, requirements, and designs emerge from self-organizing teams.

12. At regular intervals, the team reflects on how to become more effective, then tunes and adjusts its behavior accordingly.

Agile approaches focus on sustainable development; as knowledge workers, our brains are the value we bring to a project. If only for selfish reasons, organizations should want fresh, well-rested brains working for them. Maintaining a regular work pace, rather than having periods of intense overwork, helps keep team members' minds sharp and code quality high.

Here are some practices you can adopt to make this vision of teamwork a reality:

- ✔ Agile approaches require properly skilled, trained, and motivated development team members.

- ✔ Provide training sufficient to the task.

- ✔ Support the self-organizing development team's decisions about what to do and how to do it; don't have managers tell the team what to do.

- ✔ Hold project team members responsible as a single team, not individuals.

- ✔ Use face-to-face communication to quickly, efficiently convey information.

  Suppose that you usually communicate by e-mail to Sharon. You take time to craft your message and then send it. The message sits in Sharon's inbox, and she eventually reads it. If Sharon has any questions, she writes another e-mail in response and sends it. That message sits in your inbox until you eventually read it. And so forth. This type of table tennis communication is too inefficient to use in the middle of a rapid iteration.

- ✔ Spontaneous conversations throughout the day build knowledge, understanding, and efficiency.

- ✔ The closer teammates are located, the clearer and more efficient communication will be. If collocation isn't possible, use video chat rather than e-mail.

- ✔ *Lessons learned* must be an ongoing feedback loop. Retrospectives should be held at the end of each iteration, when reflection and adaptation can improve development team productivity going forward, creating ever higher levels of efficiency. A lessons learned meeting at the end of a project is of minimal value.

- ✔ The first retrospective is often the most valuable because, at that point, the project team has the opportunity to make changes to benefit the rest of the project moving forward.

The following strategies promote effective teamwork:

✔ Place the development team in the same location — this is called *collocation*.

✔ Put together a physical environment that's conducive for collaboration: a team room with white boards, colored pens, and other tactile tools for developing and conveying ideas.

✔ Create an environment where project team members are encouraged to speak their minds.

✔ Meet face-to-face whenever possible. Don't send an e-mail if a conversation can handle the issue.

✔ Get clarifications throughout the day as they're needed.

✔ Encourage the development team to solve problems rather than having managers solve problems for the development team.

Agile principles of project management

The role of project management in agile encompasses three key areas:

✔ Making sure the development team can be productive and can increase productivity over long periods of time.

✔ Ensuring that information about the project's progress is available to stakeholders without interrupting the flow of development activities by asking the development team for updates.

✔ Handling requests for new features as they occur and integrating them into the product development cycle.

An agile approach focuses on planning and executing the work to produce the best product that can be released. The approach is supported by communicating openly, avoiding distractions, and ensuring that the progress of the project is clear to everyone.

While all 12 Principles support project management, principles 2, 8, and 10 stand out for me:

2. Welcome changing requirements, even late in development. Agile processes harness change for the customer's competitive advantage.

8. Agile processes promote sustainable development. The sponsors, developers, and users should be able to maintain a constant pace indefinitely.

10. Simplicity — the art of maximizing the amount of work not done — is essential.

Following are some project management advantages of adopting agile:

- ✔ Agile project teams achieve time-to-market, and consequentially cost savings. They start development earlier than in traditional approaches because agile approaches minimize the exhaustive planning and documentation that is conventionally part of the early stages of a project.

- ✔ Agile development teams are self-organizing and self-managing. The managerial effort normally put into telling developers how to do their work can be applied to removing impediments and organizational distractions that slow down the development team.

- ✔ Agile development teams determine how much work they can accomplish in an iteration and commit to achieving those goals. Ownership is fundamentally different because the development team is establishing the commitment, not complying with an externally developed commitment.

- ✔ An agile approach asks, "What is the minimum I can do to achieve the goal?" instead of focusing on including all the features that could possibly be needed. The agile approach usually means streamlining: less documentation, fewer meetings, reduced e-mail, and even less coding.

Creating complicated documents that aren't useful for product development is a waste of effort. It's okay to document a decision, but you don't need multiple pages on the history and nuances of how the decision was made. Keep the documentation barely sufficient, and you will have more time to focus on supporting the development team.

- ✔ By encapsulating development into short sprints that last four weeks or less, you can adhere to the goals of the current iteration while accommodating change within subsequent iterations. The length of each sprint remains the same throughout the project.

- ✔ Planning, elaborating on requirements, developing, testing, and demonstrating occur within the confines of an iteration, lowering the risk of heading in the wrong direction or developing something that the customer doesn't want.

- ✔ Agile practices encourage a steady pace of development that is productive and healthy. For example, in the popular agile development methodology called extreme programming (XP), the maximum work week is 40 hours, and the preferred work week is 35 hours. Agile projects are sustainable and more productive.

Traditional approaches routinely feature a *death march,* in which the project team puts in extremely long hours for days and even weeks at the end of a project to meet a previously unidentified, unrealistic deadline. As the death march goes on, productivity tends to drop dramatically. More bugs are introduced, and because bugs need to first be found, then corrected in a way that doesn't break a different piece of functionality, correcting defects is the most expensive work that can be performed. When you overload a system, it breaks down.

- ✔ Priorities, previous realities on the existing project, and, eventually, the speed at which development will likely occur within each sprint are clear, making for good decisions about how much can or should be accomplished in a given amount of time.

If you've worked on a project before, you might have a basic understanding of project management activities. In Table 2-4, I've listed a few traditional project management tasks, along with how you would meet those needs with agile approaches. Use Table 2-4 to capture your thoughts about your prior experiences and how agile looks different from traditional project management.

A blank version of Table 2-4 is available at `www.dummies.com/go/agile` `projectmanagementfd`

Table 2-4	Contrasting Historical Project Management with Agile Project Management
Traditional Project Management Tasks	**Agile Approach to the Project Management Task**
Create a fully detailed project requirement document at the beginning of the project. Try to control requirement changes throughout the project.	Create a product backlog — a simple list of requirements by priority. Quickly update the product backlog as requirements and priorities change throughout the project.
Conduct weekly status meetings with all project stakeholders and developers. Send out detailed meeting notes and status reports after each meeting.	The development team meets quickly, for no longer than 15 minutes, at the start of each day to discuss that day's work and any roadblocks. They can update the centrally visible burndown chart in under a minute at the end of each day.
Create a detailed project schedule with all tasks at the beginning of the project. Try to keep the project tasks on schedule. Update the schedule on a regular basis.	Work within sprints and identify only specific tasks for the active sprint.
Assign tasks to the development team.	Support the development team by helping remove impediments and distractions. On agile projects, development teams define their own tasks.

Project management is facilitated by the following:

- ✔ Supporting the development team
- ✔ Producing barely sufficient documents
- ✔ Streamlining status reporting so that information is pushed out by the development team in seconds rather than pulled out by a project manager over longer periods of time
- ✔ Minimizing nondevelopment tasks

- ✔ Setting expectations that change is normal and beneficial, not something to be feared or evaded

- ✔ Adopting a just-in-time requirements refinement to minimize change disruption and wasted effort

- ✔ Collaborating with the development team to create realistic schedules, targets, and goals

- ✔ Protecting the development team from organizational disruptions that could undermine project goals by introducing work not relevant to the project objectives

- ✔ Understanding that an appropriate balance between work and life is a component of efficient development

Adding the Platinum Principles

Through in-the-trenches experience working with teams transitioning to agile project management — and field testing in large, medium, and small organizations worldwide — I developed three additional principles of agile software development that I call the Platinum Principles. They are

- ✔ Resist formality.
- ✔ Think and act as a team.
- ✔ Visualize rather than write.

You can explore each principle in more detail in the following sections.

Resisting formality

Even the most agile project teams can drift toward excessive formalization. For example, it isn't uncommon for me to find project team members waiting until a scheduled meeting to discuss simple issues that could be solved in seconds. These meetings often have an agenda and meeting minutes and require a certain level of mobilization and demobilization just to attend. In an agile approach, this level of formalization isn't required.

You should always question formalization and unnecessary, showy displays. For example, is there an easier way to get what you need? How does the current activity support the development of a quality product as quickly as possible? Answering these questions helps you focus on productive work and avoid unnecessary tasks.

In an agile system, discussions and the physical work environment are open and free-flowing; documentation is kept to the lowest level of quantity and complexity such that it contributes value to the project, not hampers it; flashy displays, such as well-decorated presentations, are avoided. Professional, frank communications are best for the project team, and the entire environment has to make that openness available and comfortable.

Strategies for success with resisting formality include the following:

- ✔ Reducing organizational hierarchy wherever possible by eliminating titles within the project team
- ✔ Avoiding aesthetic investments such as elaborate PowerPoint presentations or extensive meeting minute forms
- ✔ Identifying and educating stakeholders who may request complicated displays of work on the costs of such displays

Thinking and acting as a team

Project team members should focus on how the team as a whole can be most productive. This focus can mean letting go of individual niches and performance metrics. In an agile environment, the entire project team should be aligned in its commitment to the goal, its ownership of the scope of work, and its acknowledgment of the time available to achieve that commitment.

Following are some strategies for thinking and acting as a team:

- ✔ Develop in pairs and switch partners often. Both pair programming (both partners are knowledgeable in the area) and shadowing (only one partner is knowledgeable in the area) raise product quality. You can learn more about pair programming in Chapter 15.
- ✔ Replace individual work titles with a uniform "product developer" title.
- ✔ Report at the project team level only, as opposed to creating special management reports that subdivide the team.
- ✔ Replace individual performance metrics with project team performance metrics.

Visualizing rather than writing

An agile project team should use visualization as much as possible, whether through simple diagrams or computerized modeling tools. Images are much more powerful than words. When you use a diagram or mockup instead of a document, your customer can relate better to the concept and the content.

Our ability to define the features of a system increases exponentially when we step up our interaction with the proposed solution: A graphical representation is almost always better than a textual one, and experiencing the functionality hands-on is best.

Even a sketch on a piece of paper can be a more effective communication tool than a formal text-based document. A textual description is the weakest form of communication if you are trying to ensure common understanding.

Examples of strategies for visualization include

- Stocking the work environment with plenty of white boards, poster paper, pens, and paper so that drawing tools are readily available
- Using models instead of text to communicate concepts
- Reporting project status through charts, graphs, and dashboards, like those in Figure 2-2

Changes as a Result of Agile

The publication of the Agile Manifesto and the 12 Principles legitimized and focused the agile movement in the following ways:

- **Agile approaches changed attitudes toward project management processes.** In trying to improve processes, methodologists in the past worked to develop a universal process that could be used under all conditions, assuming that more process and greater formality would yield improved results. This approach, however, required more time, overhead, and cost and often diminished quality. The Manifesto and the 12 Principles acknowledged that too much process is a problem, not a solution, and that the right process in the right amount differs in each situation.

- **Agile approaches changed attitudes toward knowledge workers.** IT groups began to remember that development team members aren't disposable resources but individuals whose skills, talents, and innovation make a difference to every project. The same product created by different team members will be a different product.

- **Agile approaches changed the relationship between business and IT groups.** Agile project management addressed the problems associated with the historical separation between business and IT by bringing these contributors together on the same project team, at equal levels of involvement and with shared goals.

- **Agile approaches corrected attitudes toward change.** Historical approaches viewed change as a problem to be avoided or minimized. The Manifesto and its principles helped identify change as an opportunity to ensure that the most informed ideas were implemented.

Figure 2-2: Charts, graphs, and dashboards for reporting project status.

My XYZ Mobile Banking - Sprint 1

Sprint dates: February 4 - February 15

Sprint Goal
As a <mobile banking customer>,
I want to <log in to my account>
So I can <view my account balances and pending transactions>.

Burndown - Based on Est Hours Remaining

Number of working days

Leona (35 hrs wk)	9
Joey (35 hrs wk)	63
Bob (35 hrs wk)	63
Marie (20 hrs wk)	63
Pablo (35 hrs wk)	36
Madison (35 hrs wk)	63
Total:	360
Total per day:	40

Burndown: Est Hrs Remaining

Estimated Hrs Remaining (450–0) vs Days in Sprint (1–9)

Legend: — Actual - - Schedule

Values: 387, 344, 301, 258, 215, 172, 129, 86, 43

Feature Burndown - Based on Est Hours Remaining

Task	Priority	Status	Responsible	PO Approved?	Mo 4	Tu 5	W 6	Th 7	F 8	Mo 11	Tu 12	W 13	Th 14	F 15
User Story #1: Authenticate and Access My Accounts														
Create authentication screen for username & password with submit button	1	Completed	Madison		8	8	8	0	0	0	0	0	0	0
Create error screen for user to re-enter credentials	3	Completed	Marie		4	4	4	4	4	4	0	0	0	0
Create logged in screen	1	In progress	Pablo		16	16	16	16	16	16	16	16	12	12
Using authentication code from online banking application, develop login code for iPhone / iPad application	2	In progress	Leona		24	24	24	8	4	0	0	0	0	0
Create calls to database to verify username & password	1	Completed	Bob		24	24	26	8	4	0	0	0	0	0
Create authentication screen for username & password with submit button	3	Completed	Leona		8	8	8	8	8	0	0	0	0	0
Create error screen for user to re-enter credentials	3	Completed	Leona		16	16	16	16	4	0	0	0	0	0
Create logged in screen	2	Completed	Leona		4	4	4	4	4	0	0	0	0	0
Using authentication code from online banking application, develop login code for iPhone/iPad application	2	Completed	Leona		4	4	4	4	4	0	0	0	0	0
Create calls to database to verify username & password	2	Completed	Leona		4	4	4	4	4	0	0	0	0	0

Changes to come

Enterprises have barely begun to leverage agile techniques on a large-scale basis to solve business problems. Although the methodologies of agile IT groups have undergone radical transformation, the organizations around these groups have often continued to use historical methodologies and concepts. For example, corporate funding and spending cycles are still geared toward the following:

✔ Long development efforts that deliver working software at the end of the project

✔ Annual budgeting

✔ An assumption that certainty is possible at the beginning of a project

✔ Corporate incentive packages focused on individual rather than team performance

The resulting tension keeps organizations from taking full advantage of the efficiency and significant savings that agile techniques promise.

A truly integrated agile approach encourages organizations to move away from yesterday's traditions and develop a structure at all levels that continually asks what's best for the customer, the product, and the project team.

An agile project team can be only as agile as the organization it serves. As the movement continues to evolve, the values articulated in the Agile Manifesto and its principles provide a strong foundation for the changes necessary to make individual projects and entire organizations more productive and profitable. This evolution will be driven by passionate methodologists who continue to explore and apply agile principles and practices.

The Agile Litmus Test

To be agile, you need to be able to ask, "Is this agile?" If you're ever in doubt about whether a particular process, practice, tool, or approach adheres to the Agile Manifesto or the 12 Principles, refer to the following list of questions:

1. Does what we're doing at this moment support the early and continuous delivery of valuable software?

2. Does our process welcome change and take advantage of change?

3. Does our process lead to and support the delivery of working software?

4. Are the developers and the product owner working together daily? Are customers and business stakeholders working closely with the project team?

5. Does our environment give the development team the support it needs to get the job done?

6. Are we communicating face to face more than through phone and e-mail?

7. Are we measuring progress by the amount of working software produced?

8. Can we maintain this pace indefinitely?

9. Do we support technical excellence and good design that allows for future changes?

10. Are we maximizing the amount of work not done — namely, doing as little as necessary to fulfill the goal of the project?

11. Is this development team self-organizing and self-managing? Does it have the freedom to succeed?

12. Are we reflecting at regular intervals and adjusting our behavior accordingly?

If you answered "yes" to all of these questions, congratulations; you are truly working on an agile project. If you answered "no" to any of these questions, what can you do to change that answer to "yes"? You can come back to this exercise at any time and use the agile litmus test with your project team and the wider organization.

Chapter 3

Why Agile Works Better

*A*gile approaches work well in the real world. Why is this? In this chapter, you examine the mechanics of how agile processes improve the way people work and how they prevent burdensome overhead. Comparisons with historical methods highlight the improvements agile techniques bring.

When talking about agile project management advantages, the bottom line is project success and stakeholder satisfaction.

Evaluating Agile Benefits

The agile concept of project management is different from previous methodologies. As mentioned in Chapter 1, the agile framework addresses key challenges of historical project management methods such as waterfall, but it also goes much deeper. Agile processes provide a framework for how we *want* to work, how we naturally function when we solve problems and complete tasks.

Historical methods of project management weren't developed for contemporary development lifecycles, such as software development. Instead, they were adapted from other spheres, such as the military, construction, and manufacturing. It's no wonder that these project management methods don't fit when attempting to build modern products, such as mobile applications or web-centric, object-oriented applications. Even with older technologies, the track record of traditional methodologies is abysmal when applied to software projects. For more details on the high failure rates of projects that are traditionally run, check out the studies from the Standish Group shown in Chapter 1.

You can use agile project management techniques in many industries besides software development. If you're creating a product, you can benefit from agile processes.

When you have a critical looming deadline, your instinct is to *go agile*. Formality goes out of the window as you roll up your sleeves and focus on what has to get done. You solve problems quickly, practically, and in descending order of necessity, making sure you complete the most critical tasks.

When you go agile, you don't institute unreasonable deadlines to force greater focus. Instead, you realize that people function well as practical problem solvers, even under stress. For example, a popular team-building exercise titled the *marshmallow challenge* involves groups of four people building the tallest free-standing structure possible out of 20 sticks of spaghetti, a yard of tape, and a yard of string, and then placing a marshmallow on the top — in 18 minutes. See `www.marshmallowchallenge.com` for background information about the concept. On that site, you can also view the associated TED Talk by Tom Wujec.

Wujec points out that young children usually build taller and more interesting structures than most adults because children build incrementally on a series of successful structures in the time allotted. Adults spend a lot of time planning, produce one final version, and then run out of time to correct any mistakes. The youngsters provide a valuable lesson that *big bang development* — namely, excessive planning and then one shot at product creation — doesn't work. Formality, excessive time detailing uninformed future steps, and a single plan are often detriments to success.

The marshmallow challenge sets opening conditions that mimic those in real life. You build a structure (which equates to a software product in the IT industry) using fixed resources (four people, spaghetti, and so on) and a fixed time (18 minutes). What you end up with is anyone's guess, but an underlying assumption in historical project management approaches is that you can determine the precise destination (the features or requirements) in the beginning and then estimate the people, resources, and time required.

This assumption is upside down from how life really is. As you can see in Figure 3-1, the theories of historical methods are the reverse of agile approaches. We "pretend" that we live in the world on the left, but we actually live in the world on the right.

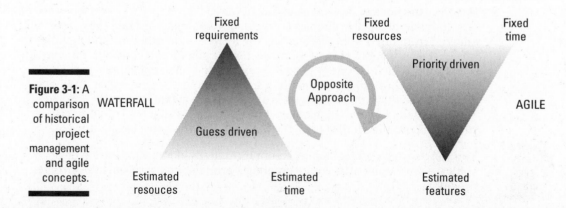

Figure 3-1: A comparison of historical project management and agile concepts.

WATERFALL

Fixed requirements

Guess driven

Estimated resouces

Opposite Approach

Fixed resources

Estimated time

Fixed time

Priority driven

AGILE

Estimated features

In the historical approach, which locks the requirements and delivers the product all in one go, the result is all or nothing. We either succeed completely or fail absolutely. The stakes are high because everything hinges on work that happens at the end (that is, putting the marshmallow on the top) of the final phase of the cycle, which includes integration and customer testing.

In Figure 3-2, you can see how each phase of a project in the most common historical project management methodology, waterfall, is dependent on the previous one. Teams design and develop all features together, meaning you don't get the highest-priority feature until you're done developing the lowest-priority feature. The customer has to wait until the end of the project to get final delivery of any element of the product.

In the testing phase of a waterfall project, the customers get to see their long-awaited product. By that time, the investment and effort have been huge, and the risk of failure is high. Finding bugs among all of the completed product requirements is like looking for a weed in a cornfield.

Agile project management turns the concept of how software development should be done upside down. Using agile methods, you develop, test, and launch small groups of product requirements in short iterative cycles, known as *iterations,* as illustrated in Figure 3-3. Testing occurs during each iteration. To find bugs, the development team looks for a weed in a flower pot, rather than in a cornfield.

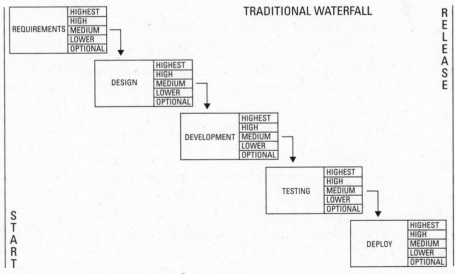

Figure 3-2: The waterfall project cycle is a linear methodology.

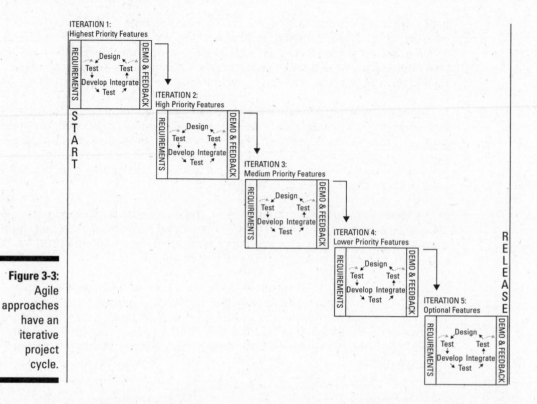

Figure 3-3:
Agile
approaches
have an
iterative
project
cycle.

Product owner, scrum master, and *sprint* are terms from *scrum,* a popular agile framework for organizing work. Scrum refers to a rugby huddle, in which a rugby team locks together over the ball. Scrum as an approach, like rugby, encourages the project team to work together closely and take responsibility for the result. You find out more about scrum and other agile methodologies in Chapter 4.

Moreover, on an agile project, the customers get to see their product at the end of every short cycle. You can create the highest-priority features first, which gives you the opportunity to ensure maximum value early on, when little of the customer's money has been invested.

The agile concept is attractive, especially to risk-averse organizations. In addition, if your product has market value, revenue can be coming in even during development. Now you have a self-funding project!

How Agile Approaches Beat Historical Approaches

The agile framework promises significant advantages over historical methods, including greater flexibility and greater stability, less nonproductive work, faster delivery with higher quality, improved development team performance, tighter project control, and faster failure detection. I describe all these results in this section.

However, these results can't be achieved without a highly competent and functional development team. The development team is pivotal to the success of the project. Agile methods emphasize the importance of the support provided to the development team as well as the importance of project team members' actions and interactions.

The first core value in the Agile Manifesto is "Individuals and interactions over processes and tools." Nurturing the development team is central to agile project management and the reason why you can have such success with agile approaches.

Agile project teams are made up of development teams (which include developers, testers, designers, and anyone else who does the actual work of creating the product), project stakeholders, and the following two important team members, without which the development team couldn't function:

- **The product owner:** The product owner is a project team member who is an expert on the product and on the customer's business needs. The product owner works with the business community and prioritizes product requirements, and supports the development team by being available to provide clarifications and final acceptance to the development team. (Chapter 2 has more on the product owner.)

- **The scrum master:** The scrum master acts as a buffer between the development team and distractions that might slow down the development effort. The scrum master also provides expertise on agile processes and helps remove obstacles that hinder the development team from making progress. The scrum master facilitates consensus building and stakeholder communication.

You can find complete descriptions of the development team, the product owner, and the scrum master in Chapter 6. Later in this chapter, however, you see how the product owner and scrum master can facilitate the development team's performance.

Where the waterfall falls short

As I mention in Chapter 1, prior to 2008, waterfall was the most widely used traditional project management methodology. The following list summarizes the major aspects of the waterfall approach to project management:

✔ The team must know all requirements up front to estimate time, budgets, team members, and resources. Knowing all the requirements at the project start means you have a high investment in detailed requirements gathering before any development begins.

✔ Estimation is complex and requires a high degree of competence and experience and a lot of effort to complete.

✔ The customer and stakeholders may not be available to answer questions during the development period, because they may assume that they provided all the information needed during the requirements-gathering and design phases.

✔ The team needs to resist the addition of new requirements or document them as change orders, which adds more work to the project and extends the schedule and budget.

✔ The team must create and maintain volumes of process documentation to manage and control the project.

✔ Although some testing can be done as you go, final testing can't be completed until the end of the project, when all functionality has been developed and integrated.

✔ Full and complete customer feedback is not possible until the end of the project, when all functionality is complete.

✔ Funding is ongoing, but the value appears only at the end of the project, creating a high level of risk.

✔ The project has to be fully complete for value to be achieved. If funding runs out prior to the end of the project, the project delivers zero value.

Greater flexibility and stability

By way of comparison, agile projects offer both greater flexibility and greater stability than traditional projects. First, you find out how agile projects offer flexibility, and then I discuss stability.

A project team, regardless of its project management approach, faces two significant challenges at the beginning of a project:

✔ The project team has limited knowledge of the product end state.

✔ The project team cannot predict the future.

This limited knowledge of the product and of future business needs almost guarantees project changes.

The fourth core value in the Agile Manifesto is "Responding to change over following a plan." The agile framework was created with flexibility in mind.

With agile approaches, project teams can adapt to new knowledge and new requirements that emerge as the project progresses. I provide many details about the agile processes that enable flexibility throughout this book. Here's a simple description of some processes that help agile project teams manage change:

- At the start of an agile project, the product owner gathers high-level product requirements from project stakeholders and prioritizes them. The product owner doesn't need all the requirements — just enough to have a good understanding of what the product needs to accomplish.

- The development team and the product owner work together to break the initial highest-priority requirements down into more detailed requirements. The result is small chunks of work that the development team can start developing immediately.

- You focus on the top priorities in each sprint regardless of how soon before the sprint those priorities were set.

    Iterations, or sprints, on agile projects are short — they only last up to eight weeks, and are often one to four weeks. You can find details about sprints, in Chapters 8, 9, and 10.

- The development team works on groups of requirements within sprints and learns more about the product with each successive sprint.

- The development team plans one sprint at a time and drills further into requirements at the beginning of each sprint. The development team generally works only on the highest-priority requirements.

- Concentrating on one sprint at a time and on the highest-priority requirements allows the project team to accommodate new high-priority requirements at the beginning of each sprint.

- When changes arise, the product owner updates a list of requirements that remains to be dealt with in future sprints. The product owner reprioritizes the list regularly.

- The product owner can financially invest in high-priority features first and can choose which features to fund throughout the project.

- The product owner and development team collect client feedback at the end of each sprint and act on that feedback. Client feedback often leads to changes to existing functionality or to new, valuable requirements. Feedback can also lead to removing or reprioritizing requirements that are not really necessary.

- The product owner can stop the project once he or she deems that the product has sufficient functionality to fulfill project goals.

Figure 3-4 illustrates how making changes on agile projects can be more stable. Think of the two images in the figure as steel bars. In the top image, the bar represents a two-year project. The bar's length makes it much easier to distort, bend, and break. Project changes can be thought of in the same way — long projects are structurally vulnerable to instability because the planning stage of a project is different than the execution where reality sets in, and there is no natural point of give in a long project.

Now look at the bottom image in Figure 3-4. The small steel bars represent two-week iterations within a project. It is much easier for those small bars to be stable and unchanging, than it is for the larger bar. In the same manner, it is easier to have project stability in smaller increments with known flexibility points. Telling a business there can be no changes for two weeks is much easier and more realistic than telling them there can be no changes for two years.

Agile projects are great at accommodating change because the means for regular change are built into everyday processes. At the same time, iterations on agile projects offer distinct areas for project stability. Agile project teams accommodate changes to the product backlog anytime but do not generally accommodate external changes to scope during the sprint. The product backlog may be constantly changing, but, except in emergencies, the sprint is generally very stable.

At the beginning of the iteration, the development team plans the work it will complete for that sprint. After the sprint begins, the development team works only on the planned requirements. A couple of exceptions to this plan can occur — if the development team finishes early, it can request more work; if an emergency arises, the product owner can cancel the sprint. In general, however, the sprint is a time of great stability for the development team.

This stability can lead to innovation. When development team members have stability — that is, they know what they will be working on in a set period of time — they will think about their tasks consciously at work. They may also think about tasks unconsciously away from work and tend to come up with solutions at any given time.

Agile projects provide a constant cycle of development, feedback, and change, allowing project teams the flexibility to create products with only the right features and the stability to be creative.

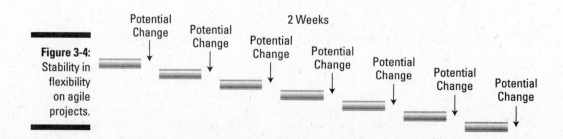

Figure 3-4: Stability in flexibility on agile projects.

2 Years - no change

2 Weeks

Potential Change

Potential Change

Potential Change

Potential Change

Potential Change

Potential Change

Potential Change

Potential Change

Reduced nonproductive tasks

When you're creating a product, at any point in your working day, you can work either on developing the product or on the peripheral processes that are supposed to manage and control the creation of the product. Clearly, there's more value in the first, which you should try to maximize, than in the second, which you want to minimize.

To finish a project, you have to work on the solution. As obvious as this statement sounds, it's routinely neglected on traditional projects. Programmers on some software projects spend only 20 percent of their time generating code, with the rest of the time in meetings, writing e-mails, or creating unnecessary presentations and documentation.

Product development can be an intense activity that requires sustained periods of focus. Many developers can't get enough development time during their normal workday to keep up with the schedule of a project because they're doing other types of tasks. The following causal chain is the result:

> Long workday = tired developers = unnecessary bugs = more bug fixing = delayed release = longer time to value

To maximize productive work, the goal is to eliminate overtime and have developers coding during the working day. To increase productive work, you have to reduce unproductive tasks, period.

Meetings

Meetings can be a large waste of valuable time. On traditional projects, development team members may find themselves in long meetings that provide little or no benefit to the developers. The following agile approaches can help ensure that development teams spend time only in productive, meaningful meetings:

- Agile processes include only a few formal meetings. These meetings are very focused, with specific topics and limited time. On agile projects, you generally don't need to attend non-agile meetings.

- Part of the scrum master's job is to prevent disruptions to the development team's working time, including requests for non-agile meetings. When there's a demand to pull developers away from coding, the scrum master asks "why" to understand the true need. The scrum master then may figure out how to satisfy that need without disrupting the development team.

- On agile projects, the current project status is often visually available to the entire organization, removing the need for status meetings. You can find ways to streamline status reporting in Chapter 14.

E-mail

E-mail is not an efficient mode of communication; agile project teams aim to use e-mail only sparingly. The e-mail process is asynchronous and slow: You send an e-mail, you wait for an answer; you have another question, you send another e-mail. This process eats up time that could be spent more productively.

Instead of sending e-mails, agile project teams use face-to-face discussions to resolve questions and issues on the spot.

Presentations

When preparing for a presentation of the code to the customer, agile project teams often use the following techniques:

- **Demonstrate, don't present.** In other words, show the customer what you've coded, rather than describing what you've coded.

- **Show how the software delivers on the requirement and fulfills the acceptance criteria.** In other words, say: "This was the requirement. These are the criteria needed to indicate the feature was complete. Here is the resulting feature meeting those criteria."

- **Avoid formal slide presentations and all the preparation they involve.** When you demonstrate the working software, it will speak for itself.

Process documentation

Documentation has been the burden of project managers and developers for a long time. Agile project teams can minimize documentation with the following approaches:

- **Use iterative development.** A lot of documentation is created to reference decisions months or years after those decisions are made. Iterative development shortens the time between decision and developed product from months or years to days. The product and associated automated tests, rather than extensive paperwork, documents the decisions made.

- **One size doesn't fit all.** You don't have to create the same documents for every project. Choose what you need to fit the particular project.

- **Use informal, flexible documentation tools.** White boards, sticky notes, charts, and other visual representations of the work plan are great tools.

- **Include simple tools that provide adequate information for management about project progress.** Don't create special project progress reports, such as extensive status reports, for the sake of reporting. Agile teams use visual charts, such as burndown charts, to readily convey project status.

Higher quality, delivered faster

On traditional projects, the period from completion of requirements gathering to the beginning of customer testing can be painfully long. During this time, the customer is waiting to see some sort of result, and the development team is wrapped up in coding. The project manager is making sure that the project team is following the plan, keeping changes at bay, and updating everyone with an interest in the outcome by providing frequent and detailed reports.

When testing starts, near the end of the project, code defects can cause budget increases, schedule delays, and even kill a project. Testing is a project's largest unknown, and in traditional projects, it is an unknown carried until the end.

Agile project management is designed to deliver high-quality, shippable code quickly. Agile projects achieve better quality and quick delivery with the following:

- Short development iterations limit the number and complexity of features, making the finished work easier to test. Only so much can be created in each sprint. Development teams break down features too complex for one sprint.

- The development team writes and tests code daily, creates builds frequently, and maintains a working product throughout the project.

- The product owner is involved daily to answer questions and clarify misunderstandings quickly.

- The development team is motivated and has a reasonable workday. Because the development team is not worn out, the code has fewer bugs.

- Errors are detected quickly because the code is tested as it's written. Extensive automated testing happens frequently, at least every night.

- Modern tools allow many requirements to be written as test scripts, without needing any programming knowledge, which makes automated testing quicker.

- The client reviews working functionality at the end of each sprint.

Improved team performance

Central to agile project management is the experience of the project team members. Compared with traditional approaches such as waterfall, agile project teams get more support, can spend more time focusing on their work, and can contribute to continuous improvement of the process. To find out what these characteristics mean in practice, continue reading.

Support for the team

The development team's ability to deliver code is central to getting results with agile approaches. This is achieved with the following support mechanisms:

- A common agile practice is *collocation* — keeping the development team together in one place and physically close to the customer. Collocation encourages collaboration and makes communication faster, clearer, and easier. You can get out of your seat, have a direct conversation, and eliminate any vagueness or uncertainty immediately.

- The product owner can respond to development team questions and requests for clarification without delay, eliminating confusion and allowing work to proceed smoothly.

- The scrum master removes impediments and ensures that the development team has everything it needs to focus and achieve maximum productivity.

Focus

Using agile processes, the development team can focus as much of its work time as possible on the development of the product. The following approaches help agile development teams focus:

- Development team members are allocated 100 percent to one project, eliminating the time and focus lost by switching context among different projects.

- Development team members know that their co-workers will be fully available.

- Developers focus on small units of functionality that are as independent as possible from other functionality.

- The scrum master has an explicit responsibility to help protect the development team from organizational distractions.

- The time the development team spends on coding and related productive activities increases because nonproductive work decreases.

Continuous improvement

The agile framework isn't a mindless check-the-box approach. Different types of projects and different project teams are able to adapt around their specific situation, as you see in the discussion of sprint retrospectives in Chapter 10. Here are some ways that agile project teams can continuously improve:

- Iterative development makes continuous improvement possible because each new iteration involves a fresh start.

- Because sprints happen over only a few weeks, project teams can incorporate process changes quickly.

> ✔ A review process called the *retrospective* takes place at the end of each iteration and gives all scrum team members a specific forum for identifying and planning improvements.

> ✔ The entire scrum team — development team members, product owner, and scrum master — reviews aspects of the work it feels might need improvement.

> ✔ The scrum team applies the lessons it learns from the retrospective to the sprints that follow, which thus become more productive.

Tighter project control

The work goes more quickly under agile projects than under waterfall conditions. Elevated productivity helps increase project control with the following:

> ✔ Agile processes provide a constant flow of information. Development teams plan their work together every morning in daily scrum meetings, and they update task status throughout each day.

> ✔ For every sprint, the customer has the opportunity to reprioritize product requirements based on business needs.

> ✔ After you deliver working software at the end of each sprint, you finalize the workload for the next iteration according to current priorities. It makes no difference whether the priorities were set weeks or minutes before the next sprint.

> ✔ When the product owner sets priorities for the next sprint, this action has no effect on the current sprint. On an agile project, a change in requirements adds no administrative costs or time and doesn't disrupt the current work.

> ✔ Agile methodologies make project termination easier. At the end of each iteration, you can determine whether the features of the product are now adequate. Low-priority items may never be developed.

In waterfall, project metrics may be outdated by weeks, and demonstrable software may be months away. In an agile context, metrics are fresh every day, code is often compiled daily, and working software is demonstrated every few weeks. From the first sprint to the close of the project, every project team member knows whether the project team is delivering. Up-to-the-minute project knowledge and the ability to quickly prioritize create the ability for high levels of project control.

Faster and less costly failure

In a waterfall project, opportunities for failure detection are theoretical until close to the end of the project schedule, when all the code comes together and when most of the investment is gone. Waiting until the final weeks or days of the project to find out that the software has serious issues is risky for all concerned. Figure 3-5 compares the risk and investment profile for the waterfall with that for agile approaches.

Along with opportunities for tighter project control, the agile framework offers you

- Earlier and more frequent opportunities to detect failure
- An assessment and action opportunity every few weeks
- Reduction in failure costs

What sorts of failures have you seen on projects? Would agile approaches have helped? You can find out more about risk on agile projects in Chapter 15.

Figure 3-5: A risk and investment chart comparing waterfall and agile methodologies.

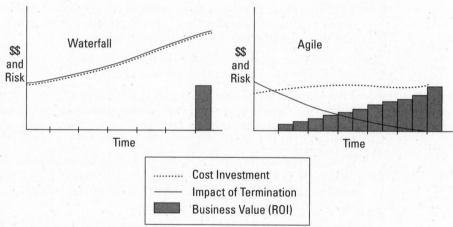

Why People Like Agile

You've seen how an organization can benefit from agile project management with faster product delivery and lower costs. In the following sections, you find out how the people involved in a project can benefit as well, whether directly or indirectly.

Executives

Agile project management provides two benefits that are especially attractive to executives: efficiency and higher, quicker return on investment.

Efficiency

Agile practices allow for vastly increased efficiency in the development process in the following ways:

- Agile development teams are very productive. They organize the work themselves, focus on development activities, and are protected from distractions by the scrum master.
- Nonproductive efforts are minimized. The agile approach eliminates unfruitful work; the focus is on development.
- By using simple, visual aids — such as graphs and diagrams — to display what's been done, what's in progress, and what's to come, the progress of the project is easier to understand at a glance.
- Through continuous testing, defects are detected and corrected early.
- An agile project can be halted when it has enough functionality.

Increased ROI opportunity

ROI is significantly enhanced using agile approaches for the following reasons:

- **Software is delivered to the marketplace earlier.** Features are fully completed and then released in groups, rather than waiting until the end of all development and releasing 100 percent of the code at once.
- **Product quality is higher.** The scope of development is broken down into manageable chunks that are tested and verified on an ongoing basis.
- **Revenue opportunity can be accelerated.** The product is released to the market earlier than with traditional approaches to project management.
- **Projects can self-fund.** A software release might generate revenue while development of further features is ongoing.

Product development and customers

Customers like agile projects because they can accommodate changing requirements and generate higher-value products.

Improved adaptation to change

Changes to product requirements, priorities, timelines, and budgets can greatly disrupt traditional projects. In contrast, agile processes handle project and product changes in beneficial ways. For example:

- Agile projects create an opportunity for increased customer satisfaction and return on investment by handling change effectively.
- Changes can be incorporated into subsequent iterations routinely and smoothly.

✔ Because the team members and the sprint length remain constant, project changes pose fewer problems than with traditional approaches. Necessary changes are slotted into the features list based on priority, pushing lower-priority items down the list. Ultimately, the product owner chooses when the project will end, at the point where future investment won't provide enough value.

✔ Because the development team develops the highest-value items first and the product owner controls the prioritization, the product owner can be confident that business priorities are aligned with developer activity.

Greater value

With iterative development, product features can be released as the development team completes them. Iterative development and releases provide greater value in the following ways:

✔ Project teams deliver highest-priority product features earlier.

✔ Project teams can deliver complete products earlier.

✔ Project teams can adjust requirements based on market changes and customer feedback.

Management

People in management tend to like agile projects for the higher quality of the software, the decreased waste of time and effort, and the emphasis on the value of the product over checking off lists of features of dubious usefulness.

Higher quality

Through such techniques as test-driven development, continuous integration, and frequent customer feedback on working software, you can build higher quality into the product.

Less product and process waste

In agile projects, wasted time and features are reduced through a number of strategies, including the following:

✔ **Just-in-time (JIT) elaboration:** Amplification of only the currently highest-priority requirements means that time isn't spent working on details for features that might never be developed.

✔ **Customer and stakeholder participation:** Customers and other stakeholders can provide feedback in each sprint, and the development team incorporates that feedback into the project. As the project and feedback continue, value to the customer increases.

✔ **A bias for face-to-face conversation:** Faster, clearer communication saves time and confusion.

✔ **Built-in exploitation of change:** Only high-priority features and functions are developed.

✔ **Emphasis on the evidence of working software:** If a feature doesn't work or doesn't work in a valuable way, it's discovered early at a lower cost.

Emphasis on value

The agile principle of simplicity supports the elimination of processes and tools that don't support development directly and efficiently, and the exclusion of features that add little tangible value. This principle applies to administration and documentation as well as development in the following ways:

✔ Fewer, shorter, more focused meetings

✔ Reduction in pageantry

✔ Barely sufficient documentation

✔ Joint responsibility between customer and project team for the quality and value of the product

Development teams

Agile approaches empower development teams to produce their best work under reasonable conditions. Agile methods give development teams

✔ A clear definition of success through joint sprint goal creation and identification of the acceptance criteria during requirements development

✔ The power and respect to organize development as they see fit

✔ The customer feedback they need to provide value

✔ The protection of a dedicated scrum master to remove impediments and prevent disruptions

✔ A humane, sustainable pace of work

✔ A culture of learning that supports both personal development and project improvement

✔ A structure that minimizes noncoding time

Under the preceding conditions, the development team thrives and delivers results faster and with higher quality.

On Broadway and in Hollywood, the performers who are on stage and onscreen to connect with the audience are often referred to as "the talent." They are the reason many entertainment customers come to a show, and the supporting writers, directors, and producers ensure that they shine. In an agile environment, the development team is "the talent."

Part II
Being Agile

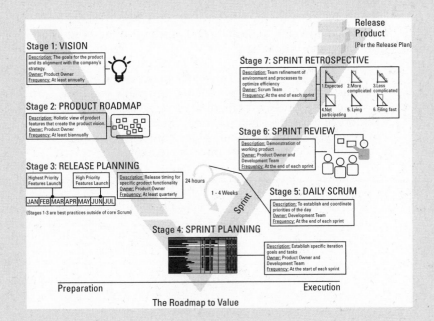

Stage 1: VISION
Description: The goals for the product and its alignment with the company's strategy.
Owner: Product Owner
Frequency: At least annually

Stage 2: PRODUCT ROADMAP
Description: Holistic view of product features that create the product vision.
Owner: Product Owner
Frequency: At least biannually

Stage 3: RELEASE PLANNING
Highest Priority Features Launch
High Priority Features Launch
Description: Release timing for specific product functionality
Owner: Product Owner
Frequency: At least quarterly

JAN FEB MAR APR MAY JUN JUL

(Stages 1-3 are best practices outside of core Scrum)

Stage 4: SPRINT PLANNING
Description: Establish specific iteration goals and tasks
Owner: Product Owner and Development Team
Frequency: At the start of each sprint

24 hours
1 - 4 Weeks
Sprint

Stage 5: DAILY SCRUM
Description: To establish and coordinate priorities of the day
Owner: Development Team
Frequency: At the end of each sprint

Stage 6: SPRINT REVIEW
Description: Demonstration of working product
Owner: Product Owner and Development Team
Frequency: At the end of each sprint

Stage 7: SPRINT RETROSPECTIVE
Description: Team refinement of environment and processes to optimize efficiency
Owner: Scrum Team
Frequency: At the end of each sprint

1.Expected 2.More complicated 3.Less complicated
4.Not participating 5. Lying 6. Filing fast

Release Product
[Per the Release Plan]

Preparation
Execution
The Roadmap to Value

In this part . . .

*B*efore you start an agile project, you need to know what it means to be agile and how you should put agile practices into action.

In the upcoming chapters, I give you an overview of the three most popular agile approaches and show you how to create the right environment of physical space, communication, and tools to facilitate agile interactions. Finally, I examine the behavior shift in values, philosophy, roles, and skills needed to operate on an agile team.

Chapter 4

Agile Frameworks

So where did agile product development come from? What are the sources and influences that created the agile product development framework? What does an approach based on agile look like?

In this chapter, you get an overview of three leading approaches used today to implement an agile project.

Diving Under the Umbrella of Agile Approaches

The Agile Manifesto and the Agile Principles on their own wouldn't be enough to launch you into an agile project, eager as you might be to do so. The reason is that principles and practices are different. The approaches described in this book provide you with the necessary practices to be successful on an agile project.

Agile is a descriptive term for a number of techniques and methods that have the following similarities:

✔ Development within multiple iterations, called *iterative development*

✔ Emphasis on simplicity, transparency, and situation-specific strategies

✔ Cross-functional, self-organizing teams

✔ Working software as the measure of progress

Agile project management is an empirical project management approach. In other words, you do something in practice and adjust your approach based on experience rather than theory.

The empirical approach is braced by the following tenets:

- ✔ **Transparency:** Everyone involved in the process understands and can contribute to the development of the process.

- ✔ **Inspection:** The inspector must inspect the product regularly and possess the skills to identify variances from acceptance criteria.

- ✔ **Adaptation:** The development team must be able to adjust quickly to minimize further product deviations.

A host of approaches have agile characteristics. However, three work well together and are common to many agile projects: lean software development, extreme programming (XP), and scrum. These three approaches share many common elements, although they use different terminology or have a slightly different focus. Broadly, lean and scrum focus on structure. Extreme programming does that, too, but is more prescriptive about development practices, focusing more on technical design, coding, testing, and integration. From an approach called extreme programming, this type of focus is to be expected, I suppose.

Like any systematic approach, agile techniques didn't arise out of nothing. The concepts have historical precedents, some of which have origins outside software development, which isn't surprising, given that software development hasn't been around for that long in the history of human events.

The basis for agile approaches is not the same as that of traditional project management methodologies, such as waterfall, which was rooted in a defined control method used for World War II materials procurement. Early computer hardware pioneers used the waterfall process to manage the complexity of the first computer systems, which were mostly hardware: 1,600 vacuum tubes but only 30 or so lines of hand-coded software. (See Figure 4-1.) An inflexible process is effective when the problems are simple and the market-place is static, but today's product development environment is too complex for such an outdated model.

Enter Dr. Winston Royce. In his article, "Managing the Development of Large Systems," published in 1970, Dr. Royce codified the step-by-step software development process known as waterfall. When you look at his original diagram in Figure 4-2, you can even see where that name came from.

Over time, however, the computer development situation reversed. Hardware became repeatable through mass production, and software became the more complex and diverse aspect of a complete solution.

Kilburn Highest Factor Routine (amended)

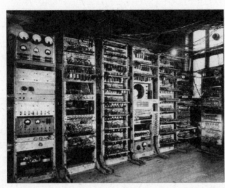

Figure 4-1: Early hardware and software.

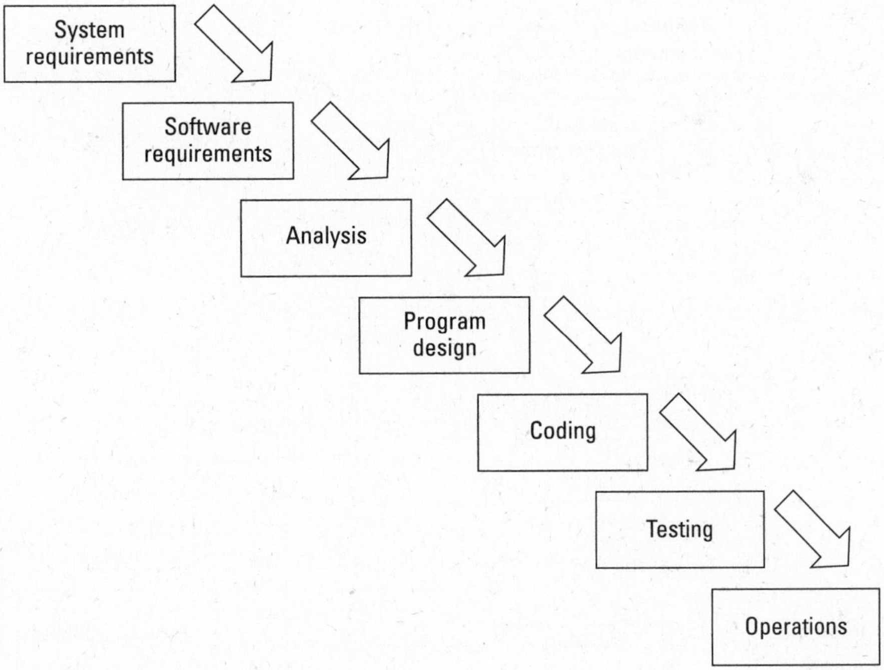
System requirements
Software requirements
Analysis
Program design
Coding
Testing
Operations

Figure 4-2: The origins of waterfall.

The irony here is that, even though the diagram implies that you complete tasks step by step, Dr. Royce himself added the cautionary note that you need iteration. Here's how he stated it:

> "If the computer program in question is being developed for the first time, arrange matters so that the version being delivered to the customer for operational deployment is actually the second version insofar as critical design/operations areas are concerned."

Royce even included the diagram shown in Figure 4-3 to illustrate that iteration.

Now, I'm not sure if the diagram was stuck with chewing gum to other pages, but the software development community by and large lost this part of the story. After you allow the idea that you might not know everything when you first start developing a software component and might have to revisit the code to ensure that it's appropriate, you have the ray of light that lets in agile concepts. Agile might have come to prominence 40 years earlier if people had taken Dr. Royce's actual advice to heart!

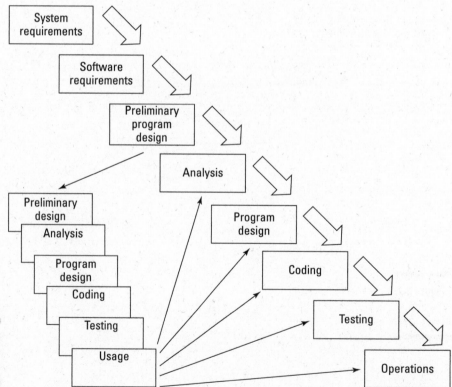

Figure 4-3:
Iteration in waterfall.

Reviewing the Big Three: Lean, Extreme Programming, and Scrum

Now that you have a brief history behind project management, you're ready to jump into three popular agile approaches: lean, extreme programming, and scrum.

An overview of lean

Lean has its origins in manufacturing. Mass production methods, which have been around for more than 100 years, were designed to simplify assembly processes (for example, putting together a Model-T Ford). These processes use complex, expensive machinery and low-skilled workers to inexpensively churn out an item of value. The idea is that if you keep the machines and people working and stockpile inventory, you generate a lot of efficiency.

The simplicity is deceptive. Mass production requires wasteful supporting systems and large amounts of indirect labor to ensure that manufacturing continues without pause. It generates a huge inventory of parts, extra workers, extra space, and complex processes that don't add direct value to the product. Sound familiar?

Cutting the fat as lean emerges in manufacturing

In the 1940s in Japan, a small company called Toyota wanted to produce cars for the Japanese market but couldn't afford the huge investment that mass production requires. The company studied supermarkets, noting how consumers buy just what they need because they know there will always be a supply and how the stores restock shelves only as they empty. From this observation, Toyota created a just-in-time process that it could translate to the factory floor.

The result was a significant reduction in inventory of parts and finished goods and a lower investment in the machines, people, and space.

One byproduct of the just-in-time process was the adoption of *kanban* boards to control production. (*Kanban* is Japanese for "visual signal.") Hanging on the factory wall where everyone can see it, the kanban board (see Figure 4-4) shows the items that teams need to produce next. Slotted into the board are cards representing units of production. As production progresses, the workers remove, add, and move cards.

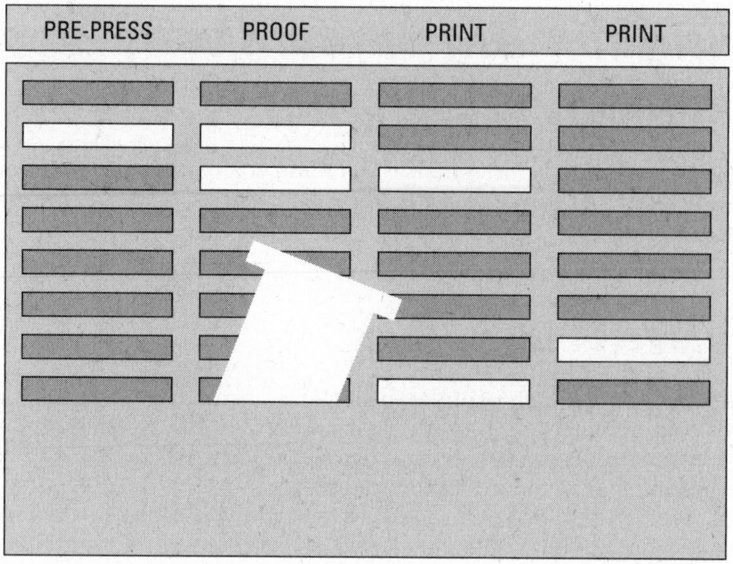

Figure 4-4:
A modern kanban board.

One big cost of the mass production processes at the time was that humans on the production line were treated like machines: People had no autonomy and could not solve problems, make choices, or improve processes. The work was boring and set aside human potential. By contrast, the just-in-time process gives workers the ability to make decisions about what is most important to do next. The workers take responsibility for the results. Toyota's success with just-in-time processes has helped change mass manufacturing approaches globally.

Understanding lean and software development

The term *lean* was coined in the 1990s in *The Machine That Changed the World: The Story of Lean Production* by James P. Womack, Daniel T. Jones, and Daniel Roos. eBay was an early adopter of lean principles for software development. The company led the way with an approach that responded daily to customers' requests for changes to the website, developing high-value features in a short time period.

The focus of lean is business value and minimizing activities outside of product development. Mary and Tom Poppendieck discuss a group of lean principles on their blog and in their books on lean software development. The lean principles are

- ✔ **Optimize the whole.** Solve problems, not just symptoms. Deliver working products. Think long-term when creating solutions.
- ✔ **Eliminate waste.** Waste includes failing to learn from work, building the wrong thing, and thrashing — only partially creating lots of product features.

- ✔ **Build quality in.** Correct defects before final verification. Use test-first development practices. Break dependencies, so you can develop any feature at any time.

- ✔ **Learn constantly.** Learning drives predictability. Enable improvement with flexible code. Make decisions at the last responsible minute.

- ✔ **Deliver fast.** Speed, cost, and quality are compatible. Work on fewer things at once. Manage workflow, rather than schedules.

- ✔ **Engage everyone.** Working autonomously, mastering skills, and believing in the purpose of work can motivate development teams.

- ✔ **Keep getting better.** Learn from failure. Challenge standards. Use the scientific method — experiment with hypotheses to find solutions.

You might have listed any number of issues in the preceding exercise. Here are a few ways you can use lean to support good product development practices:

- ✔ Don't develop features that you're unlikely to use.

- ✔ Make the development team central to the project because it adds the biggest value.

- ✔ Have the customers prioritize features — they know what's most important to them. Tackle high-priority items first to deliver value.

- ✔ Use tools that support great communication across all parties.

Today, lean principles continue to influence the development of agile techniques — and to be influenced by it. As you might expect, any approach should be agile and adapt over time.

An overview of extreme programming

Another popular approach to product development, specific to software, is extreme programming (XP). Extreme programming takes the best practices of software development to an extreme level. Created in 1996 by Kent Beck, with the help of Ward Cunningham and Ron Jeffries, the principles of XP are described in Beck's 1999 book, *Extreme Programming Explained*.

The focus of extreme programming is customer satisfaction. XP teams achieve high customer satisfaction by developing features when the customer needs them. New requests are part of the development team's daily routine, and the team is empowered to deal with these requests whenever they crop up. The team organizes itself around any problem that arises and solves it as efficiently as possible.

As XP has grown as a practice, XP roles have blurred. A typical project now consists of people in customer, management, technical, and project support groups. Each person may play a different role at different times.

Discovering extreme programming principles

Basic approaches in extreme programming are based on Agile Principles. These approaches are

- ✔ **Coding is the core activity.** Code not only delivers the solution but can also be used to explore problems. For example, a programmer can explain a problem using code.

- ✔ **XP teams do lots of testing.** If doing just a little testing helps you identify some bugs, a lot of testing will help you find more. In fact, developers don't start coding until they've worked out the success criteria for the requirement and designed the unit tests. A bug is not a failure of code; it's a failure to define the right test.

- ✔ **Communication between customer and programmer is direct.** The programmer must understand the business requirement to design a technical solution.

- ✔ **For complex systems, some level of overall design, beyond any specific function, is necessary.** In XP projects, the overall design is considered during regular *refactoring* — namely, using the process of systematically improving the code to enhance readability, reduce complexity, improve maintainability, and ensure extensibility across the entire code base.

You may find extreme programming combined with lean or scrum because the process elements are so similar that they marry well.

Getting to know some extreme programming practices

In XP, some practices are similar to other agile approaches, but others aren't. Table 4-1 lists a few key XP practices, most of which are common-sense practices and many of which are reflected in the Agile Principles.

Extreme programming intentionally pushes the limits of development customs by dramatically increasing the intensity of best practice rituals, which has resulted in a strong track record of XP improving development efficiency and success.

An overview of scrum

Scrum is the most popular agile framework in software development. Scrum is an iterative approach that has at its core the *sprint* — the scrum term for iteration. To support this process, scrum teams use specific roles, artifacts, and events. Scrum teams use inspection throughout the project to make sure that they meet the goals of each part of the process. The scrum approach is shown in Figure 4-5.

Table 4-1	Key Practices of Extreme Programming
XP Practice	**Underpinning Assumption**
Planning game	All members of the team should participate in planning. No disconnect exists between business and technical people.
Whole team	The customer needs to be collocated (physically located together) with the development team and be available. This accessibility enables the team to ask more minor questions, quickly get answers, and ultimately deliver a product more aligned with customer expectations.
Coding standards	Use coding standards for consistency; don't constantly reinvent the basics of how to develop products within your organization. Standard code identifiers and naming conventions are two examples of having coding standards.
System metaphor	When describing how the system works, use an implied comparison, a simple story that is easily understood (for instance, "the system is like cooking a meal").
Collective code ownership	The entire team is responsible for the quality of code. Any engineer can modify another engineer's code to enable progress to continue.
Sustainable pace	Overworked people are not effective. Too much work leads to mistakes, which leads to more work, which leads to more mistakes. Avoid working more than 40 hours per week for an extended period of time.
Pair programming	Two people work together on a programming task. One person is strategic, and one person is tactical. They explain their approach to each other. No piece of code is understood by only one person.
Design improvement	Continuously improve design by refactoring code — removing duplications within the code.
Simple design	The simpler the design, the lower the cost to change the software code.
Test-driven development (TTD)	Write automated customer acceptance and unit tests before you code anything. Test your success before you claim progress.
Continuous integration	Team members should be working from the latest code. Integrate code components across the development team as often as possible to identify issues and take corrective action before problems build on each other.
Refactoring	Expect to improve code constantly. The fewer dependencies, the better.
Small releases	Release value to the customer often. Avoid going more than three to four months without a customer release. Some organizations release daily.

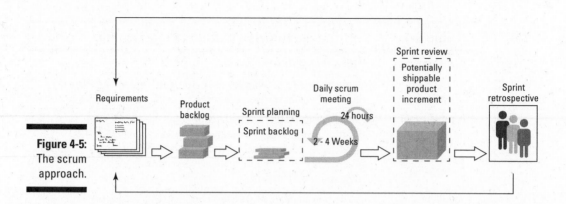

Figure 4-5:
The scrum
approach.

Going the distance with the sprint

Within each sprint, the development team develops and tests a functional part of the product until the product owner accepts it and the functionality becomes a potentially shippable product. When one sprint finishes, another sprint starts. Scrum teams deliver product features in increments at the end of each sprint. A product release occurs at the end of a sprint or after several sprints.

A core principle of the sprint is its cyclical nature: The sprint, as well as the processes within it, repeats over and over, as shown in Figure 4-6.

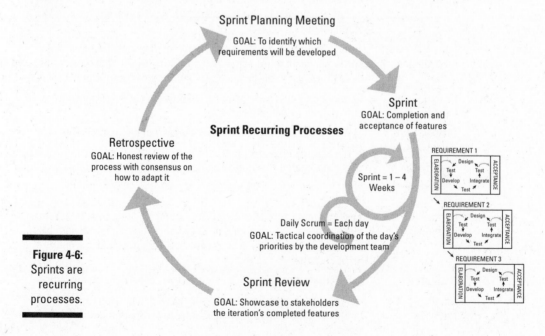

Figure 4-6:
Sprints are
recurring
processes.

You use the tenets of inspection and adaptation on a daily basis as part of a scrum project:

- ✔ During a sprint, you conduct constant inspections to assess progress toward the sprint goal, and consequentially, toward the release goal.

- ✔ You hold a *daily scrum meeting* to organize the day by reviewing what the team completed yesterday and what it will work on today. Essentially, the scrum team inspects its progress toward the sprint goal.

- ✔ At the end of the sprint, you use a *retrospective meeting* to assess performance and plan necessary adaptations.

The inspection and adaptation may sound formal and process-laden, but they aren't. Use inspection and adaptation to solve issues and don't over think this process. The problem you're trying to solve today will often change in the future anyway.

Understanding scrum roles, artifacts, and events

The scrum framework defines specific roles, artifacts, and events for projects.

Scrum's three *roles* — people on the project — are

- ✔ **Product owner:** Represents and speaks for the business needs of the project.

- ✔ **Development team:** Performs the day-to-day work. The development team is dedicated to the project and *cross-functional* — that is, although team members may have strengths, each member is capable of doing multiple jobs on the project.

- ✔ **Scrum master:** Responsible for protecting the team from organizational distractions, clearing roadblocks, and keeping the process consistent.

Additionally, scrum teams find that they're more effective and efficient when they work closely with two non-scrum–specific roles:

- ✔ **Stakeholders:** A stakeholder is anyone who is affected by or has input on the project. While stakeholders are not official scrum roles, it is essential for scrum teams and stakeholders to work closely together throughout a project.

- ✔ **Agile mentor:** This mentor is an experienced authority on agile techniques and the scrum framework. Often this person is external to the project's department or organization, so he or she can support the team objectively with an outsider's point of view.

In the same way scrum has specific roles, scrum also has three tangible deliverables, called *artifacts*:

✔ **Product backlog:** The full list of requirements, often documented as user stories, that defines the product. The product backlog can be fluid throughout the project. All scope items, regardless of level of detail, are in the product backlog.

✔ **Sprint backlog:** The list of requirements and tasks in a given sprint. The product owner and the development team select the requirements for the sprint in sprint planning, with the development team breaking these requirements down into tasks. Unlike the product backlog, only the development team can change the sprint backlog.

✔ **Product increment:** The usable product. Whether the product is a website or a new house, the product increment should be complete enough to demonstrate its working functionality. A scrum project is complete after a product contains enough shippable functionality to meet the customer's business goals for the project.

Finally, scrum also has four key meetings, called *events:*

✔ **Sprint planning meetings:** Take place just before each sprint starts. In sprint planning meetings, scrum teams decide what goals, scope, and tasks will be part of the fixed sprint backlog.

✔ **Daily scrum meeting:** Takes place daily for no more than 15 minutes. During the scrum meeting, scrum team members make three statements:

- What the team member completed yesterday

- What the team member will work on today

- A list of items impeding the team member

✔ **Sprint review meeting:** Takes place at the end of each sprint. In this meeting, the development team demonstrates to the stakeholders and the organization as a whole the accepted parts of the product they completed during the sprint.

✔ **Sprint retrospective:** Takes place at the end of each sprint. The sprint retrospective is an internal team meeting in which the scrum team members (product owner, scrum master, and development team) discuss what went well during the sprint, what didn't work well, and how they can make improvements for the next sprint. This meeting is action-oriented (that is, frustrations should be vented elsewhere) and ends with tangible improvement plans for the next sprint.

Putting It All Together

All three agile approaches — lean, extreme programming (XP), and scrum — have common threads. The biggest thing these approaches have in common is adherence to the Agile Manifesto and the 12 Agile Principles. Table 4-2 shows a few more of the similarities among the three approaches.

Table 4-2 Similarities Between Lean, Extreme Programming, and Scrum

Lean	Extreme Programming	Scrum
Engaging everyone	Entire team	Cross-functional development team
	Collective ownership	
Optimizing the whole	Test-driven development	Product increment
	Continuous integration	
Delivering fast	Small release	One- to four-week sprints

Essential credentials

If you are — or want to be — an agile practitioner, you may consider getting one or more of the agile certifications available today. The certification training alone can provide valuable information and the chance to practice agile processes — lessons you can use in your everyday work. Certification can also boost your career, as many organizations want to hire people with proven agile knowledge.

There are a number of well-recognized certifications to choose from, including

✔ **PMI Agile Certified Practitioner (PMI-ACP)**

The Project Management Institute (PMI) is the largest professional organization for project managers in the world. In 2012, PMI introduced the PMI-ACP certification. The PMI-ACP requires training, general project management experience, experience working on agile projects and passing an exam on your knowledge of agile fundamentals. See `pmi.org/ Certification/New-PMI-Agile- Certification.aspx`.

✔ **Certified ScrumMaster (CSM)**

The Scrum Alliance, a professional organization that promotes the understanding and use of scrum, offers a certification for scrum masters. The CSM requires a two-day training class, provided by a Certified Scrum Trainer and completing a CSM evaluation. CSM training provides an overall view of scrum and is a good starting point for people starting their agile journey. See `scrumalliance.org/pages/CSM`.

✔ **Certified Scrum Product Owner (CSPO)**

The Scrum Alliance also provides a certification for product owners. Like the CSM, the CSPO requires two days of training from a Certified Scrum Trainer. CSPO training provides a deep dive into product owner role. See `scrumalliance. org/pages/certified_scrum_ product_owner`.

✔ **Certified Scrum Developer (CSD)**

For development team members, the Scrum Alliance offers the CSD. The CSD is a technical-track certification, dependent on five days of training from a Certified Scrum Trainer and passing an exam on agile engineering techniques. CSM or CSPO training can count toward a CSD; the remaining three days are a technical skills course. See `scrumalliance.org/pages/ certified_scrum_product_owner`.

Chapter 5

Putting Agile into Action: The Environment

Conjure up a mental picture of your current working environment. Perhaps it looks like the following setup. The IT team sits in cube city in one departmental area with the project manager somewhere within walking distance. You work with an offshore development team eight time zones away. The business customer is on the other side of the building. Your manager has a small office tucked away somewhere. Conference rooms are usually fully booked, and even if you were to get into one, someone would chase you out within the hour.

Your project documents are stored in folders on a shared drive. The development team gets at least 100 e-mails a day. The project manager holds a team meeting every week and, referring to the project plan, tells the developers what to work on. The project manager also creates a weekly status report and posts it on the shared drive. The product manager is usually too busy to talk to the project manager to review progress, but periodically sends e-mails with some new thoughts about the application.

Although the description in the preceding paragraphs may not describe your particular situation, you can see something like it in any given corporate setting. To benefit from agile fully, your working environment is going to have to change.

This chapter shows you how to create a working space that facilitates communication, one that will help you best take advantage of agile.

Creating the Physical Environment

Agile flourishes when scrum team members work closely together in an environment that supports the process. As noted in other chapters, the development team members are central to the success of agile. Creating the right environment for them to operate in goes a long way toward supporting their success. You can even hire people who specialize in designing optimal work environments for agile.

Collocating the team

If at all possible, the scrum team needs to be *collocated* — that is, physically located together. When a scrum team is collocated, the following practices are encouraged:

- Communicating face to face
- Physically standing up — rather than sitting — as a group for the daily scrum meeting
- Using simple, low-tech tools for communication
- Getting clarifications from scrum team members
- Being aware of what others are working on
- Asking for help with a task
- Supporting others with their tasks

All these practices uphold agile processes. When everyone resides in the same area, it's much easier for one person to lean over, ask a question, and get an immediate answer. If the question is complex, a face-to-face conversation, with all the synergy it creates, is much more productive than an e-mail exchange.

This improved communication effectiveness is due to *communication fidelity* — the degree of accuracy between the meaning intended and the meaning interpreted. Albert Mehrabian, Ph.D., a professor at UCLA, has shown that for complex, incongruent communication, 55 percent of meaning is conveyed by physical body language, 38 percent is conveyed through cultural-specific voice tonality interpretation, and only 7 percent is conveyed by words. That's something to keep in mind during your next voice-over IP or cell phone conference call to discuss the design nuances of a system that doesn't exist.

Alistair Cockburn, one of the Agile Manifesto signatories, created the graph in Figure 5-1. This graph shows the effectiveness of different forms of communication. Notice the difference in effectiveness between paper communication and two people at a white board — with collocation, you get the benefit of better communication.

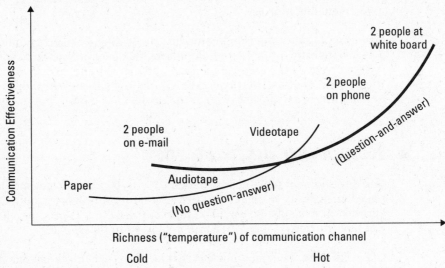

Figure 5-1:
Better communication through collocation.

Setting up a dedicated area

If the scrum team members are in the same physical place, you want to create as ideal a working environment for them as you can. The first step is to create a dedicated area.

Set up an environment where the scrum team can work in close physical proximity. If possible, the scrum team should have its own room, sometimes called a *project room* or *scrum room*. The scrum team members create the setup they need in this project room, putting whiteboards and bulletin boards on the walls and moving the furniture. By arranging the space for productivity, it becomes part of how they work. If a separate room isn't possible, a *pod* — with workspaces around the edges and a table or collaboration center in the middle — works well.

If you're stuck in cube city and can't tear down walls, ask for some empty cubes in a group and remove the dividing panels. Create a space that you can treat as your project room.

The right space allows the scrum team to be fully immersed in solving problems and crafting solutions.

The situation you have may be far from perfect, but it's worth the effort to see how close you can get to the ideal. Before you implement agile in your organization, ask management for the resources necessary to create an optimal condition. Resources will vary from project to project, but at a minimum, they can include white boards, bulletin boards, markers, pushpins, and sticky notes. You'll be surprised at how quickly the efficiency gains pay for the investment and more.

For example, with one client company, dedicating a project room and making a $6,000 investment in multiple monitors for developers increased productivity, which saved the company almost two months and $60,000 over the life of the project. That's a pretty good return on investment. We show you how to quantify these savings early on in the project in Chapter 13.

Removing distractions

The development team needs to focus, focus, focus. The methodologies based on agile are designed to create structure for highly productive work carried out in a specific way. The biggest threat to this productivity is distraction, such as . . . hold on a minute, I need to take a call.

Okay, I'm back. The good news is that an agile team has someone dedicated to deflecting or eliminating distractions: the scrum master. Whether you're going to be taking on a scrum master role or some other role, you need to understand what sorts of distractions can throw the development team off course and how to handle them. Table 5-1 is a list of common distractions and do's and don'ts for dealing with distractions.

Table 5-1	Common Distractions	
Distraction	*Do*	*Don't*
Multiple projects	Do make sure that the development team is dedicated 100 percent to a single project — this one!	Don't fragment the development team between multiple projects, operations support, and special duties.
Multitasking	Do keep the development team focused on a single task, ideally coding one piece of functionality at a time. A task board can help keep track of the tasks in progress and quickly identify whether someone is working on multiple tasks at once.	Don't let the development team switch requirements. Switching tasks creates a huge overhead in lost productivity.

Distraction	Do	Don't
Over-supervising	Do leave development team members alone after you collaborate on iteration goals; they can organize themselves. Watch their productivity skyrocket.	Don't interfere with the development team or allow others to do so. The daily scrum meeting provides ample opportunity to assess progress.
Outside influences	Do redirect any distracters. If another task surfaces, ask the product owner to decide whether the task's priority is worth sacrificing sprint functionality.	Don't mess with the development team members and their work. They're pursuing the sprint goal, which is the top priority during an active sprint. Even a seemingly quick task can throw off work for an entire day.
Management	Do shield the development team from direct requests from management (unless management wants to give team members a bonus for their excellent performance).	Don't allow management to negatively affect the productivity of the development team. Make interrupting the development team the path of greatest resistance.

Distractions sap the development team's focus, energy, and performance. The scrum master needs strength and courage to manage and deflect interruptions. Every distraction averted is a step toward success.

Going mobile

Judging by the "Going mobile" heading, you might have thought this section was about smartphone teleconferencing, but it isn't. Agile is a responsive approach, and scrum team members require an environment that helps them respond to the project needs of the day. An agile team environment should be mobile — literally:

- ✔ Use moveable desks and chairs so that people can move about and reconfigure the space.

- ✔ Get wirelessly connected laptops so that scrum team members can pick them up and move them about easily.

- ✔ Have a large mobile white board. Also see the next section on low-tech communication.

With this movable environment, scrum team members can configure and reconfigure their arrangement as needed. Given that scrum team members will be working with different members from day to day, mobility is important. Fixed furniture tends to dictate the communications that take place. Being mobile allows for freer collaboration and more freedom overall.

Low-Tech Communicating

When a scrum team is collocated, the members can communicate in person with ease and fluidity. Particularly when you first implement agile, you want to keep the communication tools low-tech. Rely on face-to-face conversations and good old-fashioned pen and paper. Low-tech promotes informality, allowing scrum team members to feel that they can change work processes and be innovative as they learn about the product.

The primary tool for communication should be face-to-face conversation. Tackling problems in person is the best way to accelerate production:

- Have short daily meetings in person. Some scrum teams stand throughout to discourage meetings from running longer than 15 minutes.

- Ask the product owner questions. Also, make sure he or she is involved in discussions about product features to provide clarity when necessary.

- Communicate with your co-workers. If you have questions about features, the project's progress, or integrating code, communicate with co-workers. The entire development team is responsible for creating the product, and team members need to talk throughout the day.

As long as the scrum team is in close proximity, you can use physical and visual approaches to keep everyone on the same page. The tools should enable everyone to see

- The goal of the sprint
- The functionality necessary to achieve the sprint goal
- What has been accomplished in the sprint
- What's coming next in the sprint
- Who is working on which task
- What remains to be done

Only a few tools are needed to support this low-tech communication:

- A white board or two (mobile — on wheels or lightweight). Nothing beats a white board for collaboration. The scrum team can use one for brainstorming solutions or sharing ideas.

- A huge supply of sticky notes in different colors (including poster-sized ones for communicating critical information you want readily visible — such as architecture, coding standards, and the project's definition of done).

  A personal favorite is giving each developer at least one tabletop dry erase/sticky note easel pad combination, with a lightweight easel. These tools are very low cost and facilitate communication fantastically.

- Lots of colorful pens.

- (Optional) A sprint-specific kanban board (described in Chapter 4) for tracking progress tactility.

If you decide to have a sprint-specific kanban board, use sticky notes to represent *units of work* (features broken down into tasks). For your work plan, you can place sticky notes on a large surface (a wall or your second white board), or you can use a kanban board with cards. You can customize a kanban board in many ways, such as using different-colored sticky notes for different types of tasks, red flag stickers for features that have an impediment, and resource stickers to easily see who is working on which task.

An *information radiator* is a tool that physically displays information to the scrum team and anyone else in the scrum team's work area. Information radiators can include kanban boards, white boards, bulletin boards, *burndown charts* that show the iteration's status, and any other sign with details about the project, the product, or the scrum team.

Basically, you move sticky notes or cards around the board to show the status. Everyone knows how to read the board and how to act on what it shows. Figure 5-2 shows a few examples. In Chapter 10, you find out the details of what to put on the boards.

Whatever tools you use, avoid spending time making things look neat and pretty. Formality in layout and presentation (what you would often call *pageantry*) can give an impression that the work is tidy and elegant. However, the work is what matters, so focus your energy on activities that support the work.

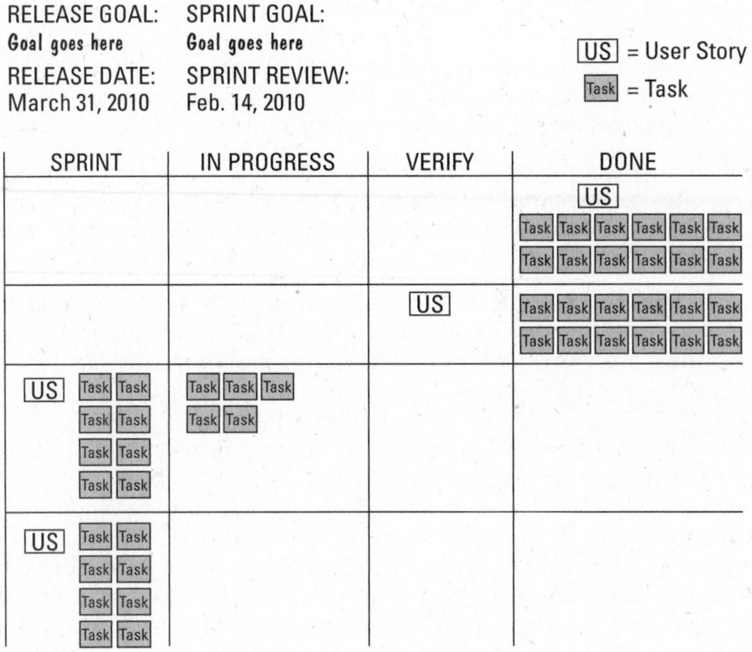

RELEASE GOAL:
Goal goes here
RELEASE DATE:
March 31, 2010

SPRINT GOAL:
Goal goes here
SPRINT REVIEW:
Feb. 14, 2010

US = User Story

Task = Task

SPRINT	IN PROGRESS	VERIFY	DONE
			US Task Task Task Task Task Task Task Task Task Task Task Task
		US	Task Task Task Task Task Task Task Task Task Task Task Task
US Task Task Task Task Task Task Task Task	Task Task Task Task Task		
US Task Task Task Task Task Task Task Task			

Figure 5-2:
A white board and kanban board used in agile.

High-Tech Communicating

Although collocation almost universally improves effectiveness, many scrum teams can't be collocated. Some projects have teammates scattered across multiple offices; others have off-shore development teams around the world. If your scrum team can't be collocated, don't give up on agile. Instead, simulate collocation as much as possible.

When scrum team members work in different places, you have to make a greater effort to set up an environment that creates a sense of connectedness. To span distance and time zones, you need more sophisticated communication mechanisms.

Don't reinvent the wheel!

In the past, manufacturing processes often involved partially completed items being shipped to another location for completion. In these situations, the kanban board on a factory wall in the first location needed to be seen by shop floor management at the second location.

Electronic kanban board software was developed to resolve this problem, but interestingly, the software looked like a literal kanban board on the wall and was used in the same way. Don't fix what's working.

When determining which types of high-tech communication tools to support, you should first consider the loss of face-to-face discussions. Some tools you can use are

- ✔ Video conferencing and webcams: These tools can create a sense of being together.

- ✔ Instant messaging: Although instant messaging doesn't convey nonverbal communication, it is real time, accessible, and easy to use. Several people can also share a session and share files.

- ✔ Web-based desktop sharing: Especially for the development team, sharing your desktop allows you to highlight issues and updates visually in real time. Seeing the problem is always better than just talking it out over the phone.

- ✔ Collaboration websites: These sites allow you to do everything from sharing simple documentation so that everyone has the latest information to using a virtual white board for brainstorming.

Using a collaboration site allows you to post documents that show the status of the sprint. When managers request status updates, you can simply direct them to the collaboration site. By updating these documents daily, you provide managers with better information than they would have under a traditional project management cycle. Avoid creating separate status reports for management; these reports duplicate information in the sprint burndowns and don't support production.

Choosing Tools

As noted throughout the chapter, low-tech tools are best suited to agile, especially initially, while the scrum team gets used to the process. The following sections discuss a few points to consider when choosing agile tools: the purpose of the tool and organizational and compatibility constraints.

The purpose of the tool

When choosing tools, the primary question you need to ask is, "What is the purpose of the tool?" Tools should solve a specific problem and support agile processes, the focus of which is pushing forward with the work.

Above all, don't choose anything more complicated than you need. Some tools are sophisticated and take time to learn before you can use them to be productive. If you're working with a collocated scrum team, the training and adoption of agile practices can be enough of a challenge without adding a suite of complicated tools to the mix. If you're working with a dislocated scrum team, introducing new tools can be even more difficult.

You can find a lot of agile-centric websites, software, and other tools on the market. Many are very useful, but you shouldn't invest in expensive agile tools in your early days of implementing agile. This investment is unnecessary and adds another level of complexity to adoption. As you go through the first few iterations and modify your approach, the scrum team will start identifying procedures that can be improved or need to change. One of these improvements might be the need for additional tools or replacement tools. When a need emerges naturally, from the scrum team, finding organizational support for purchasing the necessary tools is often easier because the need can be tied to an actual project issue.

Organizational and compatibility constraints

Beyond the initial considerations noted in the preceding section, the tools you choose must operate within your organization. Unless you're using solely non-electronic tools, you'll likely have to take into account organizational policies with respect to hardware, software, and services as well as cloud computing, security, and telephony systems.

If you're part of a distributed organization, some scrum teams may not be able to support complex solutions, maintain the latest versions of desktop software, or have the robust Internet bandwidth you take for granted.

As with other organizational constraints, budget is always a consideration when choosing tools. Some tools are costly, so you have to show significant value of a complex tool over, say, Microsoft Excel.

Chapter 6

Putting Agile into Action: The Behaviors

*I*n this chapter, you look at the behavioral dynamics that need to shift for your organization to benefit from the performance advantages that agile techniques enable. You find out what the different roles on an agile project are and see how you can change a project team's values and philosophy about project management. Finally, I discuss some ways for a project team to hone key skills for agile project success.

Establishing Agile Roles

In Chapter 4, I describe scrum, one of the most popular agile approaches in use today. The scrum framework defines common agile roles in an especially succinct manner. I use scrum terms to describe agile roles throughout this book. These roles are

✔ Development team member

✔ Product owner

✔ Scrum master

The term *scrum* comes from the sport of rugby. During rugby games, players can form tight huddles, called *scrums*, to gain control of the ball. In rugby games, as on agile projects, team members must work together closely to succeed. The Harvard Business Review first used the rugby scrum metaphor in "New New Product Development Game," an early concept framework for the scrum development approach discussed in this book.

The development team, product owner, and scrum master together make up the *scrum team*.

The development team, product owner, and scrum master are all roles in the scrum framework. The following roles are not part of the scrum framework but are still critically important to agile projects:

- Stakeholders
- Agile mentor

The scrum team, together with the stakeholders, makes up the agile *project team*. Figure 6-1 shows how these roles and teams fit together. This section discusses these roles in detail.

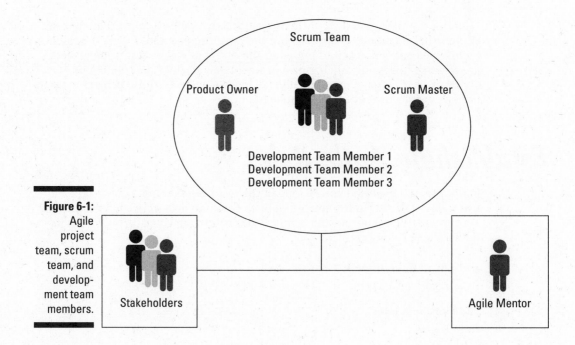

Figure 6-1:
Agile project team, scrum team, and development team members.

Development team

Development team members are the people who create the product. Programmers, testers, designers, writers, and anyone else who has a hands-on role in product development are development team members.

On an agile project, the development team is

✔ **Directly accountable for creating project deliverables.**

✔ **Self-organizing and self-managing.** The development team members determine their own tasks and how they want to complete those tasks.

✔ **Cross-functional.** Development team members are not tied to a single skillset. They have existing skills to immediately contribute at the beginning of the project, but they are also willing to learn new skills and to teach what they know to other development team members.

✔ **Ideally dedicated to one project for the duration of the project.**

✔ **Ideally collocated.** The team should be working together in the same area of the same office.

What makes a good agile team member? Take a look at the team responsibilities and matching characteristics in Table 6-1.

Table 6-1   Characteristics of a Good Agile Team Member

Responsibility	*A Good Agile Team Member . . .*
Creates the product.	Enjoys creating products.
	Is skilled in at least one of the jobs necessary to create the product.
Is self-organizing and self-managing.	Exudes initiative and independence.
	Understands how to work through impediments to achieve goals.
Is cross-functional.	Has curiosity.
	Willingly contributes to areas outside his or her mastery.
	Enjoys learning new skills.
	Enthusiastically shares knowledge.
Is dedicated and collocated.	Is part of an organization that understands the gains in efficiency and effectiveness associated with focused, collocated teams.

The two other members of the scrum team, the product owner and the scrum master, help support the development team's efforts in creating the product. The following section explains how the product owner helps ensure the development team understands the product it will create.

Product owner

The product owner, sometimes called the *customer representative* in non-scrum environments, is responsible for bridging the gaps between the customer, business stakeholders, and the development team. The product owner is an expert on the product and the customer's needs and priorities. The product owner is a member of the scrum team and works with the development team daily to help clarify requirements.

Product owners make the decisions about what the product does and does not include. Add to that the responsibility of deciding what to release to the market and when to do it, and you see that you need a smart and savvy person to fill this role.

On an agile project, the product owner

- Develops strategy and direction for the project and sets long- and short-term goals.
- Provides or has access to product expertise.
- Understands and conveys the customer's and other business stakeholders' needs to the development team.
- Gathers, prioritizes, and manages product requirements.
- Takes responsibility for the product's budget and profitability.
- Decides on the release date for completed functionality.
- Works with the development team on a daily basis to answer questions and make decisions.
- Accepts or rejects completed work during the sprint.
- Presents the scrum team's accomplishments at the end of each sprint, before the development team demonstrates these accomplishments.

What makes a good product owner? Good product owners understand the customer thoroughly. Although able to gather requirements from stakeholders, product owners are knowledgeable about the product in their own right. They can prioritize features with confidence.

Good product owners interact well with the business stakeholder community, the scrum master, and the development team. They are pragmatic and able to make trade-offs based on reality. They are decisive and ask for what they need. They are patient, especially with questions.

Table 6-2 outlines the responsibilities and their matching characteristics of a product owner.

Table 6-2	Characteristics of a Good Product Owner
Responsibility	*A Good Product Owner . . .*
Supplies project strategy and direction.	Envisions the completed product.
	Firmly understands company strategy.
Provides product expertise.	Has worked with similar products in the past.
	Understands needs of the people who will use the product.
Understands customer and other stakeholder needs.	Understands relevant business processes.
	Creates a solid customer input and feedback channel.
	Works well with business stakeholders.
Manages and prioritizes product requirements.	Focuses on efficiency.
	Remains flexible.
	Is decisive.
	Turns stakeholder feedback into valuable, customer-focused features.
	Is practical about prioritizing financially valuable features, high-risk features, and strategic system improvements.
Is responsible for budget and profitability.	Understands which product features can deliver the best return on investment.
	Manages budgets effectively.
Decides on release dates.	Understands business needs regarding timelines.
Works with development team.	Works with the development team to understand capabilities.
	Works well with developers.
	Adeptly describes product features.
	Avails himself or herself for questions and clarification every day.
Accepts or rejects work.	Understands requirements and ensures that completed features work correctly.
Presents completed work at the end of each sprint.	Clearly introduces the accomplishments of the sprint before the development team demonstrates the sprint's working functionality.

The product owner takes on a great deal of business-related responsibility during the project. While the product owner focuses on the product and the budget, the scrum master helps clear the way for the development team to work as efficiently as possible.

Scrum master

A scrum master, sometimes called a *project facilitator* in non-scrum environments, is responsible for supporting the development team, clearing organizational roadblocks, and keeping processes true to agile principles.

A scrum master is different from a project manager. Teams using traditional project approaches work for a project manager. A scrum master, on the other hand, is a servant-leader who supports the team so that it is fully functional and productive. The scrum master role is an enabling role, rather than an accountability role. You can find more about servant leadership in Chapter 14.

On an agile project, the scrum master

- ✔ Acts as a process coach, helping the project team and the organization follow scrum values and practices.
- ✔ Helps remove project impediments — both reactively and proactively — and shields the development team from external interferences.
- ✔ Fosters close cooperation between stakeholders and the scrum team.
- ✔ Facilitates consensus building within the scrum team.
- ✔ Protects the scrum team from organizational distractions.

One of the most significant parts of a scrum master's role is removing roadblocks and preventing distractions to the development team's work. A scrum master who is really good at these tasks is priceless to the project and to the team.

The product owner may never have participated in an agile project, but the scrum master likely has. As such, a scrum master may coach new product owners and development teams and does everything possible to help them succeed.

What makes a good scrum master? A scrum master doesn't need project manager experience. A scrum master is an expert in agile processes and can coach others. The scrum master must also work collaboratively with the product owner and the stakeholder community.

Facilitation skills cut through the noise of group gatherings and ensure that everyone on the scrum team is focused on the right priority at the right time.

Scrum masters have strong communication skills, with enough organizational clout to secure the conditions for success by negotiating for the right environment, protecting the team from distractions, and removing impediments. Scrum masters are great facilitators and great listeners. They can negotiate their way through conflicting opinions and help the team help itself. Review the scrum master's responsibilities and matching characteristics in Table 6-3.

Table 6-3	Characteristics of a Good Scrum Master
Responsibility	*A Good Scrum Master . . .*
Upholds scrum values and practices.	Is an expert on scrum processes.
	Is passionate about agile techniques.
Removes roadblocks and prevents disruptions.	Has organizational clout and can resolve problems quickly.
	Is articulate, diplomatic, and professional.
	Is a good communicator and a good listener.
	Is firm about the development team's need to focus only on the project and the current sprint.
Fosters close cooperation between external stakeholders and the scrum team.	Looks at the needs of the project as a whole.
	Avoids cliques and helps break down group silos.
Facilitates consensus building.	Understands techniques to help groups reach agreements.
Is a servant-leader.	Does not need or want to be in charge or be the boss.
	Ensures that all members of the development team have the information they need to do the job, use their tools, and track progress.
	Truly desires to help the scrum team.

The members of the scrum team — the development team, the product owner, and the scrum master — work together on the project every day.

As I mentioned earlier in the chapter, the scrum team plus stakeholders make up the project team. The stakeholders sometimes have less active participation than the scrum team members, but still can have considerable impact and provide a great deal of value to a project.

Gaining consensus: The fist of five

Part of working as a team means agreeing on decisions as a team. An important part of being a scrum master is helping the team build consensus. We have all worked with groups in which consensus was difficult to build on anything from how long a task will take to where to go for lunch. A quick, casual way to find out whether a group agrees with an idea is to use the *fist of five,* which is similar to rock-paper-scissors.

On the count of three, each person holds up a number of fingers, reflecting the degree of comfort with the idea in question:

> 5: I love the idea.
>
> 4: I think it's a good idea.
>
> 3: I can support the idea.
>
> 2: I have reservations, so let's discuss.
>
> 1: I am opposed to the idea.

If some people have three, four, or five fingers up, and some have only one or two, discuss the idea. Find out why the people who support the idea think it will work, and what reservations the people who oppose the idea have. You want to get all group members showing at least three fingers up — they don't need to love the idea, but they need to support it. The scrum master's consensus-building skills are essential for this task.

You can also quickly get an idea of consensus on a decision by asking for a simple thumbs up (support), thumbs down (don't support), and thumb to the side (undecided). It's quicker than a fist of five, and is great for answering yes/no questions.

Stakeholders

Stakeholders are anyone with an interest in the project. They are not ultimately responsible for the product, but they provide input and are affected by the project's outcome. The group of stakeholders is diverse and can include people from different departments, or even different companies.

On an agile project, stakeholders

- Include the customer.
- May include technical people, such as infrastructure architects or system administrators.
- May include the legal department, account managers, sales people, marketing experts, and customer service representatives.
- May include product experts besides the product owner.

Stakeholders may help provide key insights about the product and its use. Stakeholders might work closely with the product owner during the sprint, and will give feedback about the product during the sprint review at the end of each sprint.

The stakeholders and the part they play will vary among projects and organizations. Almost all agile projects have stakeholders outside the scrum team.

Some projects also have agile mentors, especially projects with project teams that are new to agile processes.

Agile mentor

A mentor is a great idea for any area in which you want to develop new expertise. The agile mentor, sometimes called an agile coach, is someone who has experience implementing agile projects and can share that experience with a project team. The agile mentor can provide valuable feedback and advice to new project teams and to project teams that want to perform at a higher level.

On an agile project, the agile mentor

- ✔ Serves in a mentoring role only and is not part of the scrum team.

- ✔ Is often a person from outside the organization, and can provide objective guidance, without personal or political considerations.

- ✔ Is an agile expert with significant experience in implementing agile techniques and running agile projects of different sizes.

You may want to think of an agile mentor the way you think of a golf coach. Most people use a golf coach not because they don't know how to play the game of golf, but because a golf coach objectively observes things that a player engaged in the game never notices. Golf, like implementing agile techniques, is an exercise where small nuances make a world of difference in performance.

Establishing New Values

Lots of organizations post their core values on the wall. Here, however, I am talking about values that represent a way of working together every day, supporting each other, and doing whatever it takes to achieve the scrum team's commitments.

In addition to the values from the Agile Manifesto, the five core values for scrum teams are

- ✓ Commitment
- ✓ Focus
- ✓ Openness
- ✓ Respect
- ✓ Courage

The following sections provide details about each of these values.

Commitment

Commitment implies engagement and involvement. On agile projects, the scrum team pledges to achieve specific goals. Confident that the scrum team will deliver what it promises, the organization mobilizes around the pledge to meet each goal.

Agile processes, including the idea of self-organization, provide people with all the authority they need to meet commitments. However, commitment requires a conscious effort. Consider the following points:

- ✓ Scrum teams must be realistic when making commitments, especially for sprints.

   It is easier, both logistically and psychologically, to bring new features into a sprint than it is to take unachievable features out of a sprint.

- ✓ Scrum teams must fully commit to goals. This includes having consensus among the team that the goal is achievable.

   Once the scrum team agrees upon a goal, the team does whatever it takes to reach that goal.

- ✓ The scrum team is pragmatic but ensures that every sprint has a tangible value.

   Achieving a goal and completing every item in the goal's scope are different. For example, a sprint goal of proving that a product can perform a specific action is much better than a goal stating that exactly seven requirements will be complete during the sprint. Effective scrum teams focus on the goal and remain flexible in the specifics of how to reach that goal.

- ✓ Scrum teams are willing to be accountable for results.

   The scrum team has the power to be in charge of the project. As a scrum team member, you can be responsible for how you organize your day, the day-to-day work, and the outcome.

Consistently meeting commitments is central to using agile approaches for long-term planning. In Chapter 13, you read about how to use performance to accurately determine project schedules and budgets.

Focus

Working life is full of distractions. A thousand people in your organization would love to use your time to make their day easier. Disruptions, however, are costly. Jonathan Spira from the consulting firm Basex recently published a report called "The Cost of Not Paying Attention: How Interruptions Impact Knowledge Worker Productivity." His report details how businesses in the United States lose close to $600 *billion* a year through workplace distractions.

Scrum team members can help change those dysfunctions by insisting on an environment that allows them focus. To reduce distractions and increase productivity, scrum team members can

- ✔ **Physically separate themselves from company distracters.** One of my favorite techniques for ensuring high productivity is to find an annex away from the company's core offices and have that be the scrum team's work area. Sometimes the best defense is distance.

- ✔ **Ensure that you are not spending time on activities unrelated to the sprint goal.** If someone tries to distract you from the sprint goal with something that "has to be done," explain your priorities. Ask, "How will this request move the sprint goal forward?" This simple question can push a lot of activities off the to-do list.

- ✔ **Figure out what needs to be done and do only that.** The development team determines the tasks necessary to achieve the sprint goal. If you are a development team member, use this ownership to drive your focus to the priority tasks at hand.

- ✔ **Balance focused time with accessibility to the rest of the scrum team.** Francesco Cirillo's Pomodoro technique — splitting work into 25-minute time blocks, with breaks in between — helps achieve balance between focus and accessibility. I often recommend giving development team members noise-canceling headsets, the wearing of which is a "do not disturb" sign. However, I also suggest a team agreement that all scrum team members have a minimum set of office hours in which they are available for collaboration.

- ✔ **Check that you are maintaining your focus.** If you're unsure of whether you are maintaining focus — it can be hard to tell — go back to the basic question, "Are my actions consistent with achieving the overall goal and the near-term goal (such as completing the current task)?"

As you can see, task focus is not a small priority. Extend the effort upfront to create a distraction-free environment that helps your team succeed.

Openness

Secrets have no place on an agile team. If the team is responsible for the result of the project, it only makes sense that they have all the facts at their disposal. Information is power, and ensuring that everyone has access to the information necessary to make the right decisions requires a willingness to be transparent. To leverage the power of openness, you can

- **Ensure that everyone on the team has access to the same information.** Everything from the vision for the project down to the smallest detail about the status of tasks needs to be in the public domain as far as the team is concerned. Use a centralized repository as the single source for information, and then avoid the distraction of "status reporting" by putting all status (burndowns, impediment list, and so forth) and information in this one place. I often send a link to this repository to the project stakeholders and say, "All the information I have is a click away. There is no faster way to get updated."

- **Be open and encourage openness in others.** Team members must feel free to speak openly about problems and opportunities to improve, whether the issues are something that they are dealing with themselves or see elsewhere in the team. Openness requires trust within the team, and trust takes time to develop.

- **Defuse internal politics by discouraging gossip.** If someone starts talking to you about what another team member did or didn't do, ask him or her to take the issue to the person who can resolve it. Don't gossip yourself. Ever.

- **Always be respectful.** Openness is never an excuse to be destructive or mean. Respect is critical to an open team environment.

Small problems unaddressed often grow to be become crises. Use an open environment to benefit from the input of the entire team and ensure that your development efforts are focused on the project's true priorities.

Respect

Each individual on the team has something important to contribute. Your background, education, and experiences have a distinctive influence on the team. Share your uniqueness and look for, and appreciate, the same in others. You encourage respect when you

✔ **Foster openness.** Respect and openness go hand in hand. Openness without respect causes resentment; openness with respect generates trust.

✔ **Encourage a positive work environment.** Happy people tend to treat one another better. Encourage positivity, and respect will follow.

✔ **Seek out differences.** Don't just tolerate differences; try to find them. The best solutions come from diverse opinions that have been considered and appropriately challenged.

✔ **Treat everyone on the team with the same degree of respect.** All team members should be accorded the same respect, regardless of their role, level of experience, or immediate contribution. Encourage everyone to give his or her best.

Respect is the safety net that allows innovation to thrive. When people feel comfortable raising a wider range of ideas, the final solution can improve in ways that would never be considered without a respectful team environment. Use respect to your team's advantage.

Courage

We all experience fear. We all have certain things we don't want to do, whether asking a team member to explain something we don't understand or confronting the boss. Embracing agile techniques is a change for many organizations. In addition to commitment, focus, openness, and respect, successfully making changes requires courage in the face of resistance. Following are some tips that foster courage:

✔ **Realize that the processes that worked in the past won't necessarily work now.** Sometimes you need to remind people of this fact. If you want to be successful with agile techniques, your everyday work processes need to change to improve.

✔ **Be ready to buck the status quo.** The status quo will push back. Some people have vested interests and will not want to change how they work.

✔ **Temper challenge with respect.** Senior members of the organization might be especially resistant to change; they often created the old rules for how things were done. Now you are challenging those rules. Respectfully remind these individuals that you can achieve the benefits of agile techniques only by following the 12 Agile Principles faithfully. Ask them to give change a try.

✔ **Embrace the other values.** Have the courage to make commitments and stand behind those commitments. Have the courage to focus and tell distracters "no." Have the courage to be open and acknowledge there is always an opportunity to improve. And have the courage to be respectful and tolerant of other people's views, even when they challenge your views.

As you replace your organization's antiquated processes with more modern approaches, expect to be challenged. Take on that challenge; the rewards can be worth it in the end.

Changing Team Philosophy

An agile development team operates differently from a team using a waterfall approach. Development team members must change their roles based on each day's priorities, organize themselves, and think about projects in a whole new way to achieve their commitments.

To be part of a successful agile project, development teams should embrace the following attributes:

- ✔ **Cross-functionality:** The willingness and ability to work on different types of tasks to create the product.
- ✔ **Self-organization:** The ability and responsibility to determine how to go about the work of product development.
- ✔ **Self-management:** The ability and responsibility to keep work on track.
- ✔ **Size-limited teams:** Ensure development teams have between five and nine people.
- ✔ **Mature behavior:** Take initiative for work and responsibility for results.

The following sections look at each of these ideas in more detail.

Cross-functionality

On traditional projects, experienced team members are often typecast as having a single skill. For example, a .NET programmer may always do .NET work, and a tester may always do quality assurance work. Team members with complementary skills are often considered to be part of separate groups, like the programming group or the testing group.

Agile approaches bring the people who create products together into a cohesive group — the development team. People on agile development teams try to avoid titles and limited roles. Development team members may start a project with one skill, but throughout the project, learn to perform many different jobs to help create the product.

Cross-functionality makes development teams more efficient. For example, suppose a daily scrum meeting uncovers testing as the highest priority task to complete the requirement. A programmer might help test to finish the task quickly. When the development team is cross-functional, they can *swarm* on product features, with as many people working on a single requirement as possible, to quickly complete the feature.

Cross-functionality also helps eliminate single points of failure. Consider traditional projects, where each person knows how to do one job. When a team member gets sick, goes on vacation, or leaves the company, no one else may be capable of doing his or her job. The tasks that person was doing are delayed. By contrast, cross-functional agile development team members are capable of doing many jobs. When one person is unavailable, another can step in.

Cross-functionality encourages each team member to

- ✔ **Set aside the narrow label of what he or she can do.** Titles have no place on an agile team. Skills and an ability to contribute are what matter. Start thinking of yourself as a Special Forces commando — knowledgeable enough in different areas that you can take on any situation.

- ✔ **Work to expand skills.** Don't work only in areas you already know. Try to learn something new each sprint. Techniques like pair programming — where two developers work together to code one item — or shadowing other developers can help you learn new skills quickly and increase overall product quality.

- ✔ **Step up to help someone who has run into a roadblock.** Helping someone with a real-world problem is a great way to learn a new skill.

- ✔ **Be flexible.** A willingness to be flexible helps to balance workloads and makes the team more likely to reach its sprint goal.

With cross-functionality in place, you avoid waiting for key people to work on tasks. Instead, a motivated, even if somewhat less knowledgeable, development team member can work on a piece of functionality today. That development team member learns and improves, and the workflow continues to be balanced.

One big payback of cross-functionality is that the development team gets work done fast. Post-sprint review afternoons are often celebration time. Go to the movies together. Head to the beach or the bowling alley. Go home early.

Self-organization

Agile techniques emphasize self-organizing development teams to take advantage of development team members' varied knowledge and experience.

If you've read Chapter 2, you may recall Agile Principle #11: The best architectures, requirements, and designs emerge from self-organizing teams.

Self-organization is an important part of the agile framework. Why? In a word — ownership. Self-organized teams are not complying with orders from others; they own the solution developed and that makes a huge difference in team member engagement and solution quality.

For development teams used to a traditional command-and-control project management model, self-organization may take some extra effort at first. Agile projects do not have a project manager to tell the development team what to do. Instead, self-organizing development teams

- **Commit to their own sprint goals.** At the beginning of each sprint, the development team works with the product owner to identify an objective it can reach, based on project priorities.

- **Identify their tasks.** Development team members determine the tasks necessary to meet each sprint goal. The development team works together to figure out who takes on which task, how to get the work done, and how to address risks and issues.

- **Estimate the effort necessary for requirements and related tasks.** The development team knows the most about how much effort it will take them to create specific product features.

- **Focus on communication.** Successful agile development teams hone their communication skills by being transparent, communicating face-to-face, being aware of nonverbal communication, participating, and listening.

The key to communication is clarity. With complex topics, avoid one-way, potentially ambiguous modes of communication, such as e-mail. Face-to-face communication prevents misunderstandings and frustration. You can always summarize the conversation in a quick e-mail later if details need to be retained.

- **Collaborate.** Getting the input of a diverse scrum team almost always improves the product but requires solid collaboration skills. Collaboration is the foundation of an effective agile team.

No successful project is an island. Collaboration skills help scrum team members take risks with ideas and bring innovative solutions to project problems. A safe and comfortable environment is a cornerstone of a successful agile project.

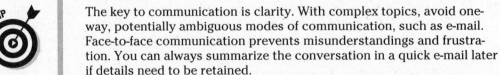

✔ **Decide with consensus.** For maximum productivity, the entire development team must be on the same page and committed to the goal at hand. The scrum master often plays an active role in building consensus, but the development team ultimately takes responsibility for reaching agreement on decisions.

✔ **Actively participate.** Self-organization may be challenging for the shy. All development team members must actively participate. No one is going to tell the development team what to do to create the product. The development team members tell themselves what to do. And when. And how.

In my experience as an agile coach, I have heard new agile development team members ask questions like, "So, what should I do now?" A good scrum master answers by asking the developer what does he or she need to do to achieve the sprint goal, or by asking the rest of the development team what they suggest. Answering questions with questions can be a helpful way to guide a development team toward being self-organizing.

Being part of a self-organizing development team takes responsibility, but it also has its rewards. Self-organization gives development teams the freedom to succeed. Self-organization increases ownership, which can result in better products, which can help development team members find more satisfaction in their work.

Self-management

Self-management is closely related to self-organization. Agile development teams have lot of control over how they work; that control comes with the responsibility for ensuring the project is successful. To succeed with self-management, development teams

✔ **Allow leadership to ebb and flow.** On agile projects, each person on the development team has the opportunity to lead. For different tasks, different leaders will naturally emerge; leadership will shift throughout the team based on skill expertise and previous experiences.

✔ **Rely on agile processes and tools to manage the work.** Agile methods are tailored to make self-management easy. With an agile approach, meetings have clear purposes and time limits, and artifacts expose information but rely on minimal effort to create and maintain. Taking advantage of these processes allows development teams to spend most of their time creating the product.

✔ **Report progress regularly and transparently.** Each development team member is responsible for accurately updating work status on a daily basis. Luckily, progress reporting is a quick task on agile projects. In

Chapter 9, you find out about burndown charts that provide status but only require a few minutes each day to update. Keeping status current and truthful makes planning and issue management easier.

✔ **Manage issues within the development team.** Many obstacles can arise on a project: Development challenges and interpersonal problems are a couple of examples. The development team's first point of escalation for most issues is the development team itself.

✔ **Create a team agreement.** Development teams sometimes make up a team agreement, a document that outlines the expectations each team member will commit to meet.

✔ **Inspect and adapt.** Figure out what works for your team. Best practices differ from team to team. Some teams work best by coming early, some teams work best by coming in late. The development team is responsible for reviewing its own performance and identifying techniques to continue and techniques to change.

✔ **Actively participate.** As with self-organization, self-management only works when development team members join in and commit to guiding the project's direction.

The development team, naturally, is primarily responsible for self-organization and self-management. However, the scrum master can assist the development team in a number of ways. When development team members look for specific directions, the scrum master can remind them that they have the power to decide what to do and how to do it. If someone outside the development team tries to give orders, insist on tasks, or dictate how to create the product, the scrum master can intervene. The scrum master can be a powerful ally in development team self-organization and self-management.

Size-limited teams

Agile development teams are intentionally small. A small development team is a nimble team. As the development team size grows, so does the overhead associated with orchestrating task flow and communication flow.

Ideally, agile development teams have seven people, plus or minus two people. Keeping the development team size between five and nine people helps teams act as cohesive teams, and avoids creating subgroups, or *silos*.

Limiting development team size

✔ Encourages diverse skills to be developed

✔ Facilitates good team communication

> ✔ Maintains the team in a single unit
>
> ✔ Promotes joint code ownership, cross-functionality, and face-to-face communication

When you have a small development team, a similarly limited and focused project scope follows. Development team members are in close contact throughout the day as tasks, questions, and peer reviews flow back and forth among teammates. This cohesiveness ensures consistent engagement, increases communication, and reduces project risk.

When you have a large project and a correspondingly large development team, split the work between multiple scrum teams. For more on scaling agile projects across the enterprise, see Chapter 13.

Mature behavior

Being part of a cross-functional, self-organized, self-managing development team requires responsibility and maturity. The top-down management approaches on traditional projects do not always foster the maturity necessary for taking responsibility for projects and results. Even seasoned development team members may need to adjust behavior to get used to making decisions on agile projects.

Development teams can adapt behavior and increase their level of maturity by doing the following:

> ✔ **Take initiative.** Instead of waiting for someone else to tell you what to work on, take action. Do what is necessary to help meet commitments and goals.
>
> ✔ **Succeed and fail as a team.** On agile projects, accomplishments and failures alike all belong to the project team. If problems arise, be accountable as a group, rather than finding blame. When you succeed, recognize the group effort necessary for that success.
>
> ✔ **Trust the ability to make good decisions.** Development teams can make mature, responsible, sound decisions about product development. This takes a degree of trust as team members become accustomed to having more control in a project.

Behavioral maturity doesn't mean that agile development teams are perfect. Rather, they take ownership for the scope they commit to, and they take responsibility for meeting those commitments. Mistakes happen. If they don't, you aren't pushing yourself outside your comfort zone. A mature development team identifies mistakes honestly, accepts responsibility for mistakes openly, and learns and improves from their mistakes consistently.

Part III
Working in Agile

The 5th Wave   By Rich Tennant

"Before we write the vision statement, I'd like to clarify what metaphors we'll be speaking in. Last time we used sports metaphors. How about using cooking metaphors? 'Half baked,' 'burnt,' 'simmering,' that sort of thing?"

In this part . . .

Your team is ready, your tools are in place, and everyone is excited about starting to work in a more agile environment. You even have a pilot project in mind.

In the next few chapters, I show you the nuts and bolts of working on an agile project. To make things simple and uniform throughout this section and the rest of the book, I largely use terminology from the scrum framework that's introduced earlier in Chapter 4.

Using the Roadmap to Value — a visual overview of an agile project — I walk you through more agile processes, artifacts, and events. You see how to quickly start an agile project with a cohesive product vision and find out how to define and estimate product requirements. You walk through a typical day in the life of a scrum team. You see how to create working product features in regular iterations, and how to showcase that work throughout your project. You also see how agile project teams constantly inspect their work and processes and adapt for improvement. Finally, you find out how to release features to product users.

Chapter 7

Defining the Product Vision and Product Roadmap

*T*o start, let's dispel a common myth. If you've heard that agile projects don't include planning, dismiss that thought right now. Not only will you plan the overall project, you also will plan every release, every sprint, and every day. Planning is fundamental to agile project success.

If you're a project manager, you probably do the bulk of your planning at the beginning of a project. You may have heard the phrase, "Plan the work, then work the plan," which sums up non-agile project management approaches.

Agile projects, in contrast, involve planning up front and throughout the entire project. By planning at the last responsible moment, right before an activity starts, you know the most about that activity. This type of planning, called *just-in-time planning* or a *situationally informed strategy* (introduced in Chapter 3), is a key to agile's success.

Helmuth von Moltke, a nineteenth-century German field marshal and military strategist, once said, "No plan survives contact with the enemy." That is, in the heat of a battle — much like in the thick of a project — plans always change. The agile focus on just-in-time planning allows you to accommodate real situations and to be well informed as you plan specific tasks.

This chapter describes how just-in-time planning works with agile. You also go through the first two steps of planning an agile project: the product vision and the product roadmap.

Planning in Agile

Planning happens at a number of points in an agile project. A great way to look at the planning activities in agile projects is with the Roadmap to Value. Figure 7-1 shows the roadmap as a whole.

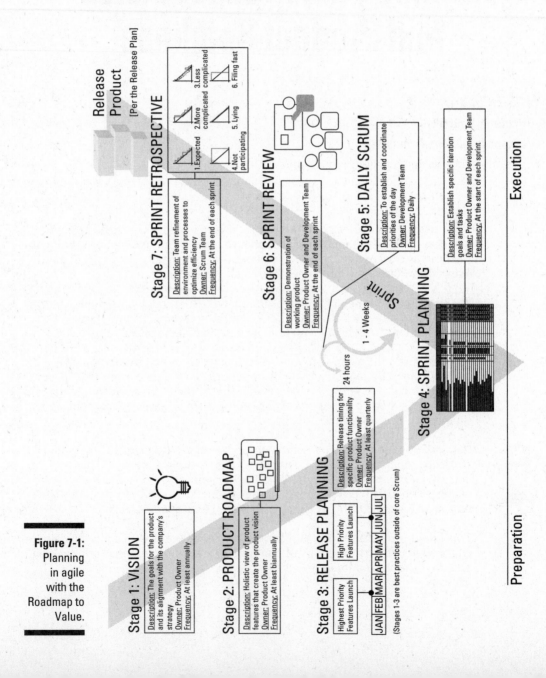

Figure 7-1:
Planning in agile with the Roadmap to Value.

Release Product [Per the Release Plan]

Stage 7: SPRINT RETROSPECTIVE
Description: Team refinement of environment and processes to optimize efficiency
Owner: Scrum Team
Frequency: At the end of each sprint

1.Expected 2.More complicated 3.Less complicated
4.Not participating 5. Lying 6. Filing fast

Stage 6: SPRINT REVIEW
Description: Demonstration of working product
Owner: Product Owner and Development Team
Frequency: At the end of each sprint

Stage 5: DAILY SCRUM
Description: To establish and coordinate priorities of the day
Owner: Development Team
Frequency: Daily

Description: Establish specific iteration goals and tasks
Owner: Product Owner and Development Team
Frequency: At the start of each sprint

Sprint
1 - 4 Weeks
24 hours

Stage 4: SPRINT PLANNING

Stage 1: VISION
Description: The goals for the product and its alignment with the company's strategy
Owner: Product Owner
Frequency: At least annually

Stage 2: PRODUCT ROADMAP
Description: Holistic view of product features that create the product vision
Owner: Product Owner
Frequency: At least biannually

Stage 3: RELEASE PLANNING
Description: Release timing for specific product functionality
Owner: Product Owner
Frequency: At least quarterly

High Priority Features Launch
Highest Priority Features Launch

JAN|FEB|MAR|APR|MAY|JUN|JUL

(Stages 1-3 are best practices outside of core Scrum)

Preparation   Execution

The Roadmap to Value has seven stages:

- ✔ In Stage 1, the product owner identifies the *product vision.* The product vision is your project's destination; it's a definition of what your product is, how it will support your company or organization's strategy, who will use the product, and why people will use the product. On longer projects, revisit the product vision about once a year.

- ✔ In Stage 2, the product owner creates a *product roadmap.* The product roadmap is a high-level view of the product requirements, with a loose time frame for when you will develop those requirements. Identifying product requirements and then prioritizing and roughly estimating the effort for those requirements allow you to establish requirement themes and identify requirement gaps. Revise the product roadmap biannually with support from the development team.

- ✔ In Stage 3, the product owner creates a release plan. The *release plan* identifies a high-level timetable for the release of working software. The release serves as a mid-term goal that the scrum team can mobilize around. An agile project will have many releases, with the highest-priority features appearing first. You create a release plan at the beginning of each release. Find out more about release planning in Chapter 8.

- ✔ In Stage 4, the product owner, the scrum master, and the development team plan sprints, also called iterations, and start creating the product within those sprints. *Sprint planning* sessions take place at the start of each sprint. During sprint planning, the scrum team determines a sprint goal, with requirements that support the goal and can be completed in the sprint, and outlines how to complete those requirements. Get more information about sprint planning in Chapter 8.

- ✔ In Stage 5, during each sprint, the development team has *daily scrum meetings* to coordinate the day's priorities. In the daily scrum meeting, you discuss what you completed yesterday, what you will work on today, and any roadblocks you have, so that you can address issues immediately. Read about daily scrums in Chapter 9.

- ✔ In Stage 6, the scrum team holds a *sprint review.* In the sprint review, at the end of every sprint, you demonstrate the working product to the product stakeholders. Find out how to conduct sprint reviews in Chapter 10.

- ✔ In Stage 7, the scrum team holds a *sprint retrospective.* The sprint retrospective is a meeting where the scrum team discusses how the sprint went and plans for improvements in the next sprint. Like the sprint review, you have a sprint retrospective at the end of every sprint. Find out how to conduct sprint retrospectives in Chapter 10.

Each stage in the Roadmap to Value is repeatable, and each stage contains planning activities. Planning in agile, like development in agile, is iterative.

The various teams on agile projects — the development team, the scrum team, and the project team — have different roles and responsibilities, as you see throughout this chapter and the rest of the book. Figure 7-2 shows how these teams fit together.

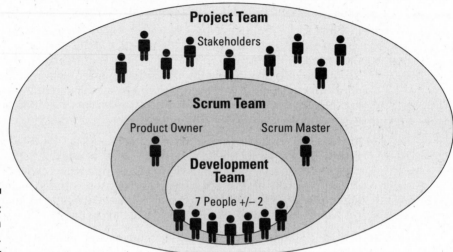

Figure 7-2:
Teams in agile.

Planning as necessary

During each stage in an agile project, you plan only as much as you need to plan. In the early stages of your project, you plan widely and holistically to create a broad outline of how the product will shape up over time. In later stages, you narrow your planning and add more details to ensure success in the immediate development effort.

Planning broadly at first and in detail later, when necessary, prevents you from wasting time on planning lower-priority product requirements that may never be implemented. This model also lets you add high-value requirements during the project without disrupting the development flow.

The more just-in-time your detailed planning is, the more efficient your planning process becomes.

Some studies show customers rarely or never use 64 percent of the features in an application. In the first few development cycles of an agile project, you complete features that are high priority and that people *will* use. Typically, you release those groups of features as early as possible.

Inspect and adapt

Just-in-time planning brings into play a fundamental tenet of agile techniques: inspect and adapt. At each stage of a project, you need to look at the product and the process (inspect) and make changes as necessary (adapt).

Planning in agile is a rhythmic cycle of inspecting and adapting. Consider the following:

- ✔ During the sprint, the product owner provides feedback to help improve the product as the development team creates the product.

- ✔ At the end of each sprint, in the sprint review, stakeholders provide feedback to further improve the product.

- ✔ Also at the end of each sprint, in the sprint retrospective, the scrum team discusses the lessons they learned during the past sprint to improve the development process.

- ✔ After a release, the customers using the product can provide feedback for improvement. Feedback might be direct, when a customer contacts the company about the product, or indirect, when potential customers either do or don't purchase the product.

Inspect and adapt is a fantastic tool for delivering the right product in the most efficient manner.

At the beginning of a project, you know the least about the product you're creating, so trying to plan fine details at that time just doesn't work. With agile, you do the detailed planning when you need it, and immediately develop the specific requirements you defined with that planning.

Now that you know a little more about how planning works in agile, it's time to complete the first step in an agile project: defining the product vision.

Defining the Product Vision

The first stage in an agile project is defining your product vision. The *product vision statement* is an elevator pitch, or a quick summary, to communicate how your product supports the company's or organization's strategies. The vision statement must articulate the goals for the product.

The product might be a commercial product for release to the marketplace or an internal solution that will support your organization's day-to-day functions. For example, say your company is XYZ Bank and your product is a mobile banking application. What company strategies does a mobile banking application support? How does the application support the company's strategies? Your vision statement clearly and concisely links the product to your business strategy.

Figure 7-3 shows how the vision statement — Stage 1 on the Roadmap to Value — fits with the rest of the stages and activities in an agile project.

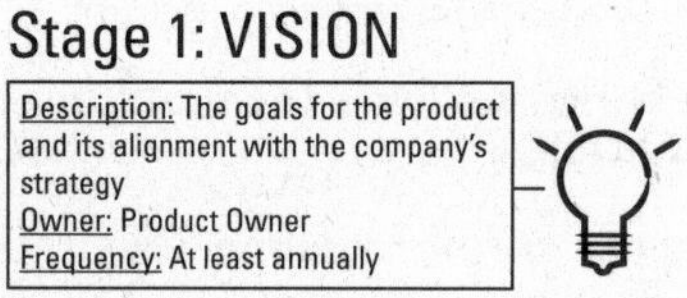

Figure 7-3:
The product vision statement as part of the Roadmap to Value.

Stage 1: VISION

Description: The goals for the product and its alignment with the company's strategy
Owner: Product Owner
Frequency: At least annually

The product owner is responsible for knowing about the product, its goals, and its requirements throughout the project. For those reasons, the product owner creates the vision statement, although other people may have input. After the vision statement is complete, it becomes a guiding light, the "what we are trying to achieve" statement that the development team, scrum master, and stakeholders refer to throughout the project.

When creating a product vision statement, follow these four steps:

1. **Develop the product objective.**

2. **Create a draft vision statement.**

3. **Validate the vision statement with product and project stakeholders. Revise the vision statement based on feedback.**

4. **Finalize the vision statement.**

The look of a vision statement follows no hard-and-fast rules. However, anyone involved with the project, from the development team to the CEO, should be able to understand the statement. The vision statement should be internally focused, clear, nontechnical, and as brief as possible. The vision statement should also be explicit and avoid marketing fluff.

Step 1: Developing the product objective

To write your vision statement, you must understand and be able to communicate the product's objective. You need to identify the following:

✔ **Key product goals:** How will the product benefit the company that is creating it? The goals may include benefits for a specific department within your company, such as customer service or the marketing department, as well as the company as a whole. What specific company strategies does the product support?

✔ **Customer:** Who will use the product? This question might have more than one answer.

✔ **Need:** Why does the customer need the product? What features are critical to the customer?

✔ **Competition:** How does the product compare with similar products?

✔ **Primary differentiation:** What makes this product different from the status quo or the competition or both?

Step 2: Creating a draft vision statement

After you have a good grasp of the product's objective, create a first draft of your vision statement.

You can find many templates for a product vision statement. For an excellent guide to defining the overall product vision, see *Crossing the Chasm,* by Geoffrey Moore (published HarperCollins), which focuses on how to bridge the gap ("chasm") between early adopters of new technologies and the majority who follow.

The adoption of any new product is a gamble. Will users like the product? Will the market take to the product? Will there be an adequate return on investment for developing the product? In *Crossing the Chasm,* Moore describes how early adopters are driven by vision, whereas the majority are skeptical of visionaries and interested in down-to-earth issues of quality, product maintenance, and longevity.

Return on investment, or ROI, is the benefit a company gets from paying for something. ROI can be quantitative, such as the additional money ABC Products makes from selling widgets online after investing in a new website. ROI can also be something intangible, such as better customer satisfaction for XYZ Bank customers who use the bank's new mobile banking application.

By creating your vision statement, you help convey your product's quality, maintenance needs, and longevity.

Moore's product vision template is pragmatic. In Figure 7-4, I expand the template to more explicitly connect the product to the company's strategies. If you use this template for your product vision statement, it will stand the test of time as your product goes from early adoption to mainstream usage.

Vision Statement for Product:

For: _____ (Target Customer)
who: _____ (needs)
the: _____ (product name)
is a: _____ (product category)
that: _____ (product benefit, reason to buy)
Unlike: _____ (competitors)
our product: (differentiation/value proposition)

Figure 7-4:
Expansion
of Moore's
template
for a vision
statement.

One way to make your product vision statement more compelling is to write it in the present tense, as if the product already exists. Using present tense helps readers imagine the product in use.

Using my expansion of Moore's template, a vision statement for a mobile banking application might look like the following:

For XYZ Bank customers

who want access to online banking capability while on the go,

the MyXYZ mobile banking application by XYZ Bank

is a mobile application that can be downloaded and used on smartphones and tablets

that allows bank customers to conduct secure, on-demand banking, 24 hours a day.

Unlike traditional banking at a branch or online banking from your home or office computer,

our product allows users immediate 24-hour access to their financial accounts wherever they have mobile carrier service.

Platinum Edge addition: **This supports our company strategy to** provide quick, convenient banking services, anytime, anywhere.

As you can see, a vision statement identifies a future state for the product when the product reaches completion. The vision focuses on the conditions that should exist when the product is complete.

Avoid generalizations in your vision statement such as "make customers happy" or "sell more products." Also watch out for too much technological specificity, such as "using release 9.x of Java, create a program with four modules that. . . ." At this early stage, defining specific technologies might limit you later.

Here are a few extracts from vision statements that should ring warning bells:

- ✔ Secure additional customers for the MyXYZ application.
- ✔ Satisfy our customers by December.
- ✔ Eliminate all defects and improve quality.
- ✔ Create a new application in Java.
- ✔ Beat the Widget Company to market by six months.

Step 3: Validating and revising the vision statement

After you draft your vision statement, review it against the following quality checklist:

- ✔ Is this vision statement clear, focused, and written for an internal audience?
- ✔ Does the statement provide a compelling description of how the product meets customer needs?
- ✔ Does the vision describe the best possible outcome?
- ✔ Is the business objective specific enough that the goal is achievable?
- ✔ Does the statement deliver value that is consistent with corporate strategies and goals?
- ✔ Is the project vision statement compelling?

These yes-or-no questions will help you determine whether your vision statement is thorough. If any answers are no, revise the vision statement.

When all answers are yes, move on to reviewing the statement with others, including the following:

- ✔ **Project stakeholders:** The stakeholders will be able to identify that the vision statement includes everything the product should accomplish.
- ✔ **Your development team:** Because the team will create the product, it must understand what the product needs to accomplish.
- ✔ **Scrum master:** A strong understanding of the product will help the scrum master remove roadblocks and ensure that the development team is on the right path later in the project.

✔ **Agile mentor:** Share the vision statement with your agile mentor, if you have one. The agile mentor is independent of the organization and can provide an external perspective, qualities that can make for a great objective voice.

See whether others think the vision statement is clear and delivers the message you want to convey. Review and revise the vision statement until the project stakeholders, the development team, and the scrum master fully understand the statement.

At this stage of your project, you might not have a development team or scrum master. After you form a scrum team, be sure to review the vision statement with it.

Step 4: Finalizing the vision statement

After you finish revising the vision statement, make sure your development team, scrum master, and stakeholders have the final copy. You might even put a copy on the wall in the scrum team's work area, where you can see it every day. You will refer to the vision statement throughout the life of the project.

If your project is more than a year long, you may want to revisit the vision statement. I like to review and revise the product vision statement once a year to make sure the product reflects the marketplace and supports any changes in the company's needs.

The product owner owns the product vision statement and is responsible for its preparation and communication across and outside the organization. The product vision sets expectations for stakeholders and helps the development team stay focused on the goal.

Congratulations. You have just completed the first stage in your agile project. Now it's time to create a product roadmap.

Creating a Product Roadmap

The product roadmap, Stage 2 in the Roadmap to Value (see Figure 7-5), is an overall view of the product's requirements and a valuable tool for planning and organizing the journey of product development. Use the product roadmap to categorize requirements, to prioritize them, and to determine a timetable for their release.

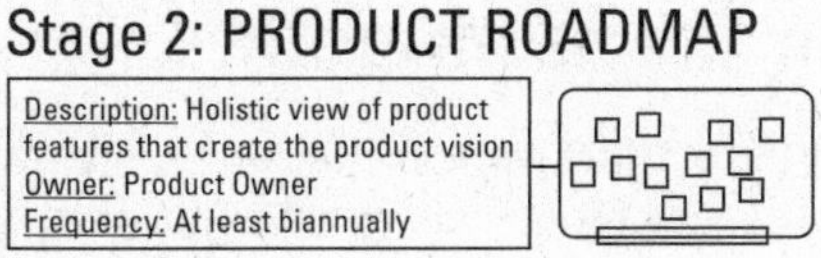

Figure 7-5:
The product
roadmap as
part of the
Roadmap to
Value.

Stage 2: PRODUCT ROADMAP

Description: Holistic view of product
features that create the product vision
Owner: Product Owner
Frequency: At least biannually

As he or she does with the product vision statement, the product owner creates the product roadmap, with help from the development team. The development team participates to a greater degree than it did during the creation of the vision statement.

Keep in mind that you will refine requirements and effort estimates throughout the project. In the product roadmap phase, it is okay for your requirements, estimates, and timeframes to be at a very high level.

To create your product roadmap, you

1. **Identify product requirements and add them to the roadmap.**

2. **Arrange the product requirements into logical groups.**

3. **Estimate requirement effort at a high level and prioritize the product's requirements.**

4. **Envision high-level time frames for the groups on the roadmap.**

Because priorities can change, expect to update your product roadmap throughout the project. I like to update the product roadmap at least twice a year.

Your product roadmap can be as simple as sticky notes arranged on a white board — which makes updates as easy as moving a sticky note from one section of the white board to another.

You use the product roadmap to plan releases — Stage 3 in the Roadmap to Value. *Releases* are groups of usable product functionality that you release to customers to gather real-world feedback and to generate return on investment.

The following section goes through the steps to create a product roadmap in detail.

Step 1: Identifying product requirements

The first step in creating a product roadmap is to identify, or define, the different requirements for your product.

Decomposing requirements

Throughout the project, you will break those requirements down into smaller, more manageable parts using a process called *decomposition.* You can break requirements down into the following sizes, listed from largest to smallest:

✔ **Themes:** A *theme* is a logical group of features and is also a requirement at its highest level. You may group features into themes in your product roadmap.

✔ **Features:** *Features* are parts of products at a very high level. Features describe a new capability the customers will have once the feature is complete. You will use features in your product roadmap.

✔ **Epic user stories:** *Epics* are very large requirements that support a feature and contain multiple actions. You need to break down your epics before you can start creating a product requirement from them. You can find out how you will use epics for release planning in Chapter 8.

✔ **User stories:** *User stories* are requirements that contain a single action and are small enough to start implementing. You will see how you define user stories and use them at the release and sprint level in Chapter 8.

✔ **Tasks:** *Tasks* are the execution steps required to develop a requirement. You break down user stories into different tasks during sprint planning. You can find out about tasks and sprint planning in Chapter 8.

Keep in mind that each requirement may not go through all these sizes. For example, you may create a particular requirement at the user story level, and never think of it on the theme or epic scale. You may create a requirement at the epic user story level, but it may be a lower-priority requirement. Because of just-in-time planning, you may not take the time to decompose that lower priority epic user story until you complete development of all the higher-priority requirements.

When you first create your product roadmap, you likely will start with large, high-level requirements. The requirements on your product roadmap will most likely be at two different levels: *themes* and *features*. Themes are logical groups of features and requirements at their highest levels. Features are parts of the product at a very high level. Features describe a new capability the customer will have once the feature is complete.

To identify product themes and features, the product owner can work with stakeholders and the development teams. It may help to have a requirements session, where the stakeholders and the development team meet and write down as many requirements as they can think of.

When you start creating requirements at the theme and feature level, it can help to write those requirements on index cards or big sticky notes. Using a physical card that you can move from one category to another and back again can make organizing and prioritizing those requirements very easy.

While you are creating the product roadmap, the features you identify start to make up your *product backlog* — the full list of what is in scope for a product, regardless of level of detail. Once you have your first requirement, you have your product backlog started.

Step 2: Arranging product features

After you identify your product requirements features, you work with the development team to group the requirements into *themes* — common, logical groups of requirements. A stakeholder meeting works well for grouping requirements, just like it works for creating requirements. You can group features by usage flow, technical similarity, or business need.

Here are questions to consider when grouping your requirements:

✔ How would customers use our product?

✔ If we offered this requirement, what else would customers need to do? What else might they want to do?

✔ Can the development team identify technical affinities or dependencies?

Use the answers to these questions to identify your themes. Then group the features by these themes. For example, in the mobile banking application, the themes might be

✔ Account information

✔ Transactions

✔ Customer service functions

✔ Mobile functions

Figure 7-6 shows features grouped by themes.

If you are using sticky notes, you can group your features on a white board, like the example in Figure 7-7.

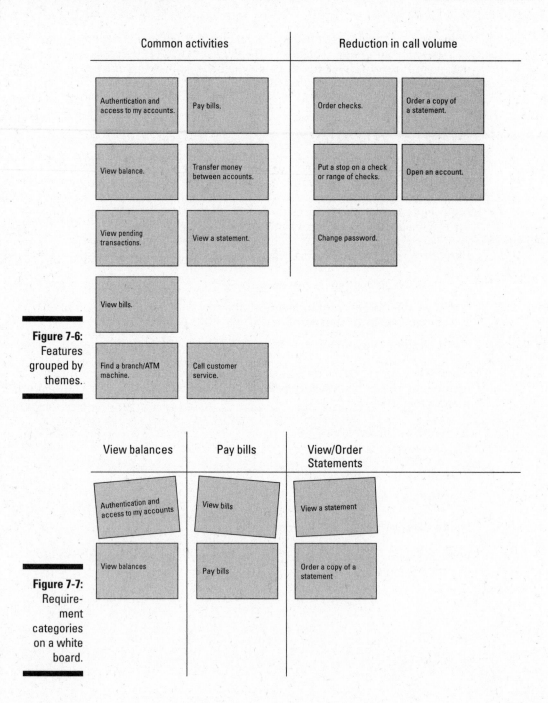

Figure 7-6:
Features
grouped by
themes.

Figure 7-7:
Require-
ment
categories
on a white
board.

Step 3: Estimating and ordering the product's features

You have identified your product requirements and arranged those requirements into logical groups. Next, you estimate and order the requirements. Here are a few terms you need to be familiar with:

- ✔ *Effort* is the ease or difficulty of creating a particular requirement.

- ✔ An *estimate,* as a noun, can be the number or description you use to express the estimated effort of a requirement.

- ✔ *Estimating* a requirement, as a verb, means to come up with an approximate idea of how easy or hard that requirement will be to create.

- ✔ *Ordering,* or *prioritizing,* a requirement means to determine that requirement's value in relation to other requirements.

- ✔ *Value* means just how beneficial a particular product requirement might be to the organization creating that product.

You can use the estimating and prioritizing techniques in this section for requirements at any level, from themes and features down to single user stories.

Scoring requirement value and effort

To order requirements, you must first estimate a score to represent the value and effort for each requirement. To order your requirements, you also want to know any dependencies. Dependencies mean that one requirement is a predecessor for another requirement. For example, if you were to have an application that needs someone to log in with a username and password, the requirement for creating the username would be a dependency for the requirement for creating the password, because you generally need a username to set up a password.

Estimating, or scoring, requirements on value and effort is a key first step to ordering those requirements.

You work with two different groups to score your requirements:

- ✔ The product owner, with support from the stakeholders, determines the value of the requirement to the customer and the business.

- ✔ The development team determines the effort to create the requirement for each requirement.

Scrum teams often use the Fibonacci sizing sequence for creating requirement scores. The Fibonacci sequence goes in a progression like this:

1, 2, 3, 5, 8, 13, 21, 34, 55, 89, 144, and so on

Each number after the first two is the sum of the prior two numbers.

The Fibonacci sequence is named after Leonardo Fibonacci, an Italian mathematician who described the sequence in his book *Liber Abaci* back in 1202!

When you are creating your product roadmap, your requirements will be on the feature scale. Most of them will have effort scores from 55 to 144. Later, when you plan releases, you break your features down to epic user stories with scores of no larger than 13 to 34. And after you start planning in sprints, your user stories should have effort scores of 1 to 8.

The concept of breaking down requirements into smaller pieces is called *decomposition*.

Use your scores relatively. Choose a requirement that the project team can agree has a small value and effort, score it, and use that requirement as a benchmark. To score other requirements, decide whether other requirements have more or less value than your benchmark requirement, and whether they are easier or harder than your benchmark requirement.

You might use two benchmark requirements, one for value and one for effort. In the end, the relative score, not the absolute score, matters. Next up is a formula for calculating relative priority.

Calculating relative priority

After you have your value and effort scores for your requirements, you can calculate the relative priority of each requirement. Relative priority helps you understand how one requirement relates to another in terms of value. Once you know the relative priority of your requirements, you can order them on your product roadmap.

Calculate relative priority with the following formula:

Relative priority = value/effort

For example, if you have a requirement with a value of 89 and an effort of 55, the relative priority would be 1.62 (89/55 = 1.62), which you could round to 2.

Using this formula

✔ A requirement with high value and low effort will have a high relative priority. For example, if the value is 144 and the effort is 3, the relative priority is 48.

✔ A requirement with a low value and high effort will have a lower relative priority. For example, if the value is 2 and the effort is 89, the relative priority is 0.0224.

✔ This formula usually produces fractional results. If you want, you can round those to the nearest whole number.

Relative priority is only a tool to help the product owner make decisions and prioritize requirements. It isn't a mathematical universal that you must follow. Make sure your tools help, rather than hinder.

Note the relative priority for each requirement. From here, you can review your requirements simultaneously and prioritize them.

Prioritizing requirements

To determine the overall priority for your requirements, answer the following questions:

✔ What is the relative priority of the requirement?

✔ What are the prerequisites for any requirement?

✔ What set of requirements belong together and will constitute a solid release?

Using the answers to these questions, you will be able to place the highest-priority requirements first in the product roadmap. When you have finished prioritizing your requirements, you will have something that looks like Figure 7-8.

Figure 7-8:
Product
roadmap
with
prioritized
require-
ments.

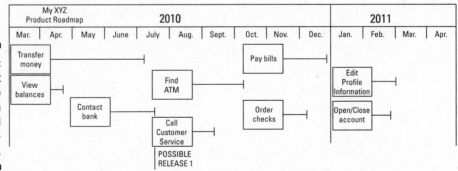

Your prioritized list of user stories is called a *product backlog*. Your product backlog is an important agile document, or in agile terms, an *artifact*. You will use this backlog throughout your entire project.

With a product backlog in hand, you can start adding target releases to your product roadmap.

Step 4: Determining high-level time frames

When you first create your product roadmap, your time frames for releasing product requirements will be at a very high level. For the initial roadmap, choose a logical time increment for your project, such as a certain number of days, weeks, months, quarters (three-month periods), or even larger increments. Using both the requirement the priority, you can add requirements to each increment of time.

Creating a product roadmap might seem like a lot of work, but after you get the hang of it, you can create one in a short time. Some scrum teams can create a product vision, product roadmap, and release plan, and be ready to start their sprint in as little as one day! To begin coding the product, you need only enough requirements for your first sprint. You can determine the rest as the project progresses.

Saving your work

Up until now, you could do all your roadmap planning with white boards and sticky notes. After your first full draft is complete, however, save the product roadmap, especially if you need to share the roadmap with remote stakeholders or development team members. You could take a photo of your sticky notes and white board, or you could type the information into a document and save it electronically.

You will update the product roadmap throughout the project, as priorities change. For now, the contents of the first release should be clear — and that's all you need to worry about at this stage.

Chapter 8

Planning Releases and Sprints

In This Chapter

▶ Decomposing requirements and creating user stories

▶ Creating a product backlog, release plan, and sprint backlog

▶ Planning agile sprints

*A*fter you create a product roadmap for your agile project (see Chapter 7), it's time to start elaborating on your product details. In this chapter, you discover how to break down your requirements to a more granular level, refine your product backlog, create a release plan, and build a sprint backlog. First, you will see how to break down the larger requirements from your product roadmap into smaller, more manageable requirements called *user stories*.

The concept of breaking down requirements into smaller pieces is called *decomposition*.

Refining Requirements and Estimates

You start agile projects with very large requirements. As the project progresses and you get closer to developing those requirements, you will break them down into smaller parts.

One clear, effective format for defining product requirements is the user story. The user story and its larger cousin, the epic user story, are good-sized requirements for release planning and sprint planning. In this section, you find out how to create a user story, how to prioritize user stories, and how to estimate user story effort.

What is a user story?

The *user story* is a simple description of a product requirement in terms of what that requirement must accomplish for whom. Your user story will have, at a minimum, the following parts:

- **Title:** *<a name for the user story>*
- **As a** *<user or persona>*
- **I want to** *<take this action>*
- **so that** *<I get this benefit>*

It will also include the following validation steps; steps to take to know that the working requirement for the user story is correct:

- **When I** *<take this action>*, **this happens** *<description of action>*

User stories may also include the following:

- **A user story ID:** A number to differentiate this user story from other user stories.
- **The user story value and effort estimate:** *Value* is how beneficial a user story might be to the organization creating that product. *Effort* is the ease or difficulty in creating that user story. You find out how to score user story value and effort later in this chapter.
- **The name of the person who thought of the user story:** Anyone on the project team can create a user story.

Agile techniques encourage low-tech tools, so try using index cards or sticky notes for your user stories. Even if you eventually want to use an electronic tool, it is a good idea to become familiar with the process of creating user stories first. Once you know how to create user stories, then consider taking on the overhead of complex electronic tools.

Agile project management approaches encourage low-tech tools, but agile approaches also encourage scrum teams to find out what works best for each team in each situation. There are a lot of electronic user story tools out there. Some cost money; some are free. Some are simple, and are just for user stories. Others are complex and will integrate with your other product documents. Personally, I love index cards, but that solution may not be for everyone. Use what works best for your scrum team and for your project.

Figure 8-1 shows a typical user story card, back and front. The front has the main description of the user story. The back shows how you will confirm that the requirement works correctly, after the development team has created the requirement.

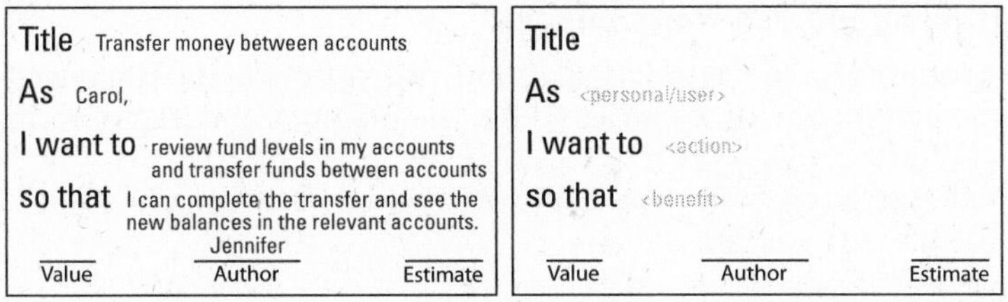

Title	Transfer money between accounts	Title	
As Carol,		As <personal/user>	
I want to review fund levels in my accounts and transfer funds between accounts		I want to <action>	
so that I can complete the transfer and see the new balances in the relevant accounts. Jennifer		so that <benefit>	
Value Author Estimate		Value Author Estimate	

Figure 8-1: Card-based user story example.

The product owner gathers and manages the user stories. However, the development team and other stakeholders also will be involved in creating and decomposing user stories.

TIP

It's important to note that user stories aren't the only way to describe product requirements. You could simply make a list of requirements without any given structure. However, because user stories include a lot of useful information in a simple, compact format, I find them to be very effective at conveying exactly what a requirement needs to do.

The big benefit of the user story format is when the development team starts to create and test requirements. The development team members know exactly whom they are creating the requirement for, what the requirement should do, and how to double-check that the requirement satisfies the intention of the requirement.

I use user stories as examples of requirements throughout this chapter and throughout the book. Keep in mind that anything I describe that you can do with user stories, you can do with more generically expressed requirements.

Steps to create a user story

When creating a user story, follow these steps:

1. **Identify the project stakeholders.**

2. **Identify who will use the product.**

3. **Working with the stakeholders, write down the requirements that the product will need and use the format I describe earlier in this chapter to create your user stories.**

Find out how to follow these three steps in the following sections.

REMEMBER

Agile is iterative. Don't spend a ton of time trying to identify every single requirement your product might have. You can always add requirements later in the project. The best changes often come at the end of a project, when you know the most about the product and the customers.

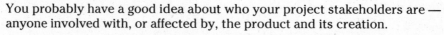

Identifying project stakeholders

You probably have a good idea about who your project stakeholders are — anyone involved with, or affected by, the product and its creation.

You will also work with stakeholders when you create your product vision and your product roadmap.

Make sure the stakeholders are available to help you create requirements. Stakeholders might include

- ✔ People who interact with customers on a regular basis, such as customer service representatives or bank branch personnel.

- ✔ Business experts for the different areas where your product's customers interact. For example, XYZ Bank, the sample company I tell you about in Chapter 7, might have one manager in charge of checking accounts, another manager in charge of savings accounts, and a third manager in charge of online bill payment services. If you're creating a mobile banking application, all these people would be project stakeholders.

- ✔ Users of your product, if they are available.

- ✔ Experts on the type of product you are creating. For example, a developer who has created mobile applications, a marketing manager who knows how to create mobile campaigns, and a user experience specialist who specializes in mobile interfaces all might be helpful on the sample XYZ Bank mobile banking project.

- ✔ Technical stakeholders, people who work with the systems that might need to interact with your product.

Identifying customers

When thinking about the customers who will use your product, it's often helpful to assign them personas, such as a salesperson or a customer service representative.

Development teams of all types often create personas, character descriptions of people who are likely to use a product. Think of a *persona* as a character in a book or a movie. You can give a persona its own background: a name, age, gender, job, likes, dislikes, and needs. Using personas can help you understand exactly what your product may need to do.

You can also think of personas in terms of specific representatives of those roles, such as someone in a particular demographic or a type of user. An example is a 30-something female marketing director who travels a lot on business.

Keep the customer you described in your product vision statement in mind when creating personas. You can find out more about the vision statement in Chapter 7.

Suppose that you are the product owner for the XYZ Bank's mobile banking project described previously. You are responsible for the department that will bring the product to market, preferably in the next six months. You have the following ideas about the application's users:

- ✔ The customers (the end users of the application) probably want quick access to up-to-date information about their balances and recent transactions.

- ✔ Maybe the customers are about to buy a large-ticket item, and they want to make sure they can charge it.

- ✔ Maybe the customers' ATM cards were just refused, but they have no idea why, and they want to check recent transactions for possible fraudulent activities.

- ✔ Maybe the customers just realized that they forgot to pay their credit card bill and will have penalty charges if they don't pay the card today.

Who are your personas for this application? Here are a few examples:

- ✔ **Persona #1:** Jason is a young, tech-savvy executive who travels a lot. When he has a spare moment, he wants to handle personal business quickly. He carefully invests his money in high-interest portfolios. He keeps his available cash low.

- ✔ **Persona #2:** Carol is a small-business owner who stages properties when clients are trying to sell their home. She shops at consignment centers and sees a couch she wants to buy for a client.

- ✔ **Persona #3:** Nick is a student who lives on student loans and a part-time job. He knows he can be flaky with money because he's flaky with everything else. He just lost his checkbook.

Your product stakeholders can help you create personas. Find people who are experts on the day-to-day business for your product. Those stakeholders will know a lot about your potential customers.

Determining product requirements and creating user stories

After you have identified your different customers, you can start to determine product requirements and create user stories for the personas. A good way to create user stories is to bring your stakeholders together for a user story creation session.

Have the stakeholders write down as many requirements as they can think of, using the user story format. One user story for the project and personas from the preceding sections might be

✔ Front side of card:

  • **Title:** See bank account balance.

  • **As a** busy, tech-savvy, on-the-go customer of XYZ Bank (Jason)

  • **I want to** see my checking account balance on my smartphone

  • **so that** I can see how much money I have in my checking account

✔ Back side of card:

  • **When I** sign into the XYZ Bank mobile application, my checking account balance appears at the top of the page.

  • **When I** sign into the XYZ Bank mobile application after making a purchase or a deposit, my checking account balance reflects that purchase or deposit.

You can see sample user stories in card format in Figure 8-2.

Title	Transfer money between accounts

| As | Carol, |

| I want to | transfer funds between accounts |

| so that | I can complete the transfer and see the new balances in the relevant accounts. |

Jennifer

| Value | Author | Estimate |

| Title | Put a stop on a check |

| As | Nick, |

| I want to | enter a check number to put a stop on a lost or stolen check |

| so that | I can see a confirmation that the check has been stopped. |

Caroline

| Value | Author | Estimate |

Figure 8-2: Sample user stories.

REMEMBER

Be sure to continuously add new user stories to your product backlog. Keeping your product backlog up-to-date will help you have the highest priority user stories when it is time to plan your sprint.

Throughout an agile project, you will create new user stories. You will also take existing large requirements and decompose them until they are manageable enough to work on during a sprint.

Breaking down requirements

You will refine requirements many times throughout an agile project. For example:

- When you create the product roadmap (see Chapter 7), you create features, a capability your customers will have after you develop the feature that they don't have prior, as well as themes, which are logical groups of features. Although features are intentionally large, at Platinum Edge, we require features at the product roadmap level to be no larger than 144 story points.

- When you plan releases, you break down the features into more concise user stories. User stories at the release plan level can be either *epics*, very large user stories with multiple actions, or individual user stories that will contain a single action. For our clients, user stories at the release plan level should be no larger than 34 story points. You find out more about releases later in this chapter.

- When you plan sprints, you can break down user stories even further. You also identify individual tasks associated with each user story in the sprint. For our clients, user stories at the sprint level should be no larger than eight story points.

A story point is a relative score to represent the value and effort for each requirement. Scrum teams often use numbers in the Fibonacci sequence — where each number after the first two is the sum of the prior two numbers — for their story points. You can find out more about story points and the Fibonacci sequence in Chapter 7.

To decompose requirements, you will want to think about how to break the requirement down into individual actions. Table 8-1 shows a requirement decomposed from the theme level down to the user story level.

Table 8-1	Decomposing a Requirement
Requirement Level	*Requirement*
Theme	See account data with a mobile application.
Features	See account balances.
	See a list of recent withdrawals or purchases.
	See a list of recent deposits.
	See my upcoming automatic bill payments.
	See my account alerts.

(continued)

Table 8-1 *(continued)*

Requirement Level	Requirement
Epic User Stories — decomposed from "see account balances"	See checking account balance.
	See savings account balance.
	See investment account balance.
	See retirement account balance.
User Stories — decomposed from "see checking account balance"	Log into mobile account.
	Securely log into mobile account.
	See a list of my accounts.
	Select and view my checking account.
	See account balance changes after withdrawals.
	See account balance changes after purchases.
	See day's end account balance.
	See available account balance.
	See mobile application navigation items.
	Change account view.
	Log out of mobile application.

Estimation poker

As you refine your requirements, you need to refine your estimates as well. It's time to have some fun!

One of the most popular ways of estimating user stories is by playing *estimation poker,* sometimes called Planning Poker, a game to determine user story size and to build consensus with the development team members.

The scrum master can help coordinate estimation, and the product owner can provide information about features, but the development team is responsible for estimating the level of effort required for the user stories. After all, the development team has to do the work to create the features that those stories describe.

User stories and the INVEST approach

You may be asking, just how decomposed does a user story have to be? Bill Wake, in his blog at XP123.com describes the INVEST approach to ensure quality in user stories. I like his method so much I include it here.

Using the INVEST approach, user stories should be

✔ **I**ndependent: To the extent possible, a story should need no other stories to implement the feature that the story describes.

✔ **N**egotiable: Not overly detailed. There is room for discussion and expansion of details.

✔ **V**aluable: The story demonstrates product value to the customer. The story describes features, not a single-thread start-to-finish user task. The story is in the user's language and is easy to explain. The people using the product or system can understand the story.

✔ **E**stimable: The story is descriptive, accurate, and concise, so the developers can generally estimate the work necessary to create the functionality in the user story.

✔ **S**mall: It is easier to plan and accurately estimate small user stories. A good rule of thumb is that a user story should not take one person on the development team longer than half of a sprint to complete.

✔ **T**estable: You can easily validate the user story, and the results are definitive.

To play estimation poker, you need a deck of cards like the one in Figure 8-3. You can get them online at my website (www.platinumedge.com/estimationpoker), or you can make your own with index cards and markers. The numbers on the cards are from the Fibonacci sequence.

Figure 8-3:
A deck of estimation poker cards.

Only the development team plays estimation poker. The scrum master and product owner don't get a deck and don't provide estimates. However, the scrum master can act as a facilitator, and the product owner will read the user stories and provide details on user stories as needed.

To play estimation poker, follow these steps:

1. **Provide each member of the development team with a deck of estimation poker cards.**

2. **Starting with a simple user story, the players decide on an estimate — as a story point — that they can all agree on for that user story.**

   This user story becomes the baseline story.

3. **The product owner reads a high-priority user story to the players.**

4. **Each player selects a card representing his or her estimate of the effort involved in the user story and lays the card face-down on the table.**

   The players should compare the user story to other user stories they have estimated. (The first time through, the players compare the user story only to the baseline story.) Make sure no other players can see your card.

5. **Once each development team member selects a card, all players turn over their cards simultaneously.**

6. **If the players have different story points:**

   a. It's time for discussion.

      The players with the highest and lowest scores talk about their assumptions and why they think the estimate for the user story should be higher or lower, respectively. The players compare the effort for the user story against the baseline story. The product owner provides more information about the story, as necessary.

   b. Once everyone agrees on assumptions and has any necessary clarifications, the players reevaluate their estimates and place their new selected cards on the table.

   c. If the story points are different, the players repeat the process, usually up to three times.

   d. If the players can't agree on the estimated effort, the scrum master helps the development team determine a score that all the players can support or determine that the user story requires more detail or needs to be further broken down.

7. **The players repeat Steps 3 through 6 for each user story.**

Consider each part of the definition of *done* — developed, integrated, tested, and documented — when you create estimates.

You can play estimation poker at any point — but definitely play during product roadmap development and as you progressively break down user stories for inclusion in releases and sprints. With practice, the development team gets into a planning rhythm and becomes more adept at quickly estimating.

On the average, development teams will spend about ten percent of their time on a project estimating and re-estimating. Make your estimation poker games fun! Bring in snacks, use humor, and keep the mood light to help speed the task of estimating.

Affinity estimating

Estimation poker can be effective, but what if you have many user stories? Playing estimation poker for, say, 500 user stories could take a long time. You need a way to focus only on the user stories you need to discuss to gain consensus.

When you have a large number of user stories, many of them are probably similar and would require a similar amount of effort to complete. One way to determine the right stories for discussion is to use affinity estimating. In *affinity estimating,* you quickly categorize your user stories and then apply estimates to these categories of stories.

When estimating by affinity, write your user stories on index cards or sticky notes. These types of user story cards work well when quickly categorizing stories.

Affinity estimating can be a fast and furious activity — the development team may choose to have the scrum master help facilitate affinity estimating sessions. To estimate by affinity, follow these steps:

1. **Taking no more than one minute for each category, the development team agrees on a single user story in each of the following categories:**

   a. Extra-small user story

   b. Small user story

   c. Medium user story

   d. Large user story

   e. Extra-large user story

   f. Epic user story that is too large to come into the sprint

   The sizes are like T-shirt sizes and should correspond to Fibonacci scale numbers, as shown in Figure 8-4. You can find out about Fibonacci scale numbers in Chapter 7.

2. **Taking no more than 30 seconds per user story, the development team puts all remaining stories into the categories listed in Step 1.**

   If you're using index cards or sticky notes for your user stories, you can physically place those cards into categories on a table or a whiteboard, respectively. If you split the user stories among the development team members, having each development team member categorize a group of stories, this step can go quickly!

SIZE	POINTS
XtraSmall (XS)	1 pt
Small (S)	2 pts
Medium (M)	3 pts
Large (L)	5 pts
XtraLarge (XL)	8 pts

Figure 8-4:
Story sizes
as T-shirt
sizes
and their
Fibonacci
numbers.

3. **Taking another 60 minutes, maximum, for each 100 stories, the development team reviews and adjusts the placement of the user stories.**

   The entire development team must agree on the placement of the user stories into size categories.

4. **The product owner reviews the categorization.**

5. **When the product owner's expected estimate and the team's actual estimate differ by more than one story size, they discuss that user story.**

   The development team may or may not decide to adjust the story size.

Note that after the product owner and the team discuss clarifications, the team has final say on the user story size.

User stories in the same size category will have the same user story score. You can play a round of estimation poker to double-check a few, but you won't need to waste time in unnecessary discussion for every single user story.

You can use the estimating and prioritizing techniques in this chapter for requirements at any level, from themes and features down to single user stories.

Release Planning

A *release,* in agile terms, is a group of usable product features that you release to production. A release does not need to include all the functionality outlined in the roadmap but should include at least the *minimal marketable features,* the smallest group of product features that you can effectively deploy and promote in the marketplace. Your early releases will exclude many of the medium- and low-priority requirements you created during the product roadmap stage.

When planning a release, you establish the next set of minimal marketable features and identify an imminent product launch date around which the team can mobilize. As when creating the vision statement and the product roadmap, the product owner is responsible for creating the release goal and establishing the release date. However, the development team, with the scrum master's facilitation, contributes to the process.

Release planning is Stage 3 in the Roadmap to Value (refer to Figure 7-1 in Chapter 7 to see the roadmap as a whole). Figure 8-5 shows how release planning fits into an agile project.

Figure 8-5:
Release
planning as
part of the
Roadmap to
Value.

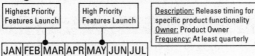

Stage 3: RELEASE PLANNING

Highest Priority Features Launch	High Priority Features Launch	Description: Release timing for specific product functionality
		Owner: Product Owner
		Frequency: At least quarterly

| JAN | FEB | MAR | APR | MAY | JUN | JUL |

(Stages 1-3 are best practices outside of core Scrum)

Release planning involves completing two key activities:

- ✔ **Revising the product backlog:** In Chapter 7, I told you that the product backlog is a comprehensive list of all the user stories you currently know for your project, whether or not they belong in the current release. Keep in mind that your list of user stories will probably change throughout the project.

- ✔ **Release plan:** The release goal, release target date, and prioritization of product backlog items that support the release goal. The release plan provides a midrange goal that the team can accomplish.

Don't create a new, separate backlog during release planning. The task is unnecessary and reduces the product owner's flexibility. Prioritizing the existing product backlog based on the release goal is sufficient and enables the product owner to have the latest information when he or she commits to scope during sprint planning.

The product backlog and release plan are some of the most important communication channels between the product owner and the team. The following sections describe how to complete a product backlog and a release plan.

Completing the product backlog

As Chapter 7 explains, the product roadmap contains themes, epic user stories, and some tentative release timelines. The requirements on your product roadmap are the first version of your *product backlog*.

The product backlog is the list of all user stories associated with the project. The product owner is responsible for creating and maintaining the product backlog by adding and prioritizing user stories. The scrum team uses the backlog during release planning and throughout the project.

Figure 8-6 shows a sample product backlog. At a minimum, when creating your product backlog, be sure to

✔ Include a description of your requirement.

✔ Order the user stories based on priority. You can find out how to determine priority in Chapter 7.

✔ Add the effort estimate.

ID	Story	Type	Status	Value
121	As an Administrator, I want to link accounts to profiles, so that customers can access new accounts.	Feature	Not started	5
113	As a Customer, I want to view my account balances, so that I know how much money is currently in each account.	Feature	Not started	3
403	As a Customer, I want to transfer money between my active accounts, so that I can adjust each account's balance.	Feature	Not started	1
97	As a Site Visitor, I want to contact the bank, so that I can ask questions and raise issues.	Feature	Not started	2
68	As a Site Visitor, I want to find locations, so that I can use bank services.	Feature	Not started	8

Figure 8-6: Product backlog sample.

In Chapter 2, I explain how documents for agile projects should be barely sufficient, with only information that is absolutely necessary to create the product. Keep your product backlog format simple and barely sufficient, and you will save time on updating it throughout the project.

The scrum team refers to the product backlog as the main source for project requirements. If a requirement exists, it is in the product backlog. The user stories in your product backlog will change throughout the project in several ways. For example, as the team completes user stories, you mark those stories as complete within the backlog. You also record any new user stories. Additionally, you update the priority and effort scores of existing user stories as needed.

The total number of story points in the product backlog — all user story points added together — is your current *product backlog estimate.* This estimate changes daily as user stories are completed and new user stories are added. Discover more about using the product backlog estimate to predict the project length and cost in Chapter 13.

Keep your product backlog up to date so that you always have accurate cost and schedule estimates. A current product backlog also gives you the flexibility to prioritize new product features — a key benefit of agile — against existing features.

After you have a product backlog, create your first release plan, as described next.

Creating the release plan

The release plan contains a release schedule for a specific set of features. The product owner creates a release plan at the start of each release. To create a release plan, follow these steps:

1. **Establish the release goal.**

   The release goal is an overall business goal for the product features in your release. The product owner and development team collaborate to create a release goal based on business priorities, the development team's development speed, and the development team's capabilities.

2. **Review the product backlog and the product roadmap to determine the highest-priority user stories that support your release goal.**

   These user stories will make up your first release. I like to have my releases be achieved with about 80 percent of the user stories, using the final 20 percent to add robust features that will meet the release goal while adding to the product's "wow" factor.

3. **Determine a date for the release.**

   The release date is typically at least three sprints out, but the actual date depends on your specific project. Some scrum teams determine release dates based on completion of functionality; others may have hard dates, like March 31 or September 1.

   Some project teams add a *release sprint* to each release in order to conduct activities that are not related to product development, but still necessary to release the product to customers. If you need a release sprint, be sure to factor that into the date you choose. You can find more about release sprints in Chapter 11.

4. **If you haven't done so already, refine the user stories in your release goal.**

   Consult the development team when updating estimates for your revised user stories.

5. **Get the development team's buy-in and commitment for the first release.**

   Be sure you have consensus on both the release date and the release goal.

TIP

Not all agile projects use release planning. Some scrum teams release functionality for customer use with every sprint. The development team, product, organization, customers, stakeholders, and technological complexity can all help determine your approach to product releases.

The planned releases now go from a tentative plan to a more concrete goal. Figure 8-7 represents a typical release plan.

Release Goal: Enable customers to access, view, and transact against their active accounts.
Release Date: March 31, 2013

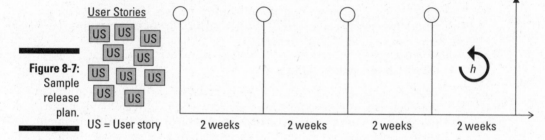

Figure 8-7:
Sample release plan.

TIP

Bear in mind the pen-pencil rule: You can commit to (write in pen) the plan for the first release, but anything beyond the first release is tentative (written in pencil). In other words, use just-in-time planning (see Chapter 7) for each release. After all, things change, so why bother getting microscopic too early?

Sprint Planning

In agile projects, a *sprint* is a consistent iteration of time in which the development team creates a specific group of product capabilities from start to finish. At the end of each sprint, the product that the development team has created should be working and ready to demonstrate.

Sprints should be the same length within a project. Keeping the sprint lengths consistent helps you measure the development team's performance and plan better at each new sprint.

Sprints generally last one, two, three, or four weeks. Four weeks is the longest amount of time any sprint should last; longer iterations make changes riskier, defeating the purpose of agile.

Each sprint includes the following:

✔ Sprint planning at the beginning of the sprint

✔ Daily scrum meetings

- ✔ Development time — the bulk of the sprint
- ✔ A sprint review and a sprint retrospective at the end of the sprint

Discover more about daily scrums, sprint development, the sprint review, and the sprint retrospective in Chapters 9 and 10. In this chapter, you find out how to plan sprints.

Sprint planning is Stage 4 on the Roadmap to Value, as you can see in Figure 8-8. The entire scrum team — the product owner, the scrum master, and the development team — works together to plan sprints.

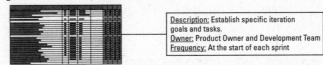

Figure 8-8:
Sprint planning as part of the Roadmap to Value.

The sprint backlog

The *sprint backlog* is a list of user stories associated with the current sprint and related tasks. When planning your sprint, you

- ✔ Establish goals for your sprint.
- ✔ Choose the user stories that support those goals.
- ✔ Break user stories into specific development tasks.
- ✔ Create a *sprint backlog*. The sprint backlog includes
  - The list of user stories within the sprint in order of priority.
  - The relative effort estimate for each user story.
  - The tasks necessary to develop each user story.
  - The effort, in hours, to complete each task.

    At the task level, you estimate the number of hours each task will take to complete, instead of using story points. Since your sprint has a specific length, and thus a set number of available working hours, you can use the time each task takes to determine whether the tasks will fit into your sprint.

    Each task should take one day or less for the development team to complete.

  - A *burndown chart,* which shows the status of the work the development team has completed.

Tasks in agile projects should take a day or less to complete for two reasons. The first reason involves basic psychology: People are motivated to get to the finish line. If you have a task that you know you can complete quickly, you are more likely to finish it on time, just to check it off your to-do list. The second reason is that one-day tasks provide good red flags that a project might be veering off course. If a development team member reports that he or she is working on the same task for more than one or two days, that team member probably has a roadblock. The scrum master should take the opportunity to investigate what might be keeping the team member from finishing work. (For more on managing roadblocks, see Chapter 9.)

The development team collaborates to create and maintain the sprint backlog, and only the development team can modify the sprint backlog. The sprint backlog should reflect an up-to-the-day snapshot of the sprint's progress. Figure 8-9 shows a sample sprint backlog. You can use this example, find other samples, or even use a white board.

The sprint planning meeting

On the first day of each sprint, often a Monday morning, the scrum team holds the sprint planning meeting.

For a successful sprint planning meeting, make sure everyone involved in the session is dedicated to the effort for the entire meeting.

Base the length of your sprint planning meeting on the length of your sprints: Meet for no more than two hours for every week of your sprints. This timebox is one of the rules of scrum. Figure 8-10 illustrates this and is a good quick reference for your meeting lengths.

On agile projects, the practice of limiting the time of your meetings is sometimes called *timeboxing*. Keeping your meetings timeboxed ensures that the development team has the time it needs to create the product.

You will split your sprint planning meetings into two parts: one to set a sprint goal and choose user stories for the sprint, and another to break down your user stories into individual tasks. The details on each part are discussed next.

Figure 8-9: Sprint backlog example.

My XYZ Mobile Banking - Sprint 1
Sprint dates: February 4 - February 15

Sprint goal
As a <mobile banking customer>,
I want to <log in to my account>
So I can <view my account balances and pending transactions>.

Burndown - Based on Est Hours Remaining

Number of working days	9
Leona (35 hrs wk)	63
Joey (35 hrs wk)	63
Bob (35 hrs wk)	63
Marie (20 hrs wk)	63
Pablo (35 hrs wk)	63
Madison (35 hrs wk)	63
Total:	**387**
Total per day:	**43**

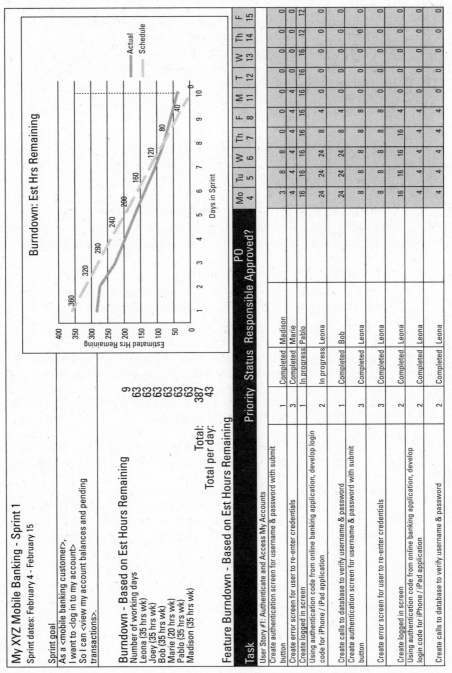

Burndown: Est Hrs Remaining — Estimated Hrs Remaining vs. Days in Sprint (Actual, Schedule)
(360, 320, 280, 240, 200, 160, 120, 80, 40, 0)

Feature Burndown - Based on Est Hours Remaining

Task	Priority	Status	Responsible	PO Approved?	Mo 4	Tu 5	W 6	Th 7	F 8	M 11	T 12	W 13	Th 14	F 15
User Story #1: Authenticate and Access My Accounts														
Create authentication screen for username & password with submit button	1	Completed	Madison		3	3	8	8	0	0	0	0	0	0
Create error screen for user to re-enter credentials	3	Completed	Marie		4	4	4	4	4	4	0	0	0	0
Create logged in screen	1	In progress	Pablo		16	16	16	16	16	16	16	16	12	12
Using authentication code from online banking application, develop login code for iPhone / iPad application	2	In progress	Leona		24	24	24	8	8	4	0	0	0	0
Create calls to database to verify username & password	1	Completed	Bob		24	24	24	8	8	8	0	0	0	0
Create authentication screen for username & password with submit button	3	Completed	Leona		8	8	8	8	8	8	0	0	0	0
Create error screen for user to re-enter credentials	3	Completed	Leona		8	8	8	8	8	8	0	0	0	0
Create logged in screen	2	Completed	Leona		16	16	16	16	16	16	0	0	0	0
Using authentication code from online banking application, develop login code for iPhone / iPad application	2	Completed	Leona		4	4	4	4	4	4	0	0	0	0
Create calls to database to verify username & password	2	Completed	Leona		4	4	4	4	4	4	0	0	0	0

If my sprint is this long...	My sprint planning meeting should last no more than...
One week	Two hours
Two weeks	Four hours
Three weeks	Six hours
Four weeks	Eight hours

Figure 8-10: Sprint planning meeting to sprint length ratio.

Part 1: Setting goals and choosing user stories

In the first part of your sprint planning meeting, the product owner and development team, with support from the scrum master, do the following:

1. Discuss and set a sprint goal.

2. Review the user stories from the product backlog that support the sprint goal and revisit their relative estimates.

3. Determine what the team can commit to in the current sprint.

At the beginning of your sprint planning meeting, the product owner and the development team should determine a goal for the sprint. The sprint goal should be an overall description supported by the highest-priority user stories in the product backlog. A sample sprint goal for the mobile banking application (refer to Chapter 7) might be

> As a mobile banking customer, I want to log in to my account so I can view my account balances and pending and prior transactions.

Using the sprint goal, you determine the user stories that belong in this sprint. You also take another look at the estimates for those stories and make changes to the estimates if you need to. For the mobile banking application sample, the group of user stories for the sprint might include

✔ Log in and access my accounts.

✔ View account balances.

✔ View pending transactions.

✔ View prior transactions

All these would be high-priority user stories that support the sprint goal.

The second part of reviewing user stories is confirming that the effort estimates for each user story look correct. Adjust the estimate if necessary. With the product owner in the meeting, resolve any outstanding questions.

Finally, once you know which user stories support the sprint goal, the development team should agree and confirm it can complete the goal planned for this sprint. If any of the user stories you discussed earlier don't fit in the current sprint, remove them from the sprint and add them back into the product backlog.

Always plan and work one sprint at a time. Don't place user stories into specific future sprints — it's an easy trap to fall into. For example, don't decide that user story X should go into sprint 3 or 4. Instead, keep the ordered list of user stories up to date in the product backlog and focus on always developing the remaining highest-priority stories. Commit only to planning for the current sprint.

Once you have a sprint goal, user stories for the sprint, and commitment to the goal, move on to the second part of sprint planning. Because your sprint planning meeting may last a few hours, you might want to take a break between the two parts of the meeting.

Part 2: Creating tasks for the sprint backlog

In the second part of the sprint planning meeting, the scrum team does the following:

1. Create the sprint backlog tasks associated with each user story. Make sure that there are tasks encompassing each part of the definition of done: developed, integrated, tested, and documented.

2. Double-check that the team can complete the tasks in the time available in the sprint.

3. Each development team member should choose his or her first task to accomplish.

Development team members should work on only one task on one user story at a time to enable *swarming* — the practice of having the whole development team work on one requirement until completion. Swarming can be a very efficient way to complete work in a short amount of time.

At the beginning of part two of the meeting, break the user stories into individual tasks and allocate a number of hours to each task. The development team should target being able to complete a task in a day or less. For example, a user story for the XYZ Bank mobile application might be

Log in and access my accounts.

The team decomposes this user story into tasks, like the following:

- Create an authentication screen for a username and password, with a Submit button.
- Create an error screen for the user to reenter credentials.

- ✔ Create a logged-in screen (includes list of accounts — to be completed in next user story).
- ✔ Using authentication code from the online banking application, rewrite code for an iPhone/iPad application.
- ✔ Create calls to the database to verify the username and password.
- ✔ Refactor code for mobile devices.

Once you know the number of hours that each task will take, do a final check to make sure that the number of hours available to the development team reasonably matches the total of the tasks' estimates. If the tasks exceed the hours available, one or more user stories will have to come out of the sprint. Discuss with the product owner what tasks or user stories are the best to remove.

If extra time is available within the sprint, the development team might be able to include another user story. Just be careful about over-committing at the beginning of a sprint, especially in the project's first few sprints.

After you know which tasks will be part of the sprint, choose what you will work on first. Each development team member should select his or her initial task to accomplish for the sprint. Team members should focus on one task at a time.

As the development team thinks about what they can complete in a sprint, use the following guidelines to ensure that they don't take on more work than they can handle:

- ✔ **Sprint 1:** 25 percent of what the team thinks it can accomplish. Include overhead for learning the new process and starting a new project.
- ✔ **Sprint 2:** 50 percent of what the team thinks it can accomplish.
- ✔ **Sprint 3:** 75 percent of what the team thinks it can accomplish.
- ✔ **Sprint 4 and forward:** 100 percent. The team will have developed a rhythm, gained insight into agile and the project, and will be working at close to full pace.

The team should constantly evaluate the sprint backlog against the development team's progress on the tasks. At the end of the sprint, the team can also assess estimation skills and capacity for work. This evaluation is especially important for the first sprint.

For the sprint, how many total working hours are available? In a 40-hour week, you could wisely assume, for a two-week sprint, that nine working days are available to develop user stories. If you assume each full-time team member has 35 hours per week (seven productive hours per day) to focus on the project, the number of working hours available is

Number of team members × 7 hours × 9 days

Why nine days? Half of day one is taken up with planning, and half of day ten is taken up with the sprint review (when the stakeholders review the completed work) and the sprint retrospective (when the team identifies improvements for future sprints). That leaves nine days of development.

After the sprint planning is finished, the development team can immediately start working on the tasks to create the product!

The scrum master should make sure the product roadmap, product backlog, and sprint backlog are all in a prominent place and accessible to everyone. This allows managers and other interested parties to view the artifacts and get status on progress without interrupting the development team.

Chapter 9

Working Through the Day

*I*t's Tuesday, 9 a.m. You completed sprint planning yesterday, and the development team started work. For the rest of the sprint, you'll be working *cyclically*, where each day follows the same pattern.

In this chapter, you find out how to use Agile Principles daily throughout each sprint. You see the work that you will do every day as part of a scrum team: planning your day, tracking progress, creating and verifying usable functionality, and identifying and dealing with impediments to your work. You see how the different scrum team members work together each day during the sprint to help create the product.

Planning the Day: The Daily Scrum

On agile projects, you make plans throughout the entire project — and on a daily basis. Agile development teams start each workday with a *daily scrum* meeting to note completed items, to identify impediments, or roadblocks, requiring scrum master involvement, and to plan their day.

The daily scrum is Stage 5 on the Roadmap to Value. You can see how the sprint and the daily scrum fit into an agile project in Figure 9-1. Note how they both repeat.

Figure 9-1:
The sprint
and the
daily scrum
in the
Roadmap to
Value.

24 hours

1 - 4 Weeks

Sprint

Stage 5: DAILY SCRUM

<u>Description:</u> To establish and coordinate priorities of the day
<u>Owner:</u> Development Team
<u>Frequency:</u> Daily

In the daily scrum meeting, each development team member makes the following three statements, which enable team coordination:

✔ Yesterday, I completed *[state items completed]*.

✔ Today, I'm going to take on *[state task]*.

✔ My impediments are *[state impediments, if any]*.

Other names you might hear for the daily scrum meeting are the *daily huddle* or the *daily standup* meeting. Daily scrum, daily huddle, and daily standup all mean the same thing.

One of the rules of scrum is that daily scrum meetings last 15 minutes or less. Meetings that last longer eat into the development team's day. You can use props to keep daily scrum meetings quick. I start meetings by tossing a squeaky burger-shaped dog toy — don't worry; it's clean — to a random development team member. Each person makes their three statements and then passes the squeaky toy to someone else. If people are long-winded, I change the prop to a 500-page ream of copy paper, which weighs about five pounds. Each person can talk for as long as he or she can hold the ream out to one side. Either meetings will quickly become shorter, or development team members will quickly build up their arm strength — in my experience, it's the former.

To keep daily scrums brief and effective, the scrum team can follow several guidelines:

✔ **Anyone may attend a daily scrum, but only the development team, the scrum master, and the product owner may talk.** Stakeholders can discuss questions with the scrum master or product owner afterward, but stakeholders should not approach the development team.

✔ **The focus is on immediate priorities.** The scrum team should review only completed tasks, tasks to be done, and roadblocks.

✔ **Daily scrum meetings are for coordination, not problem-solving.** The development team and the scrum master are responsible for removing roadblocks during the day.

✔ **To keep meetings from drifting into problem-solving sessions, scrum teams can**

- Keep a list on a white board to keep track of issues that need immediate attention, and then address those issues directly after the meeting.

- Hold a meeting, called an *after-party,* to solve problems once the daily scrum is finished. Some scrum teams schedule time for an after-party every day; others only meet as needed.

✔ **The daily scrum is for peer-to-peer coordination, rather than individuals reporting status to one person, such as the scrum master or product owner.** Status is reported at the end of each day in the sprint backlog.

✔ **With such a short meeting, you need to start on time.** It is not unusual for the scrum team to have creative punishments for tardiness (such as doing pushups or adding penalty money into a team celebration fund or another inconvenience).

✔ **The scrum team may request that daily scrum attendees stand up — rather than sit down — during the meeting.** Standing up makes people eager to finish the meeting and get on with the day's work.

When you only have 15 minutes to meet, every minute counts. Scrum teams should not be afraid to make the punishment for being late to the daily scrum appropriately unpleasant. If members of the team love to sing, for example, performing a karaoke song shouldn't be the punishment. I've helped cure perpetual tardiness problems overnight by suggesting the tardy punishment change from adding $1 to a team celebration fund to adding $20 to the fund.

Daily scrum meetings are effective for keeping the development team focused on the right tasks for any given day. Because the development team members are accountable for their work in front of their peers, they are less likely to stray from their daily commitments. Daily scrum meetings also help ensure that the scrum master and development team can deal with roadblocks immediately. These meetings are so useful that even organizations that are not using any other agile techniques sometimes adopt daily scrums.

I like to hold daily scrum meetings one hour after the development team's normal start time to allow for traffic jams, e-mails, coffee, and other rituals of starting the day. Having a later scrum meeting also allows the development team time to review bug reports from automated testing tools that ran the night before.

The daily scrum is for discussing progress and planning each upcoming day. As you see next, you also track progress — not just discuss it — every day.

Tracking Progress

You also need to track the progress of your sprint daily. This section discusses ways to keep track of the tasks within your sprint.

Two tools for tracking progress are the sprint backlog and a task board. Both the sprint backlog and the task board enable the scrum team to show the sprint's progress to anyone at any given time.

 The Agile Manifesto values individuals and interactions over processes and tools. Make sure your tools support, rather than hinder, your scrum team. Modify or even replace tools if you have to. Read more about the Agile Manifesto in Chapter 2.

The sprint backlog

Chapter 8 discusses details of the sprint backlog. During sprint planning, you concentrate on adding user stories and tasks to the backlog. During the sprint itself, you update the sprint backlog daily, tracking progress of the development team's tasks for each working day. Figure 9-2 shows the sprint backlog for this book's sample application, the XYZ Bank's mobile banking application.

Make the sprint backlog available to the entire project team every day. That way, anyone who needs to know the sprint status can find it instantly.

In the top right of Figure 9-2, note the *sprint burndown chart,* which shows the progress that the development team is making. You can include burndown charts on your sprint backlog and on your product backlog. (This chapter concentrates on the sprint backlog.) Figure 9-3 shows the burndown chart in detail.

A burndown chart is a powerful tool for visualizing progress and the work remaining. The chart shows the following:

- ✔ The outstanding work (in hours) on the first vertical axis
- ✔ Time, in days along the horizontal axis

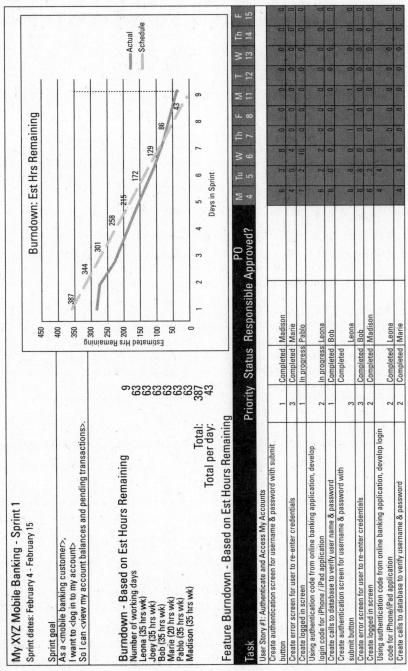

Figure 9-2: Sample sprint backlog.

My XYZ Mobile Banking - Sprint 1
Sprint dates: February 4 - February 15

Sprint goal
As a <mobile banking customer>,
I want to <log in to my account>
So I can <view my account balances and pending transactions>.

Burndown - Based on Est Hours Remaining

Number of working days	9
Leona (35 hrs wk)	63
Joey (35 hrs wk)	63
Bob (35 hrs wk)	63
Marie (20 hrs wk)	63
Pablo (35 hrs wk)	63
Madison (35 hrs wk)	63
Total:	387
Total per day:	43

Burndown: Est Hrs Remaining

Actual — Schedule

387, 344, 301, 258, 215, 172, 129, 86, 43, 9 (Estimated Hrs Remaining, Days in Sprint 1–9)

Feature Burndown - Based on Est Hours Remaining

Task	Priority	Status	Responsible	PO Approved?	M 4	Tu 5	W 6	Th 7	F 8	M 11	Tu 12	W 13	Th 14	F 15
User Story #1: Authenticate and Access My Accounts														
Create authentication screen for username & password with submit button	1	Completed	Madison		8	3	8	0	0	0	0	0	0	0
Create error screen for user to re-enter credentials	3	Completed	Marie		4	0	4	0	0	0	0	0	0	0
Create logged in screen	1	In progress	Pablo		7	2	16	0	0	0	0	0	0	0
Using authentication code from online banking application, develop login code for iPhone / iPad application	2	In progress	Leona		6	2	2	0	0	0	0	0	0	0
Create calls to database to verify user name & password	1	Completed	Bob		8	0	0	0	0	0	0	0	0	0
Create authentication screen for username & password with submit button	3	Completed	Leona		8	8	8	0	1	0	0	0	0	0
Create error screen for user to re-enter credentials	3	Completed	Bob		6	2	0	0	0	0	0	0	0	0
Create logged in screen	2	Completed	Madison		4	4		0	0	0	0	0	0	0
Using authentication code from online banking application, develop login code for iPhone/iPad application	2	Completed	Leona		4	4	4	0	0	0	0	0	0	0
Create calls to database to verify username & password	2	Completed	Marie											

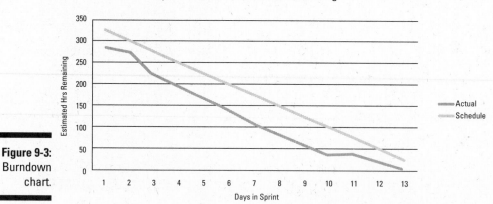

Figure 9-3:
Burndown
chart.

Some sprint burndown charts also show the outstanding story points on a second vertical axis that is plotted against the same horizontal time axis as hours of work remaining.

A burndown chart enables anyone, at a glance, to see the status of the sprint. Progress is clear. By comparing the realistic number of hours available to the actual work remaining, you can find out daily whether the effort is going as planned, is in better shape than expected, or is in trouble. That information helps you determine whether the development team is likely to accomplish the targeted number of user stories and helps you make informed decisions early in the sprint.

You can create a sprint backlog using a spreadsheet and charting program like Microsoft Excel. You can also download my sprint backlog template, which includes a burndown chart, from www.dummies.com/go/agile projectmanagementfd.

Figure 9-4 shows samples of burndown charts for sprints in different situations. Looking at these charts, you can tell how the work is progressing:

1. **Expected:** This chart shows a normal sprint pattern. The remaining work hours rise and fall as the development team completes tasks, ferrets out details, and identifies tactical work it may not have initially considered. Although work occasionally increases, it is manageable, and the team mobilizes to complete all user stories by the end of the sprint.

2. **More complicated:** In this sprint, the work increased beyond the point in which the development team felt it could accomplish everything. The team identified this issue early, worked with the product owner to remove some user stories, and still achieved the sprint goal. The key to scope changes within a sprint is that they are always initiated by the development team — no one else.

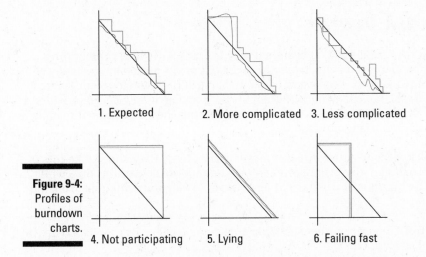

1. Expected   2. More complicated   3. Less complicated

Figure 9-4:
Profiles of
burndown
charts.

4. Not participating   5. Lying   6. Failing fast

3. **Less complicated:** In this sprint, the development team completed some critical user stories faster than anticipated and worked with the product owner to identify additional user stories it could add to the sprint.

4. **Not participating:** A straight line in a burndown means that the team didn't update the burndown or made zero progress that day. Either case is a red flag for future problems.

   Just like on a heartbeat graph, a horizontal straight line on a sprint burndown chart is never a good thing.

5. **Lying (or conforming):** This burndown pattern is common for new agile development teams that might be used to reporting the hours that management expects, instead of the time the work really takes, and consequently tend to adjust their work estimates to the exact number of remaining hours. This pattern often reflects a fear-based environment, where the managers lead by intimidation.

6. **Failing fast:** One of the strongest benefits of agile is the immediate proof of progress, or lack thereof. This pattern shows an example of a team that wasn't participating or progressing. Halfway through the sprint, the product owners cut their losses and killed the sprint. Only product owners can end a sprint early.

The sprint backlog helps you track progress throughout each sprint. You can also refer to earlier sprint backlogs to compare progress from sprint to sprint. You will make changes to your process in each sprint (read more about the concept of inspect and adapt in Chapter 7). Constantly inspect your work and adapt to make it better. Hold on to those old sprint backlogs. Find out more about inspect and adapt in Chapter 10.

Another way to keep track of your sprint is by using a task board. Read on to find out how to create and use a task board.

The task board

Although the sprint backlog is a great way to track and show project progress, it's probably in an electronic format, so it might not be immediately accessible to anyone who wants to see it. Some scrum development teams also use a task board, along with their sprint backlog. A *task board* provides a quick, easy view of the items within the sprint that the development team is working on and has completed.

I like task boards because you cannot deny the status they show. Like the product roadmap, the task board can be made up of sticky notes on a white board. The task board will have at least the following four columns, from left to right:

- **To Do:** The user stories and tasks that remain to be accomplished are in the far left column.

- **In Progress:** User stories and tasks that the development team is currently working on are in the In Progress column. Only one user story or two should be in this column. Having more user stories in progress is an alert that development team members are not working cross-functionally and, instead, are hoarding desired tasks. You risk having multiple user stories partially done instead of more user stories completely done by the end of the sprint.

- **Accept:** After the development team completes a user story, it moves it to the Accept column. User stories in the Accept column are ready for the product owner to review and either provide feedback or accept.

- **Done:** When the product owner has reviewed a user story and verifies that the user story is complete, the product owner can move that user story to this column.

Limit your work in progress! Only select one task at a time. Leave other tasks available in the To Do column. Ideally, a development team will work on only one user story at a time and swarm on that user story to complete it quickly.

Because the task board is tactile — people physically move a user story card through its completion — it can engage the development team more than an electronic document ever could. The task board encourages thought and action just by existing in the scrum team's work area, where everyone can see the board.

Allowing only the product owner to move user stories to the Done column prevents misunderstandings about user story status.

Figure 9-5 shows a typical task board. As you can see, the task board is a strong visual representation of the work in progress.

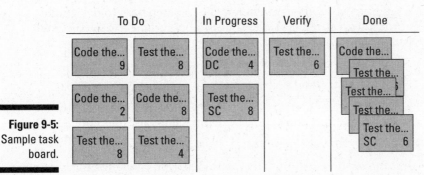

Figure 9-5:
Sample task
board.

The task board is a lot like a kanban board. *Kanban* is a Japanese term that means *visual signal.* (For more on kanban boards, see Chapter 4.) Toyota created these boards as part of its lean manufacturing process.

Day-to-day work on an agile project involves more than just planning and tracking progress. In the next section, you see what most of your day's work will include, whether you are a member of the development team, a product owner, or a scrum master.

Some development teams report status only with a task board and ask the scrum master to convert status into the sprint backlog. This process helps the scrum master see trends and potential issues.

Agile Roles Within the Sprint

Each member of a scrum team has specific daily roles and responsibilities during the sprint. The day's focus for the development team is producing shippable functionality. For the product owner, the focus is on preparing the product backlog for future sprints while supporting the development team with real-time clarifications. The scrum master is the agile coach and maximizes the development team's productivity by removing roadblocks and protecting the development team from external distractions.

Following are descriptions of the tasks each member of the scrum team performs during the sprint. If you're a member of the development team, you also perform the following tasks during the sprint.

✔ Select the tasks of highest need and complete them as quickly as possible.

✔ Request clarification from the product owner when you are unclear about a user story.

✔ Collaborate with other development team members to design the approach to a specific user story, seek help when you need it, and provide help when another development team member needs it.

✔ Conduct peer reviews on one another's work.

✔ Take on tasks beyond your normal role as the sprint demands.

✔ Fully develop functionality as agreed to in the definition of done (described in the next section, "Creating Shippable Functionality").

✔ Report daily on your progress.

✔ Alert the scrum master to any roadblocks you can't effectively remove on your own.

✔ Achieve the sprint goal you committed to during sprint planning.

The product owner has the following tasks during the sprint:

✔ Make investments required to keep development speed high.

✔ Prioritize product functionality.

✔ Represent the product stakeholders to the development team.

✔ Report on cost and schedule status to product stakeholders.

✔ Elaborate user stories with the development team so that the team clearly understands what it is creating.

✔ Provide immediate clarification and decisions about requirements to keep the development team developing.

✔ Remove business impediments brought to you by the scrum master.

✔ Review complete functionality for user stories and provide feedback to the development team.

✔ Add new user stories to the product backlog as necessary and ensure that new user stories support the product vision, the release goal, or the sprint goal.

✔ Look forward to the next sprint and elaborate user stories in readiness for the next sprint planning meeting.

 Nonverbal communication says a lot. Scrum masters can benefit from understanding body language to identify unspoken tensions within the scrum team.

If you are a scrum master, you do the following during the sprint:

✔ Uphold agile values and practices by coaching the product owner, development team, and the organization when necessary.

✔ Shield the development team from external distractions.

✔ Remove roadblocks, both tactically for immediate problems and strategically for potential long-term issues.

✔ Facilitate consensus-building within the scrum team.

✔ Build relationships to foster close cooperation with people working with the scrum team.

I often tell scrum masters, "Never lunch alone. Always be building relationships." You never know when you will need to call in a favor on a project.

As you can see, each scrum team member has a specific job within the sprint. In the next section, you see how the product owner and the development team work together to create the product.

Creating Shippable Functionality

The objective of the day-to-day work of a sprint is to create shippable functionality for the product in a form that can be delivered to a customer or user.

Within the context of a single sprint, a *product increment* or *shippable functionality* means that a work product has been developed, integrated, tested, and documented according to the project definition of done, and is deemed ready to release. The development team may or may not actually release that product at the end of the sprint — release timing depends on the release plan. The project may require multiple sprints before the product contains the set of minimum marketable features necessary to justify a market release.

It helps to think about shippable functionality in terms of user stories. A user story starts out as a written requirement on a card. As the development team creates functionality, each user story becomes an action a user can take. Shippable functionality equals completed user stories.

To create shippable functionality, the development team and the product owner are involved in three major activities:

✔ Elaborating

✔ Developing

✔ Verifying

During the sprint, any or all of these activities can be happening at any given time. As you review them in detail, remember that they don't always occur in a linear way.

Elaborating

In an agile project, *elaboration* is the process of determining the details of a product feature. Whenever the development team tackles a new user story, elaboration ensures that any unanswered questions about a user story are answered so that the process of development can proceed.

The product owner works with the development team to elaborate user stories, but the development team should have the final say on design decisions. The product owner should be available for consultation if the development team needs further clarification on requirements throughout the day.

Collaborative design is a major part of agile's success. Watch out for development team members who have a tendency to try to work alone on elaborating user stories. If a member of the development team separates himself or herself from the team, perhaps part of the scrum master's job should be coaching that person on upholding agile values and practices.

Developing

During product development, most of the activity, naturally, falls to the development team. The product owner continues to work with the development team on an as-needed basis to provide clarification and to approve developed functionality. The scrum master should focus on protecting the development team from outside disruptions and removing impediments that the development team encounters.

To sustain agile practices during development, be sure to

- **Pair up development team members to complete tasks.** Doing so enhances the quality of the work and encourages the sharing of skills.

- **Follow the development team's agreed-upon design standards.** If you can't, revisit these standards and improve them.

- **Start development by setting up automated tests.** You can find more about automated testing in the following section and in Chapter 15.

- **If new, nice-to-have features become apparent during development, add them to the product backlog.** Avoid coding new features that are outside the sprint goal.

- **Integrate changes that were coded during the day, one set at a time.** Test for 100 percent correctness. Integrate changes at least once a day; some teams integrate several times a day.

✔ **Undertake code reviews to ensure that the code follows development standards.** Identify areas that need revising. Add the revisions as tasks in the sprint backlog.

✔ **Create technical documentation as you work.** Don't wait until the end of the sprint or, worse still, the end of the sprint prior to a release.

Continuous integration is the term used in software development for integrating and comprehensively testing with every code build. Continuous integration helps identify problems before they become crises.

Verifying

Verifying the work done in a sprint has three parts: automated testing, peer review, and product owner review.

Automated testing

Automated testing means using a computer program to do the majority of your code testing for you. With automated testing, the development team can quickly develop and test code, which is a big benefit for agile projects.

Often, agile project teams code during the day and let the tests run overnight. In the morning, the project team can review the bug report that the testing program generated, report on any problems during the daily scrum, and correct those issues immediately during the day.

Automated testing can include

✔ **Unit testing:** Testing source code in its smallest parts — the component level.

✔ **System testing:** Testing the code with the rest of the system.

✔ **Static testing:** Static testing verifies that the product's code meets standards based on rules and best practices that the development team has agreed upon.

Peer review

Peer review simply means that development team members review one another's code. If Sam writes program A and Joan writes program B, Sam could review Joan's code, and vice versa. Objective peer review helps ensure code quality.

The development team can conduct peer reviews during development. Collocation helps make this easy — you can turn to the person next to you and ask him or her to take a quick look at what you just completed. The development team can also set aside time during the day specifically for reviewing code. Self-managing teams should decide what works best for their specific team.

Product owner review

When a user story has been developed and tested, the development team moves the stories to the Accept column on the task board. The product owner then reviews the functionality and verifies that it meets the goals of the user story, per the user story's acceptance criteria. The product owner verifies user stories throughout each day.

As discussed in Chapter 8, the back side of each user story card has verification steps. These steps allow the product owner to review and confirm that the code works and supports the user story. Figure 9-6 shows a sample user story card's verification steps.

When I do this:	This happens:
When I go to the accounts page	I am able to see my active account balance.
When I select transfer funds	I am able to select "Transfer to Account" and amount.
When I submit transfer requests	I get an account confirmation funds were transferred.

Figure 9-6:
User story
verification.

Finally, the product owner should run through some checks to verify that the user story in question meets the definition of done. When a user story meets the definition of done, the product owner updates the task board by moving the user story from the Accept column to the Done column.

While the product owner and the development team are working together to create shippable functionality for the product, the scrum master helps the scrum team to identify and clear roadblocks that appear along the way.

Identifying roadblocks

It's a major part of the scrum master's role to manage and help resolve roadblocks that the team identifies. Roadblocks are anything that thwarts a team member from working to full capacity.

While the daily scrum is the best place for the development team to identify roadblocks, the development team may come to the scrum master with issues throughout the day.

Examples of roadblocks could be

✔ Local, tactical issues like

- A manager trying to pull away a team member to work on a "priority" sales report.

- The development team needs additional hardware or software to facilitate progress.

- A development team member doesn't understand a user story and says the product owner isn't available to help.

✔ Organizational impediments, such as

- An overall resistance to agile techniques, especially when the company established and maintained prior processes at significant cost.

- Managers might not be in touch with the work on the ground. Technologies, development practices, and project management practices are always progressing.

- External departments may not be familiar with scrum needs and pace of development when using agile techniques.

- The organization can enforce policies that don't make sense for agile project teams. Centralized tools, budget restrictions, and standardized processes that don't align with agile processes can all cause issues for agile teams.

The most important trait a scrum master can have is organizational clout. Organizational clout gives the scrum master the ability to have difficult conversations and make the small and large changes necessary for the scrum team to be successful.

Beyond the primary focus of creating shippable functionality, other things happen during the day on an agile project. Many of these tasks fall to the scrum master.

Table 9-1 shows potential roadblocks and the action that the scrum master can take to remove the impediments.

Table 9-1	Common Roadblocks and Solutions
Roadblock	*Action*
The development team needs simulation software for a range of mobile devices so that it can test the user interface and code.	Do some research to estimate the cost of the software, prepare a summary of that for the product owner, and have a discussion about funding. Process the purchase through procurement, and deliver the software to the development team.
Management wants to borrow a development team member to write a couple of reports. All your development team members are fully occupied.	Tell the requesting manager that person is not available, and is not likely to be for the duration of the project. As you're likely a problem solver, you may want to suggest alternative ways in which the manager could get what he or she needs. You may also have to justify why you cannot pull the person off the project, even for half a day.
A development team member cannot move forward on a user story because he or she does not fully understand the story. The product owner is out of the office for the day on a personal emergency.	Work with the development team member to determine if any work can happen around this user story while waiting on an answer. Help locate another person who could answer the question. Failing that, ask the development team to review upcoming tasks (not related to this stopped one) and move things around to keep productivity up.
A user story has grown in complexity and now appears to be too large for the sprint length.	Have the development team work with the product owner to break the user story down so that some demonstrable value can be completed in the current sprint and the rest can be put back into the product backlog. The goal is to ensure this sprint ends with completion, even if that is a smaller user story, rather than an incomplete user story.

So far in this chapter, you have seen how the scrum team starts its day and works throughout the day. The scrum team wraps up each day with a few tasks as well. The next section shows you how to end a day within a sprint.

The End of the Day

At the end of each day, the development team reports on task progress by updating the sprint backlog with which tasks were completed and how much work, in hours, remains to be done on new tasks started. Depending on the software the scrum team uses, the sprint backlog could automatically update the sprint burndown chart as well.

Update the sprint backlog with the amount of work remaining on open tasks. If possible, avoid spending time tracking how many hours were spent working on tasks. Tracking hours spent is often to gauge initial forecast accuracy, which is less necessary with self-correcting models in agile.

The product owner should also walk by the task board and move any user stories that have passed review to the Complete column.

The scrum master can review the sprint backlog for any risks prior to the next day's daily scrum.

The scrum team follows this daily cycle until the end of the sprint, when it will be time for the sprint review and the sprint retrospective.

Chapter 10

Showcasing Work and Incorporating Feedback

*A*t the end of each sprint, the scrum team gets a chance to put the results of its hard work on display in the sprint review. The sprint review is where the product owner and the development team demonstrate the sprint's completed user stories to the stakeholders. In the sprint retrospective, the development team, product owner, and scrum master review how the sprint went and determine whether they need any adjustments for the next sprint.

Underpinning both of these events is the agile concept of inspect and adapt, which Chapter 7 explains.

In this chapter, you find out how to conduct a sprint review and a sprint retrospective.

The Sprint Review

The *sprint review* is a meeting to review and demonstrate the user stories that the development team completed during the sprint. The sprint review is open to anyone interested in reviewing the sprint's accomplishments. This means that all stakeholders get a chance to see progress on the product and provide feedback.

The sprint review is Stage 6 in the Roadmap to Value. Figure 10-1 shows how the sprint review fits into an agile project.

Figure 10-1:
The sprint
review
in the
Roadmap to
Value.

Stage 6: SPRINT REVIEW

<u>Description:</u> Demonstration of
working product
<u>Owner:</u> Product Owner and Development Team
<u>Frequency:</u> At the end of each sprint

The following sections show you what you need to do to prepare for a sprint review, how to run a sprint review meeting, and the importance of collecting feedback.

Preparing to demonstrate

Preparation for the sprint review meeting should not take more than a few minutes at most. Even though the sprint review might sound formal, the essence of showcasing in agile is informality. The meeting needs to be prepared and organized, but that doesn't require a lot of flashy materials. Instead, the sprint review focuses on demonstrating what the development team has done.

If your sprint review is overly showy, ask yourself if you are covering up for not spending enough time developing? Get back to working on value — creating a working product.

The preparation for the sprint review meeting involves the product owner and the development team. The product owner needs to know which user stories the development team completed during the sprint. The development team needs to be ready to demonstrate completed, shippable functionality.

Within the context of a single sprint, *shippable functionality* means that the product owner has verified the work product and deemed it complete per the sprint-level definition of done. The actual release may be at a later time, per the communicated release plan. Find out more about shippable functionality in Chapter 9.

For the development team to demonstrate the code in the sprint review, it must be complete according to the definition of done. This means that the code is fully

> ✔ Developed
>
> ✔ Tested

✔ Integrated

✔ Documented

As user stories are moved to a status of done throughout the sprint, the product owner and development team should check that the code meets these standards. This continuous validation throughout the sprint reduces end-of-sprint risks and helps the scrum team spend as little time as possible preparing for the sprint review.

Knowing the completed user stories and being ready to demonstrate those stories' functionality prepares you to confidently start the sprint review meeting.

The sprint review meeting

Sprint review meetings have two activities: demonstrate and showcase the scrum team's finished work, and allow stakeholders to provide feedback on that work. Figure 10-2 shows the different loops of feedback a scrum team receives about a product.

This cycle of feedback repeats throughout the project as follows:

✔ Each day, development team members work together in a collaborative environment that encourages feedback through peer reviews and informal communication.

✔ Throughout each sprint, as the development team completes each requirement, the product owner provides feedback by reviewing the working functionality for acceptance.

✔ At the end of each sprint, project stakeholders provide feedback about completed functionality in the sprint review meeting.

✔ With each release, customers who use the product provide feedback about new working functionality.

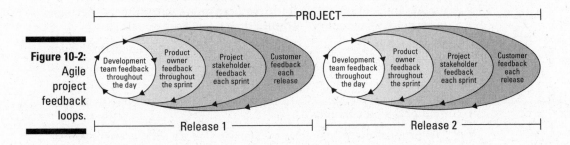

Figure 10-2:
Agile project feedback loops.

The sprint review usually takes place later in the day on the last day of the sprint, often a Friday. One of the rules of scrum is to spend no more than one hour in a sprint review meeting for every week of the sprint — Figure 10-3 shows a quick reference.

If my sprint is this long...	My sprint review meeting should last no more than...
One week	One hour
Two weeks	Two hours
Three weeks	Three hours
Four weeks	Four hours

Figure 10-3: Sprint review meeting to sprint length ratio.

Here are some guidelines for your sprint review meeting:

- ✔ No PowerPoint slides! Refer to the sprint backlog if you need to display a list of completed user stories.

- ✔ The entire scrum team should participate in the meeting.

- ✔ Anyone who is interested in the meeting may attend. The project stakeholders, the summer interns, and the CEO could all theoretically be in a sprint review.

- ✔ The product owner introduces the release goal, the sprint goal, and the new capabilities included.

- ✔ The development team demonstrates what it *completed* during the sprint. Typically, the development team showcases new features or architecture.

- ✔ The demonstration should be on equipment as close as possible to the planned production environment. For example, if you are creating a mobile application, present the features on a smartphone — perhaps hooked up to a monitor — rather than a laptop.

- ✔ The stakeholders can ask questions and provide feedback on the demonstrated product.

- ✔ No non-disclosed rigged functionality, such as hard-coded values and other programming shortcuts that make the application look more mature than it currently is.

- ✔ The product owner can lead a discussion about what is coming next based on the features just presented and new items that have been added to the product backlog during the current sprint.

By the time you get to the sprint review, the product owner has already seen the functionality for each of the user stories that are going to be presented and has agreed that they are complete.

The sprint review meeting is valuable to the development team. The sprint review provides an opportunity for the development team to show its work directly. The meeting allows the stakeholders to recognize the development team for its efforts. The meeting contributes to development team morale, keeping the team motivated to try and produce ever increasing volumes of quality work. The sprint review even establishes a certain level of friendly comparative competition between scrum teams that keeps everyone focused.

Sometimes, healthy competition can result in developers trying to create the coolest code or exceed the requirements of a user story — an issue known as *gold-plating*. A tenet of agile is to produce only what a user story needs to pass the acceptance test. There is a risk that development team members will go beyond requirement needs in their enthusiasm, essentially wasting time that should be spent on useful product functionality. The product owner should be watchful for this.

Next, you see how to note and use the stakeholders' feedback during the sprint review meeting.

Collecting feedback in the sprint review meeting

Gather sprint review feedback informally. The product owner or scrum master can take notes on behalf of the development team, as team members often will be engaged in the presentation and resulting conversation.

Keep in mind the example project I use throughout the book: a mobile application for XYZ Bank. Stakeholders responding to functionality they saw for the XYZ Bank mobile application might have comments like

- ✔ "You might want to consider letting the customers save their preferences, based on the results you showed. It will make for a more personalized experience going forward."

- ✔ "Given what I've seen, you might be able to leverage some of the code modules that were developed for the ABC project last year. They needed to do similar data manipulation."

- ✔ "I noticed your logins were pretty straightforward; will the application be able to handle special characters?"

New user stories may come out of the sprint review. The new user stories could be new features altogether, or they could be changes to the existing code.

In the first couple of sprint reviews, the scrum master may need to remind stakeholders about agile practices. Some people hear the word "demonstration" and immediately expect fancy slides and printouts. The scrum master has a responsibility to manage these expectations and uphold agile values and practices.

The product owner needs to add any new user stories to the product backlog and order those stories by priority. The product owner also adds stories that were scheduled for the current sprint, but not completed, back into the product backlog, and reorders those stories based on the most recent priorities.

The product owner needs to complete updates to the product backlog in time for the next sprint planning meeting.

Once the sprint review is over, it is time for the sprint retrospective. You may want to take a break between the sprint review and the sprint retrospective. The scrum team will want to come into the retrospective ready to inspect its processes and will have ideas for adaptation.

The Sprint Retrospective

The *sprint retrospective* is a meeting where the scrum master, the product owner, and the development team discuss how the sprint went and what they can do to improve the next sprint.

If the scrum team likes, other stakeholders can attend as well. If the scrum team regularly interacts with outside stakeholders, then those stakeholders' insights can be valuable.

The goal of the sprint retrospective is to continuously improve your processes. Improving and customizing processes according to the needs of each individual scrum team increases scrum team morale, improves efficiency, and increases *velocity* — work output. Find details on velocity in Chapter 13.

Your sprint retrospective results may be unique for your scrum team. For example, members of one scrum team I worked with in the past decided that they would like to come into work early and leave early in the day, and spend summer afternoons with their families. Another team at the same organization felt that they did better work late at night, and decided to come to the office in the afternoon and work into the evenings. The result for both teams was increased morale and increased velocity.

Use the information you learn in the retrospective to review and revise your work processes and make your next sprint better.

Agile approaches quickly reveal problems within projects. Data from the sprint backlog shows exactly where the development team has been slowed down. The development team talks and collaborates. All these tools and practices help reveal inefficiencies and allow the development team to refine practices to improve sprint after sprint.

In the following sections, you find out how to plan for a retrospective, how to run a sprint retrospective meeting, and how to use the results of each sprint retrospective to improve future sprints.

Planning for retrospectives

For the first sprint retrospective, everyone on the scrum team should think about a few key things and be ready to discuss them. What went well during the sprint? What would you change, and how?

Everyone on the scrum team may want to make a few notes beforehand, or even take notes throughout the sprint. The scrum team could keep the roadblocks from the sprint's daily scrum meetings in mind. For the second sprint retrospective forward, you can also start to compare the current sprint with prior sprints. In Chapter 9, I mention saving sprint backlogs from prior sprints; this is where they might come in handy.

If the scrum team has honestly and thoroughly thought about what went right and what could be better, they can go into the sprint retrospective ready to have a useful conversation.

The retrospective meeting

The retrospective meeting is an action-oriented meeting. The scrum team immediately applies what it learned in the retrospective to the next sprint.

The sprint retrospective meeting is an action-oriented meeting, not a justification meeting. If you are hearing words like "because…," the conversation is moving away from action and toward rationale.

One of the rules of scrum is to spend no more than 45 minutes in a sprint retrospective meeting for every week of the sprint. Figure 10-4 shows a quick reference.

If my sprint is this long...	My sprint review meeting should last no more than...
One week	45 minutes
Two weeks	1.5 hours
Three weeks	2.25 hours
Four weeks	Three hours

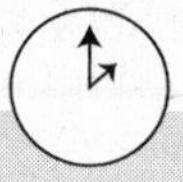

Figure 10-4:
Sprint retrospective meeting to sprint length ratio.

The sprint retrospective should cover three primary questions:

- ✔ What went well during the sprint?
- ✔ What would we like to change?
- ✔ How can we implement that change?

The following areas are also open for discussion:

- ✔ **Results:** Compare the amount of work planned with what the development team actually completed. Review the sprint burndown chart (see Chapter 9) and what it tells the development team about how they are working.

- ✔ **People:** Discuss team composition and alignment.

- ✔ **Relationships:** Talk about communication, collaboration, and working in pairs.

- ✔ **Processes:** Go over getting support, development, and code review processes.

- ✔ **Tools:** How are the different tools working for the scrum team? Think about the artifacts, electronic tools, communication tools, and technical tools.

- ✔ **Productivity:** How can the team improve productivity and get the most work done within the next sprint?

It helps to have these discussions in a structured format. Esther Derby and Diana Larsen, authors of *Agile Retrospectives: Making Good Teams Great* (Pragmatic Bookshelf, 2006), have a great agenda for sprint retrospectives that keeps the team focused on discussions that will lead to real improvement:

1. **Set the stage.**

   Establishing the goals for the retrospective up front will help keep your scrum team focused on providing the right kind of feedback later in the meeting. As you progress into later sprints, you may wish to have retrospectives that focus on one or two specific areas for improvement.

2. **Gather data.**

   Discuss the facts about what went well in the last sprint and what needed improvement. Create an overall picture of the sprint; consider using a white board to write down the input from meeting attendees.

3. **Generate insights.**

   Take a look at the information you just gathered and come up with ideas about how to make improvements for the next sprint.

4. **Decide what to do.**

   Determine — as a team — which ideas you will put into place. Decide upon specific actions you can take to make the ideas reality.

5. **Close the retrospective.**

   Reiterate your plan of action for the next sprint. Thank people for contributing. Also find ways to make the next retrospective better!

For some scrum teams, it might be difficult to open up at first. The scrum master may need to ask specific questions to start discussions. Participating in retrospectives takes practice. What matters is to encourage the scrum team to take responsibility for the sprint — to truly embrace being self-managing.

In other scrum teams, a lot of debate and discussion ensues during the retrospective. The scrum master can find it challenging to manage these discussions and keep the meeting within its allotted time, but that is what needs to be done.

Be sure to use the results from your sprint retrospectives, to inspect and adapt, throughout your project.

Inspecting and adapting

The sprint retrospective is one of the best opportunities you have to put the ideas of inspect and adapt into action. You came up with challenges and solutions during the retrospective. Don't leave those solutions behind after the meeting; make the improvements part of your work every day.

You could record your recommendations for improvement informally. Some scrum teams post the actions identified during the retrospective meeting in the team area to ensure visibility and action on the items listed.

In subsequent retrospective meetings, it's important to review the evaluations of the prior sprint and make sure you put the suggested improvements into place.

Chapter 11

Preparing for Release

Releasing new product features to customers has a special set of challenges. The development team has specific tasks for a product release that differ from the tasks involved with creating code during normal sprints. The organization sponsoring the product may need to prepare to support the product. You want customers to be able to correctly use the released product.

This chapter covers how to manage the final sprint before product release. You also learn how to prepare your organization and the marketplace for the product release.

Preparing the Product for Deployment: The Release Sprint

The work that takes place during regular development sprints should be whole and complete, including testing and technical documentation, before you demonstrate your product. The product of a development sprint is working software.

However, there are often activities, not related to creating product features, that the development team can't realistically complete within development sprints and that might even introduce unacceptable overhead. To accommodate prerelease activities and help ensure that the release goes well, scrum teams often schedule a release sprint as the final sprint prior to releasing product to customers.

Understanding the role of documentation

What's the difference between the technical documentation that you create during a sprint and the user documentation that you may create in your release sprint?

Your *technical documentation* should be barely sufficient, with no frills, and just enough information to tell the development team — and perhaps future development teams — how to create and update the product. If, on the last day of the sprint, the whole development team won the lottery and retired to Costa Rica, a new development team should be able to review the technical documentation and be able to easily pick up coding where the former team left off.

Your *user documentation* tells your customers how to use your product. You may want user documentation crafted specifically for each of your customers. For example, a mobile banking application might need a frequently asked questions (FAQs) section for banking customers. The same application may have a feature that enables marketing managers to upload ad messages to the application — you would want to make sure those managers have instructions for the upload feature as well. Because your product will have changes throughout each sprint, it will be more efficient to wait until the last responsible minute to create your user documentation.

The release sprint should contain anything that you need to do to move working software to production. Sprint backlog items in a release sprint might include

- ✔ Creating user documentation for the most recent version of the product

- ✔ Performance testing, load testing, security testing, and any other checks to ensure the working software will perform acceptably in production

- ✔ Integrating the product with enterprise-wide systems, where testing may take days or weeks

- ✔ Completing organizational or regulatory procedures that are mandatory prior to release

- ✔ Preparing release notes — final notes about changes to the product

- ✔ Preparing the deployment package, enabling all the code for the product features to move to production at one time

- ✔ Deploying your code to the production environment

Some things about a release sprint are very different from a development sprint:

- ✔ You do not develop any requirements from the product backlog.

- ✔ Based on the work you need to do, your release sprint may be a different length than your regular development sprints.

✔ The definition of done is different for work completed during a release sprint. In a development sprint, "done" means the completion of working software for a user story. In a release sprint, the definition is the completion of all tasks required for release.

✔ A release sprint includes tests and approvals that may not be practical to do within a development sprint, such as performance testing, load testing, security testing, focus groups, and legal review.

Agile development teams may create two definitions of done: one for sprints and one for releases.

Table 11-1 shows a comparison between the parts of a development sprint and a release sprint. For detailed descriptions of the key elements in a sprint, see Chapters 8 through 10.

Table 11-1	Development Sprint Elements Versus Release Sprint Elements	
Element	*Used in Development Sprint*	*Used in Release Sprint*
Sprint planning	Yes	Yes
Product backlog	Yes	No
Sprint backlog	Yes	Yes
	For a development sprint, your sprint backlog contains user stories and the tasks needed to create each user story. You estimate user stories relatively, with story points. (See Chapters 7 and 8.)	In a release sprint, you no longer need to put your requirements in the user story format. Instead, you will create only a list of tasks needed for the release. You will not use story points, either; just add the estimated hours each task will take.
Burndown chart	Yes	Yes
Daily scrum	Yes	Yes
		Involve stakeholders from outside the scrum team who have tasks associated with releasing the product, like enterprise build managers or other configuration managers.
Daily activities	In a development sprint, your daily activities focus on creating shippable code.	In a release sprint, your daily activities focus on preparing your working software for external release.

(continued)

Table 11-1 *(continued)*

Element	Used in Development Sprint	Used in Release Sprint
End-of-day reporting	Yes	Yes
Sprint review	Yes	Yes
		Some organizations use a release sprint review as a *go or no-go meeting* to authorize launching the product.
Sprint retrospective	Yes	Yes

A release sprint should not be a parking lot for tasks that the development team didn't finish in the development sprints. You may not be surprised to hear that development teams sometimes will be tempted to delay tasks until the release sprint. You can avoid this by ensuring that the product owner and the team have created a proper definition of done for requirements in development sprints, including testing, integration, and documentation.

While running a release sprint, you also need to prepare your organization for the product release. The next section discusses how to get stakeholders within your company or organization ready for product deployment.

Preparing the Organization for Product Deployment

A product release often affects a number of departments within a company or organization. To get the organization ready for the new product, the product owner and scrum master need to prepare a *sprint backlog,* or a list of the goals and tasks, for the release sprint. See how to create a sprint backlog in Chapter 9.

The release sprint backlog should cover activities by the development team. It also needs to address activities to be performed by groups within the organization, but outside of the scrum team, to prepare for the product deployment. These departments might include

✓ **Marketing:** Are there any marketing campaigns related to the new product that need to launch at the same time as the product?

✓ **Sales:** Are there specific customers who need to know about the product? Will the new product cause an increase in sales?

✔ **Manufacturing:** Is the product a physical item, such as boxed CD-ROM software?

✔ **Product support:** Does the customer service group have the information it needs to answer questions about the new product? Will they have enough people on hand in case customer questions increase when the product launches?

✔ **Legal:** Does the product meet legal standards, including pricing, licensing, and correct verbiage, for release to the public?

The departments that need to be ready for the product launch and the specific tasks these groups need to complete will, of course, vary from organization to organization. A key to release success, however, is that the product owner and scrum master involve the right people and ensure that those people clearly understand what they need to do to be ready for the product release.

As with development sprints, in your release sprint, you can effectively use daily scrums, review meetings, and retrospectives with department colleagues involved in preparing for product deployment. You can even use a task board, like the one I describe in Chapter 9.

During your release sprint, you also need to include one more group in your planning: the product customer. The next section discusses getting the marketplace ready for your product.

Preparing the Marketplace for Product Deployment

The product owner is responsible for working with other departments to ensure that the marketplace — existing customers and potential customers — is ready for what's coming. The marketing or sales teams may lead this effort; they look to the product owner to keep them informed on the release date and the features that will be part of the release.

Some software products are only for internal employee use. Certain things you are reading in this section might seem like overkill for an internal software application — an application released only within your company. However, many of these steps are still good guidelines for promoting internal applications. Preparing customers, whether internal or external, for new products can be a key part of product success.

To help prepare customers for the product release, the product owner may want to work with different teams to ensure the following:

- ✔ **Marketing support:** Whether you're dealing with a brand new product or new features for an existing product, the marketing department should leverage the excitement of the new product functionality to help promote the product and the organization.

- ✔ **Customer testing:** If possible, work with focus groups to get real-world feedback from test customers about the product. Your marketing team can translate this into testimonials for promoting the product.

- ✔ **Marketing materials:** An organization's marketing group also prepares the promotional and advertising plans, as well as packaging for physical media. Media materials, such as press releases and information for analysts, need to be ready, as do marketing and sales materials.

- ✔ **Support channels:** Ensure that customers understand the available support channels in case they have questions about the product.

Review the tasks on your release sprint backlog from the customer standpoint. Think of the personas you used when creating your user stories. Is there anything those personas might need to know about the product? Update your launch checklist with items that would be valuable to your personas. You can find more information about personas in Chapter 8.

The product release is a busy time for the entire project team, with a lot of activities going on. Use those Agile Principles.

Finally, you're there — release day. Whatever role you played along the way, this is the day you worked hard to achieve. Time to celebrate!

Part IV
Managing in Agile

The 5th Wave   By Rich Tennant

"You ever get the feeling some of the team members are beginning to lose focus?"

In this part . . .

In the following chapters, I explain how to use agile processes to manage the different areas of responsibility that most projects have in common, such as scope, procurement, time, cost, team dynamics, communication, quality, and risk.

You come to understand the important differences between historical project management and agile approaches for each project management area. You see how to apply the different 12 Agile Principles to each area and how self-organizing scrum teams can work with different agile artifacts and events to successfully manage agile projects.

Chapter 12

Managing Scope and Procurement

. . . .

In This Chapter

▶ Finding out how scope management is different on agile projects

▶ Managing scope and scope changes with agile processes

▶ Seeing the different approach agile processes bring to procurement

▶ Managing procurement on agile projects

. . . .

Scope management is part of every project. To create a product, you have to understand basic product requirements and the work it will take to create those requirements. You need to be able to prioritize and manage scope changes as new requirements arise. You have to verify that finished product features fulfill customers' needs.

Procurement is also part of many projects. If you need to look outside of your organization for help completing a project, you should know how to go about procuring goods and services. You will want to know how to collaborate with vendor teams during the project. You should also know something about creating contracts and different cost structures.

In this chapter, you find out how to manage scope within an agile project and take advantage of agile methodologies' welcoming approach to informed change. You also find out how to manage procurement of goods and services to deliver product scope on an agile project. First, I review traditional scope management.

What's Different About Scope in Agile

Historically, a large part of project management is scope management. *Product scope* is all the features and requirements that a product includes. *Project scope* is all the work involved in creating a product.

Unlike many traditional projects, agile projects have variable scope so that project teams can incorporate learning and feedback, and ultimately create better products. The methodologists who crafted the Agile Manifesto and 12 Agile Principles recognized that scope change is natural and beneficial. Agile approaches specifically embrace change and use it to make better informed, more useful products.

Chapter 2 details the Agile Manifesto and the 12 Agile Principles. (If you haven't yet checked out that chapter, flip back to it now. I'll wait.) The manifesto and the principles answer the question, "How agile are we?" The degree to which your project approach supports the manifesto and the principles helps determine how agile your methods are.

The Agile Principles that relate the most to scope management are:

1. Our highest priority is to satisfy the customer through early and continuous delivery of valuable software.

2. Welcome changing requirements, even late in development. Agile processes harness change for the customer's competitive advantage.

3. Deliver working software frequently, from a couple of weeks to a couple of months, with a preference to the shorter timescale.

10. Simplicity — the art of maximizing the amount of work not done — is essential.

Agile approaches to scope management are fundamentally different than traditional methods for scope management. Consider the differences you see in Table 12-1.

At any point in an agile project, anyone — the scrum team, stakeholders, or anyone else in the organization with a good idea — can identify new product requirements. The product owner determines the value and priority of new requirements and adds those requirements to the product backlog.

Within traditional project management, there is a term to describe requirements that change after the project's initial definition phase: *scope creep.* Waterfall doesn't have a positive way to incorporate changes mid-project, so scope changes often cause large problems with a waterfall project's schedule and budget. (For more on the waterfall methodology, see Chapter 1.) Mention "scope creep" to a seasoned project manager, and you might even see him or her shudder.

During sprint planning at the beginning of each sprint, the scrum team can use the product backlog priority to help decide whether a new requirement should be part of the sprint. Lower-priority requirements stay in the product backlog for future consideration. You can read about planning sprints in Chapter 8.

The next section addresses how to manage scope on an agile project.

Table 12-1   Historical Versus Agile Scope Management

Scope Management with Traditional Approaches	*Scope Management with Agile Approaches*
Project teams attempt to identify and document complete scope at the beginning of the project, when the teams are the least informed about the product.	You gather high level requirements at the beginning of your project, breaking down and further detailing requirements that are going to be implemented in the immediate future. Requirements are gathered and refined throughout the project as the team's knowledge of customer needs and project realities grows.
Organizations view scope change after the requirements phase is complete as negative.	Organizations view change as a positive way to improve a product as the project progresses.
	Changes late in the project, when you know the most about the product, are often the most valuable changes.
Project managers rigidly control and discourage changes once stakeholders sign off on requirements.	Change management is an inherent part of agile processes.
	You assess scope and have an opportunity to include new requirements with every sprint.
	The product owner determines the value and priority of new requirements and adds those requirements to the product backlog.
The cost of change increases over time, while the ability to make changes decreases.	You fix resources and schedule initially.
	New features with high priority don't necessarily cause budget or schedule slip; they simply push out the lowest-priority features.
	Iterative development allows for changes with each new sprint.
Projects often include *scope bloat,* unnecessary product features included out of fear of mid-project change.	You determine scope by considering which features directly support the project vision, the release goal, and the sprint goal.
	The development team creates the most valuable features first to guarantee their inclusion and to ship those features as soon as possible.
	Less valuable features might never be created.

How to Manage Scope in Agile

Welcoming scope change helps you create the best product possible. Embracing change, however, requires that you understand the current scope and know how to deal with updates as they arise. Luckily, agile projects have straightforward ways to manage new and existing requirements:

- ✔ **Product owners:** Ensure that all the rest of the project team — the scrum team plus the project stakeholders — clearly understand the existing scope for the project, the project vision, the current release goal, and the current sprint goal.

- ✔ **Product owners:** Determine the value and priority of new requirements in relation to the product vision, release, sprint goals, and existing requirements.

- ✔ **Development teams:** Create product requirements in order of priority to release the most important parts of the product first.

In the following sections, you find out how to understand and convey scope in different parts of an agile project. You see how to evaluate priorities as new requirements arise. You also find out how to use the product backlog and other agile artifacts to manage scope.

Understanding scope throughout the project

At each stage in an agile project, the scrum team manages scope in different ways. A good way to look at scope management throughout a project is by using the Roadmap to Value, shown in Figure 12-1.

Consider each part of the Roadmap to Value:

- ✔ **Stage 1 — Vision:** The product vision statement is the first step in establishing project scope. The product owner is responsible for ensuring that all members of the project team know the product vision statement and that everyone on the project team interprets the statement correctly.

- ✔ **Stage 2 — Product Roadmap:** During product roadmap creation, the product owner refers back to the vision statement and ensures that features fit the vision statement. As new features materialize, the product owner needs to understand those features and clearly communicate their scope to the development team and stakeholders.

- ✔ **Stage 3 — Release Planning:** During release planning, the product owner needs to determine a release goal and select only the scope that supports that goal.

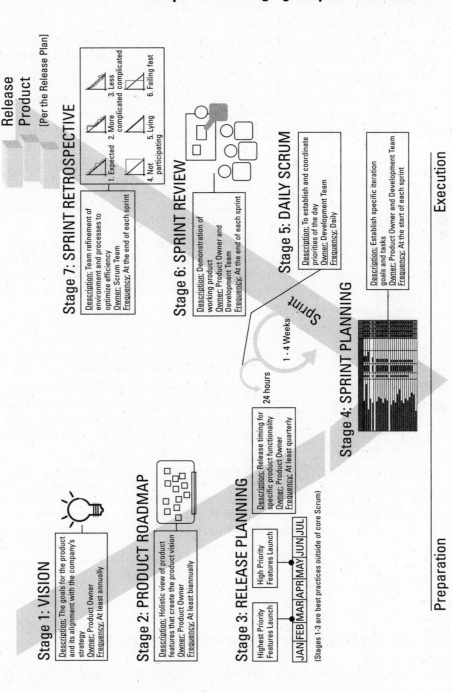

Figure 12-1:
The
Roadmap
to Value.

✔ **Stage 4 — Sprint Planning:** During sprint planning, the product owner needs to ensure that the scrum team understands the release goal and plans each sprint goal based on that release goal. The product owner also selects only the scope that supports the sprint goal. The product owner will also ensure that the development team understands the scope of the individual user stories selected for the sprint.

✔ **Stage 5 — Daily Scrum:** The daily scrum meeting can be a launching point for scope change for future sprints. The daily scrum meeting is a focused, 15-minute meeting for the development team to state three things: the preceding day's completed work, the scope of work for the coming day, and any roadblocks the development team may have. However, the three subjects of the daily scrum often reveal larger opportunities for scope changes.

When topics come up that warrant a bigger discussion than the time and format of the daily scrum meeting allows, a scrum team can decide to have an after-party meeting. In the after-party, scrum team members talk about anything, including potential changes, in detail.

✔ **Stage 6 — Sprint Review:** The product owner sets the tone of each sprint review meeting by reiterating the scope of the sprint — the sprint goals that the scrum team pursued and what was completed. It's important, especially during the first sprint reviews, that the stakeholders in the meeting have the right expectations about scope.

Sprint reviews can be inspiring. When the entire project team is in one room, interacting with the working product, they may look at the product in new ways and come up with ideas to improve the product. The product owner updates the product backlog with new scope based on discussions in the sprint review.

✔ **Stage 7 — Sprint Retrospective:** In the sprint retrospective, the scrum team can discuss how well they met the scope commitments they made at the beginning of the sprint. If the development team was not able to achieve the sprint goal identified during sprint planning, they will need to refine planning and work processes to make sure they can select the right amount of work for each sprint. If the development team met their goals, they can use the sprint retrospective to come up with ways to add more scope to future sprints. Scrum teams aim to improve productivity with every sprint.

Introducing scope changes

Many people, even people outside of the organization, can suggest a new product feature on an agile project. You might see new ideas for features from

✔ User community feedback, including groups or people who are given an opportunity to preview the product

✔ Business stakeholders who see a new market opportunity or threat

✔ Executives and senior managers who have insight into long-term organizational strategies and changes

✔ The development team, which is learning more about the product every day, and is closest to the working product

✔ The scrum master, who may find an opportunity while working with external departments or clearing development team roadblocks

✔ The product owner, who often knows the most about the product and stakeholder needs

Because you will receive suggestions for product changes throughout an agile project, you want to determine which changes are valid and manage the updates. Read on to see how.

Managing scope changes

When you get new requirements, use the following steps to evaluate and prioritize the requirements and update the product backlog.

Do not add new requirements to sprints already in progress, unless the development team requests them.

1. **Assess whether the new requirement should be part of the project, the release, or the sprint by asking some key questions about the requirement:**

   a. *Does the new requirement support the product vision statement?*

   • If yes, add the requirement to the product backlog and product roadmap.

   • If no, the requirement shouldn't be part of the project. It may be a good candidate for a separate project.

   b. *Does the new requirement support the current release goal?*

   • If yes, the requirement is a candidate for the current release plan.

   • If no, leave the requirement on the product backlog for a future release.

   c. *Does the new requirement support the current sprint goal?*

   • If yes, and the sprint has not started, the requirement is a candidate for the current sprint backlog.

   • If no, leave the requirement on the product backlog for a future sprint.

2. **Estimate the effort for the new requirement.** The development team estimates the effort. Find out how to estimate requirements in Chapter 7.

3. **Prioritize the requirement against other requirements in the product backlog and add the new requirement to the product backlog, in order of priority.** Consider the following:

   • The product owner knows the most about the product's business needs and how important the new requirement may be in relation to other requirements. The product owner may also reach out to project stakeholders for additional insight to a requirement's priority.

   • The development team may also have technical insight about a new requirement's priority. For example, if Requirement A and Requirement B have equal business value, but you need to complete Requirement B for Requirement A to be feasible, the development team will need to alert the product owner.

   • While the development team and project stakeholders can provide information to help prioritize a requirement, determining priority is ultimately the product owner's job.

   • Adding new requirements to the product backlog may mean other requirements move down the list in the product backlog. Figure 12-2 shows the addition of a new requirement in the product backlog.

The product backlog is a complete list of all known scope for the product and is your most important tool for managing scope change on an agile project.

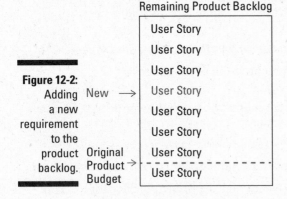

Figure 12-2: Adding a new requirement to the product backlog.

Keeping the product backlog up to date will allow you to quickly prioritize and add new requirements. With a current product backlog, you always understand the scope left in a project. Chapter 7 has more information about prioritizing requirements.

Using agile artifacts for scope management

From the vision statement through the sprint plan, all the artifacts in agile project management support you in your scope management efforts. Decompose requirements progressively as features rise to the top of the priority list. Table 12-2 reveals how each artifact, including the product backlog, contributes to ongoing scope refinement.

What's Different About Procurement in Agile

Another part of project management is *procurement,* managing the purchase of services or goods needed to deliver the product's scope. Like scope, procurement is part of the investment side of a project.

Chapter 2 explains that the Agile Manifesto values *customer collaboration over contract negotiation.* This sets an important tone for procurement relationships on agile projects.

Valuing customer collaboration more than contract negotiation doesn't mean that agile projects have no contracts: Contracts and negotiation are critical to business relationships. However, the Agile Manifesto sets forth the idea that a buyer and seller should work together to create products, and that the relationship between the two is more important than quibbling over ill-informed details and checking off contract items that may or not ultimately be valuable to customers.

All 12 Agile Principles apply to procurement on agile projects. However, the following six seem to stand out the most when securing goods and services for an agile project:

2. Welcome changing requirements, even late in development. Agile processes harness change for the customer's competitive advantage.

3. Deliver working software frequently, from a couple of weeks to a couple of months, with a preference to the shorter timescale.

4. Business people and developers must work together daily throughout the project.

5. Build projects around motivated individuals. Give them the environment and support they need, and trust them to get the job done.

10. Simplicity — the art of maximizing the amount of work not done — is essential.

11. The best architectures, requirements, and designs emerge from self-organizing teams.

Table 12-3 highlights the differences between procurement on traditional projects and procurement on agile projects.

Table 12-2	Agile Artifacts and Scope Management Roles	
Artifact	*Role in Establishing Scope*	*Role in Scope Change*
Vision Statement: A definition of the product's end goal. Chapter 7 has more about the vision statement.	Use the vision statement as a benchmark to judge whether features belong in scope for the current project.	When someone introduces new requirements, those requirements must support the project vision statement.
Product Roadmap: A holistic view of product features that create the product vision. Chapter 7 has more about the product roadmap.	Product scope is part of the product roadmap. Requirements at a feature level are good for business conversations about what it means to realize the product vision.	Update the product roadmap as new requirements arise. The product roadmap provides visual communication of the new feature's inclusion in the project.
Release Plan: A digestible mid-term target focused around a minimum set of marketable features. Chapter 8 has more about the release plan.	The release plan shows the scope of the current release. You may want to plan your releases by themes — logical groups of requirements.	Add new features that belong in the current release to the release plan. If the new user story doesn't belong in the current release, leave it on the product backlog for a future release.
Product Backlog: A complete list of all known scope for the product. Chapters 7 and 8 offer more about the product backlog.	If a requirement is in scope, it is part of the product backlog.	The product backlog contains all scope changes. New, high-priority features push lower-priority features down on the product backlog.
Sprint Backlog: The user stories and tasks within the scope of the current sprint. Chapter 8 has more about the sprint backlog.	The sprint backlog contains the user stories that are in scope for the current sprint.	The sprint backlog establishes what is allowed in the sprint. Once the development team commits to the sprint goal in the sprint planning meeting, only the development team can modify the sprint backlog.

Table 12-3   Historical Versus Agile Procurement Management

Procurement Management with Traditional Approaches	Procurement Management with Agile Approaches
The project manager and the organization are responsible for procurement activities.	The self-managing development team plays a larger part in identifying items needing procurement.
Contracts with service providers often include provisions for fixed requirements, extensive documentation, a comprehensive project plan, and other traditional deliverables based on a waterfall lifecycle.	Contracts for agile projects are based on the evaluation of working functionality at the end of each sprint, not on fixed deliverables and documentation that may or may not contribute to delivering quality products.
Contract negotiation between buyers and sellers can sometimes be challenging. Because negotiation is often a stressful activity, it can damage the relationship between the buyer and the seller before work even starts on a project.	Agile project teams focus on keeping a positive, cooperative relationship between buyers and sellers from the start of the procurement process.
Switching vendors after a project starts can be costly and time-consuming because a new vendor must try to understand the old vendor's massive amount of work in progress.	Vendors provide completed, working functionality at the end of each sprint. If vendors change mid-project, the new vendor can immediately start developing requirements for the next sprint, avoiding a long, costly transition.

Both waterfall and agile project teams are interested in vendor success. Traditional project approaches were firm in their accountability for compliance, defining success as checking off documents and deliverables from a list. Agile project approaches, by contrast, are firm in their accountability for end results, defining success with working products.

The next section shows how to manage procurement on agile projects.

How to Manage Procurement in Agile

This section focuses on how agile project teams go through the procurement process: from determining need, selecting a vendor, and creating a contract through working with a vendor and closing out the contract at the end of a buyer-seller project.

Determining need and selecting a vendor

On agile projects, procurement starts when the development team decides it needs a tool or the services of another company in order to create the product.

Agile project development teams are self-managing and self-organizing, and they get to make the decisions about what is best for maximizing development output. Self-management applies to all project management areas, including procurement. Find out more about self-managing teams in Chapters 6 and 14.

Development teams have a number of opportunities to consider outside goods and services:

- ✔ **Product vision stage:** The development team may start thinking about the tools and skills necessary to help reach the product goals. At this stage, it may be prudent to research needs, but not begin the purchase process.

- ✔ **Product roadmap stage:** The development team starts to see specific features to create and may know some of the goods or services necessary to help create the product.

- ✔ **Release planning:** The development team knows more about the product and can identify specific goods or services that will help meet release goals.

- ✔ **Sprint planning:** The development team is in the trenches of development and may identify urgent needs for the sprint.

- ✔ **Daily scrum:** Development team members state impediments. Procuring goods or services may help remove these impediments.

- ✔ **Throughout the day:** Development team members communicate with one another and collaborate on tasks. Specific needs may arise from the development team's conversations.

- ✔ **Sprint review meeting:** Project stakeholders may identify new requirements for future sprints that warrant procurement of goods or services.

- ✔ **Sprint retrospective:** The development team may discuss how having a specific tool or service could have helped the past sprint and suggest a purchase for future sprints.

Sometimes you can find the goods or services you need for a project within your organization. Before looking at buying an item or working with vendors, the scrum master determines if the tools or the person with the skills to fulfill the services the development team needs are available internally. If internal resources or people can meet the development team's needs, the scrum team saves money.

Once the development team determines it needs a good or service, the development team and the scrum master work with the product owner to procure any necessary funds. The product owner is responsible for the project budget, so the product owner is ultimately responsible for any project purchases.

When procuring goods, the development team may need to compare tools and vendors before deciding upon a purchase. When procuring goods, once you choose what to buy and where to get it, the process is usually straightforward: Make the purchase, take delivery, and procurement is then complete.

Procuring services is usually a longer and more complex process than purchasing goods. Some agile-specific considerations for selecting a services vendor include

✔ Whether the vendor can work in an agile project environment and, if so, how much experience the vendor has with agile projects

✔ Whether the vendor can work on-site with the development team

✔ Whether the relationship between the vendor and the scrum team is likely to be positive and collaborative

The organization or company you work for may be subject to laws and regulations for choosing vendors. Companies involved in government work, for example, often need to gather multiple proposals and bids from companies for work that will cost more than a certain amount of money. While your cousin or your friend from college may be the most qualified person to complete the work, you may run into trouble if you don't follow applicable laws. Check with your company's legal department if you are in doubt about how to streamline bloated processes.

After you pick a service vendor, you need to create a contract so that the vendor can start work. The next section explains how contracts work on agile projects.

Contracts and cost approaches for services

After the development team and the product owner have chosen a vendor, they need a contract to ensure agreement on the services and pricing. To start the contract process, you should know about different pricing structures and how they work with agile projects. Once you understand these approaches, you see how to create a contract.

Cost structures

When you are procuring services for an agile project, it is important to know the difference between a *fixed-price* project, a *fixed-time* project, and a *time-and-materials* project. Each approach has its own strengths in an agile setting:

✔ **Fixed-price projects:** Start out with a set budget. In a fixed-price project, a vendor works on the product and creates releases until that vendor has spent all of the money in the budget, or until you have delivered enough product features, whichever comes first.

For example, if you have a $250,000 budget, and your vendor costs are $10,000 a week, the vendor's portion of the project will be able to last

25 weeks. Within those 25 weeks, the vendor creates and releases as much shippable functionality as possible.

✔ **Fixed-time projects:** Have specific deadlines. For example, you may need to launch a product in time for the next holiday season, for a specific event, or to coincide with the release of another product. With fixed-time projects, you determine costs based on the cost of the vendor's team for the duration of the project, along with any additional resource costs, such as hardware or software.

✔ **Time-and-materials projects:** Are more open-ended than fixed-priced or fixed-time projects. Within time-and-materials projects, your work with the vendor lasts until enough product functionality is complete, without regard to total project cost. In a time-and-materials project, you know the total project cost at the end of the project, once your stakeholders have determined that the product has enough features to call the project complete.

For example, if your project costs $10,000 a week, and after 20 weeks, the stakeholders feel they have enough valuable product features, your project cost is $200,000. If the customer deems that he or she has enough value by the end of 10 weeks, the project cost is half that amount, $100,000.

✔ **Not-to-exceed projects:** Are projects in which time and materials have a fixed-price cap.

Regardless of the cost approach, on agile projects, concentrate on completing the highest value product features first.

Creating a contract

Once you know the project's cost approach, the scrum master needs to help create a contract. Contracts are legally binding agreements between buyers and sellers that set expectations about work and payment.

The person responsible for creating contracts differs by organization. In some cases, a person from the legal or procurement department drafts a contract and then asks the scrum master to review it. In other cases, the opposite occurs: The scrum master drafts the contract and has a legal or procurement expert review it.

Regardless of who creates the contract, the scrum master is generally responsible for initiating the contract creation, negotiating the contract details, and routing the contract through any necessary internal approvals.

The agile approach of placing value on collaboration over negotiation is a key to maintaining a positive relationship between a buyer and a seller while creating and negotiating a contract. The scrum master works closely with the vendor and communicates openly and often with the vendor throughout the contract creation process.

Bid it low and watch it grow: The fallacy of low-balling the vendor

Trying to bully vendors into providing the lowest possible price is always a lose-lose situation. Contractors in industries where projects always go to the lowest bidder have a saying: *Bid it low, and watch it grow.* It is common for vendors to provide a low price during a project's proposal process and then add multiple change orders until the buyer ends up paying as much or more than he or she would have for higher-priced offers.

The traditional project management model supports this practice by locking in scope and price at the project start, when you know almost nothing about the product. Change orders — and their accompanying cost increases — are inevitable.

A better model is for the vendor and buyer to collaborate on defining the product scope, within fixed cost and schedule constraints, as the project unfolds. Both parties can reap the benefits of what they learn during the project, and you end up with a better product. Instead of trying to be a tough negotiator, be a good collaborator.

Regardless of the size of your company or organization, it is a very good idea to create a contract between your company and your vendor for services. Skipping the contract can leave buyers and sellers open to confusion about expectations, unfinished work, and even legal problems.

At the very least, most contracts have legal language describing the parties and the work, the budget, the cost approach, and payment terms. A contract for an agile project may also include the following:

✔ **A description of the work that the vendor will complete:** The vendor may have its own product vision statement, which may be a good starting point to describe the vendor's work. You may want to refer to the product vision statement in Chapter 7.

✔ **Agile approaches that the vendor may use:** They may include

- Meetings that the vendor will attend, such as the daily scrum, sprint planning, sprint review, and sprint retrospective meetings

- Delivery of working functionality at the end of each sprint

- The definition of done, discussed in Chapter 9: work that is developed, tested, integrated, and documented, per an agreement between the product owner and the development team

- Artifacts that the vendor will provide, such as a sprint backlog with a burndown chart for status

- People whom the vendor will have on the project, like the development team

- Whether the vendor will work on-site at your company

> - Whether the vendor will work with its own scrum master and product owner, or if it will work with your scrum master and product owner
> - A definition of what may constitute the end of the engagement: the end of a fixed budget or fixed time, or enough complete, working functionality
>
> ✔ **If the vendor doesn't use agile approaches, describe how the vendor and the vendor's work will integrate with the buyer's development team and sprints.**

This is not a comprehensive list; contract items vary by project and organization.

The contract will likely go through a few rounds of reviews and changes before the final version is complete. One way to clearly communicate changes and maintain a good relationship with a vendor is to speak with the vendor each time you propose a change. If you e-mail a revised contract, follow up with a call to explain what you changed and why, answer any questions, and discuss any ideas for further revision. Open discussion helps the contract process to be positive.

If anything substantial about the vendor's services changes during contract discussions, it is a good idea for the product owner or the scrum master to review those changes with the development team. The development team especially needs to know and provide input about changes to the service the vendor will provide, the vendor's approach, and the people on the vendor's team.

It is quite likely that your company and the vendor will require reviews and approvals by people outside of their respective project teams. People who review contracts might include high-level managers or executives, procurement specialists, accounting people, and company attorneys. This differs by organization; the scrum master needs to ensure that anyone who needs to read the contract does so.

Now that you understand a little about how to select a vendor and create a contract, it's time to look at how procurement differs among companies and organizations.

Organizational considerations for procurement

The way your company approaches procurement will make a difference in how you go about selecting a vendor and creating and negotiating a contract. Because procurement involves money and legal contracts, purchase procedures and decisions are sometimes outside a project team's control. Considerations for procurement activities can include

✔ **Company or organization size and experience:** Smaller and newer companies may have less formality, allowing project managers autonomy over purchases. Larger and more established companies tend to have more overhead with purchasing. Some companies have whole departments with people working full-time on procurement.

✔ **Company or organization type:** Some organizations, like government agencies, have legally required procurement processes and documents to complete. Private companies may have fewer restrictions on procurement than publicly traded companies because of differences in laws for public companies.

✔ **Company or organization culture:** Many organizations involve the project team in procurement decisions. However, this is not always the case, and project teams sometimes find themselves working with goods or service providers they had no part in choosing. Some companies are rather informal and don't require much documentation or process for procurement. Other companies require documents to justify the need for a good or service, formal proposals from sellers, and multiple approvals at each step in procurement.

If you are working on an agile project in an organization with heavy procurement processes and a separate procurement department, you must balance those processes with agile processes. A good way to ensure agile processes during procurement is for the scrum master to work closely with the procurement department staffers.

In Chapter 6, I note that the scrum master makes sure that the organization follows agile practices and principles. In this role, the scrum master helps explain agile approaches to procurement specialists. The scrum master may find it worthwhile to help translate organizational requirements into agile processes.

The scrum master makes sure procurement people understand why a contract may need to accommodate changing requirements and iterations. The scrum master sets the tone for the contract creation process to be collaborative.

If an agile project team has support from an organization's upper management, it may be easier to work agile approaches into an organization's procurement processes.

One good way to get support for moving agile approaches into your organization's procurement processes is to ensure that upper management knows the benefits of agile methods. Benefits like better product quality, reduced risk, and more control and visibility of project performance help make a strong argument for using agile processes when working with vendors. Chapter 18 provides a list of key benefits of agile project management.

Organizations with light or no procurement processes provide different challenges for an agile project — or for any project, for that matter. Scrum masters may find themselves starting procurement activities from scratch, with little precedent or support.

People who sign contracts should have the authorization to make financial decisions for a company, and they often are people at the executive level. Scrum masters and product owners usually don't have this type of authorization. When in doubt, ask around. Find the right signatory.

After you choose a vendor and have a signed contract, the vendor can start work. In the next section, you see that, like the initial procurement processes, working with vendors has special considerations for agile projects.

Working with a vendor

How you work with a vendor on an agile project depends in part upon the vendor team's structure.

In an ideal situation, vendor teams are fully integrated with the buyer's organization. The vendor's team members are collocated with the buyer's scrum team. Vendor team members work as part of the buyer's development team for as long as necessary.

Some development teams include vendor team members in their daily scrum meetings. This can be a good way to get an idea of what the vendor team is doing every day and to help the development team work more closely with the vendor. You can also invite vendors to your sprint reviews to keep them informed on your progress.

Vendor teams also can be integrated but dislocated. If the vendor can't work on-site at the buyer's company, it can still be part of the buyer's scrum team. Chapter 14 has more information on team dynamics on agile projects. This information applies to internal scrum teams and vendor teams.

If a vendor can't be collocated, or if the vendor is responsible for a discrete, separate part of the product, the vendor may have a separate scrum team. The vendor's scrum team works on the same sprint schedule as the buyer's scrum team. See Chapter 13 to find out how to work with more than one scrum team on a project.

If a vendor doesn't use agile project management processes, the vendor's team works separately from the buyer's scrum team, outside of the sprints, and on its own schedule. The vendor's traditional project manager helps ensure that the vendor can deliver its services when the development team needs them. The buyer's scrum master may need to step in if the vendor's processes or timeline becomes a roadblock or disruption for the development team. See the "Managing projects with dislocated teams" section in Chapter 14 for information about working with non-agile teams.

If you are working with a vendor that does not use agile processes, the product owner may want to have the traditional team's deliverables be a dependency to adding associated requirements to sprints. Traditional teams often struggle to match the pace of agile teams.

Vendors may provide services for a defined amount of time, or for the life of the project. Once the vendor's work is complete, the buyer's scrum master often manages any closing tasks.

Closing a contract

Once a vendor completes work on a contract, the buyer's scrum master usually has some final tasks to close the contract.

If the project finishes normally, according to the contract terms, the scrum master may wish to acknowledge the end of the contract in writing. If the project is a time-and-materials project, the scrum master should definitely do so to ensure that the vendor doesn't keep working on lower-priority requirements — and billing for them.

Depending upon the organizational structure and the contract's cost structure, the scrum master may be responsible for notifying the buyer's company accounting department after work is complete to ensure that the vendor is paid properly.

If the project finishes before the contract dictates the end, the scrum master needs to notify the vendor in writing and follow any early termination instructions from the contract.

End the engagement on a positive note. If the vendor did a good job, the scrum team may want to acknowledge the people on the vendor's team at the sprint reviews. Everyone on the project could potentially work together again, and a simple, sincere "thank-you" can help maintain a good relationship for future projects.

Chapter 13

Managing Time and Cost

Managing project time and project costs are typically key aspects of managing a project. In this chapter, you see agile approaches to time and cost management. You find out how to use a scrum team's development speed to determine time and cost on a given project and how to increase development speed to lower your project's time and cost.

What's Different About Time in Agile

In project management terms, time refers to the processes that ensure timely project completion. To understand time management in agile, it helps to review some of the Agile Principles I discuss in Chapter 2:

1. Our highest priority is to satisfy the customer through early and continuous delivery of valuable software.

2. Welcome changing requirements, even late in development. Agile processes harness change for the customer's competitive advantage.

3. Deliver working software frequently, from a couple of weeks to a couple of months, with a preference to the shorter timescale.

8. Agile processes promote sustainable development. The sponsors, developers, and users should be able to maintain a constant pace indefinitely.

Table 13-1 shows some of the differences between time management on traditional projects and on agile projects.

Table 13-1	Historical Versus Agile Time Management
Time Management with Traditional Approaches	*Time Management with Agile Approaches*
Fixed scope directly drives the schedule.	Scope is not fixed on agile projects. Time can be fixed, and development teams can create the requirements that will fit into a specific time frame.
Project managers determine time based on the requirements gathered at the beginning of the project.	During the project, scrum teams assess and reassess how much work they can complete in a given time frame.
Teams work on all project requirements at one time in phases, like requirements-gathering, design, development, testing, and deployment. There is no schedule difference between critical requirements and optional requirements.	Scrum teams work in sprints and complete all the work on the highest-priority, highest-value requirements first.
Teams do not start actual product development until later in the project, after the requirements-gathering and design phases are complete.	Scrum teams start product development in the very first sprint.
Time is more variable on traditional projects.	Time-boxed sprints on agile projects stay stable.
Project managers try to predict schedules at the project start, when they know little about the product.	Scrum teams determine long-range schedules on actual development performance in sprints. Scrum teams adjust time estimates throughout the project as they learn more about the product and the development team's speed, or *velocity.* You find more about velocity later in this chapter.

Fixed-schedule and fixed-price projects have lower risk with agile techniques, because agile development teams always deliver the highest priority functionality within the time or budget constraints.

A big benefit of agile time management techniques is that agile project teams can deliver products much earlier than traditional project teams. For example, starting development earlier and completing functionality in iterations often allow agile project teams that work with my company, Platinum Edge, to bring products to the market 30 percent to 40 percent faster.

The reason agile projects finish sooner isn't complicated; they simply start development sooner.

In the next section, find out how to manage time on an agile project.

How to Manage Time in Agile

Agile methodologies support both strategic and tactical schedules and time management:

- ✔ Your early planning is strategic in nature. The high-level requirements in the product roadmap and the product backlog can help you get an early idea of the overall schedule. Find out how to create a product roadmap and backlog in Chapter 7.

- ✔ Your detailed planning for each release and at each sprint is tactical. Read more about release planning and sprint planning in Chapter 8.

  - • At release planning, you can plan your release to match a specific date, with minimal marketable features.

  - • You also can plan your release with enough time to create a specific set of features.

  - • During each sprint planning meeting, in addition to selecting the scope for the sprint, the development team estimates the time, in hours, to complete individual tasks for each of that sprint's requirements. Use the sprint backlog to manage detailed time allocations throughout the sprint.

- ✔ Once your project is underway, use the scrum team's velocity to fine-tune your scheduling.

In Chapter 8, I describe planning releases for *minimal marketable features,* the smallest group of product features that you can effectively deploy and promote in the marketplace.

To determine how much functionality an agile development team can deliver within a set amount of time, you need to know your development team's velocity. In the next section, you take a look at how to measure velocity, how to use velocity for a project timeline, and how to increase velocity throughout the project.

Introducing velocity

One of the most important things about time management on agile projects is the use of velocity, a powerful tool for forecasting long-term timelines. Velocity, in agile terms, is a development team's work speed. In Chapter 7, I describe measuring the effort for requirements, or user stories, in story points. You measure velocity by the number of user story points that the development team completes in each sprint.

Determining the length of an agile project

A few different factors determine the length of agile projects:

- **Assigned deadline:** Agile project teams may wish to set a specific end date for business reasons. For example, you may wish to get a product to market for a specific shopping season, or perhaps have it coincide with the timing of a competitor's product release. In that case, you set a specific end date, and create as much shippable functionality as possible from the project start until the end date.

- **Budget considerations:** Agile project teams may also have budget considerations that affect the amount of time a project will last. For example, if you have a $1,600,000 budget, and your project costs $20,000 a week to run, your project will be able to last 80 weeks. You will have 80 weeks to create and release as much shippable functionality as possible.

- **Functionality completed:** Agile projects may also last only until enough product functionality is complete. Project teams may run sprints until the requirements with the highest value are complete, and then determine that the lower-value requirements — the ones that few people will use or that will not generate much revenue — are not really necessary.

A user story is a simple description of a product requirement, identifying what a requirement must accomplish for whom. User story points are relative numbers that describe the amount of effort necessary to develop a user story. Chapter 8 delves into the details of creating user stories and estimating the effort using story points.

Once you know the development team's velocity, you can use velocity as a long-range planning tool. Velocity can help you forecast how long the scrum team will take to complete a certain number of requirements and how much a project may cost.

In the next section, you dive into velocity as a tool for time management. You see how scope changes affect an agile project's timeline. You also find out how to work with multiple scrum teams, and you review agile artifacts for time management.

Monitoring and adjusting velocity

Once a project starts, the scrum team starts to monitor its velocity. You measure velocity from sprint to sprint. You use velocity for long-term schedule and budget planning as well as for sprint planning.

In general, people are good at planning and estimating in the short term, so identifying hours for tasks in an upcoming sprint works well. At the same time, people are often terrible at estimating distant tasks in absolute terms like hours. Tools like velocity, which are based on actual performance, are more accurate measurements for longer-term planning.

Velocity is a good trending tool. You can use it to determine future timelines since the activities and development time within sprints is the same from sprint to sprint.

Avoid attempting to guess a scrum team's velocity before a project starts, or even in the middle of a sprint. You will only set unrealistic expectations about how much work the team can complete. Instead, use the scrum team's actual velocity to forecast how much longer the project may take and cost.

In the next section, you see how to calculate velocity, how to use velocity to predict a project's schedule, and how to increase your scrum team's velocity.

Calculating velocity

At the end of each sprint, the scrum team looks at the requirements it has finished and adds up the number of story points associated with those requirements. The total number of completed story points is the scrum team's velocity for that sprint. After the first few sprints, you will start to see a trend and will be able to calculate the average velocity.

The average velocity is the total number of story points completed, divided by the total number of sprints completed.

For example, if the development team's velocity was

> Sprint 1 = 15 points
>
> Sprint 2 = 19 points
>
> Sprint 3 = 21 points
>
> Sprint 4 = 25 points

your total number of story points completed will be 80. Your average velocity will be 20—80 story points divided by four sprints.

Once you have run a sprint and you know the scrum team's velocity, you can start forecasting the remaining time on your project.

Using velocity to estimate the project timeline

Once you know your velocity, you can determine how long your project will last. Follow these steps:

1. **Add up the number of story points for the remaining requirements in the product backlog.**

2. **Determine the number of sprints you will need by dividing the number of story points remaining in the product backlog by the velocity.**

   - To get a pessimistic estimate, use the lowest velocity the development team has accomplished.

   - To get an optimistic estimate, use the highest velocity the development team has accomplished.

   - To get a most likely estimate, use the average velocity the development team has accomplished.

3. **Determine how much time it will take to complete the story points in the product backlog by multiplying sprint length by the number of remaining sprints.**

   For example, assume that

   - Your remaining product backlog contains 800 story points.

   - Your development team velocity averages 20 story points per sprint.

   How many more sprints will your product backlog need? Divide the number of story points by your velocity, and you get your remaining sprints. In this case, 800/20 = 40.

   If you are using two-week sprints on your project, your project will last 80 weeks.

Velocity, like other tools on agile projects, is not meant to be a rigid rule to control development speed. Use velocity to measure development speed after a sprint, rather than to dictate how much work a scrum team should complete before a sprint. If velocity turns into a target, rather than a past measurement, scrum teams may be tempted to exaggerate estimated story points in order to meet that target, rendering velocity meaningless. Instead, focus on increasing velocity by removing constraints identified during the sprint and at the sprint retrospective.

Once the scrum team knows its velocity and the number of story points for the requirements, you can use the velocity to determine how long any given group of requirements will take to create. For example:

✔ You can calculate the time an individual release may take if you have an idea of the number of story points that will go into that release. At the release level, your story point estimates will be more high level than at the sprint level. If you are basing your release timing on delivering specific functionality, your release date may change as you refine your user stories and estimates throughout the project.

✔ You can calculate the time you need for a specific group of user stories, like all high-priority stories, or all stories relating to a particular theme, by using the number of story points in that group of user stories.

Velocity differs from sprint to sprint. In the first couple of sprints, when the project is new, the scrum team will typically have a low velocity. As the project progresses, velocity should increase, because the scrum team will have learned more about the product and will have matured as a team working together. Setbacks within specific sprints can temporarily decrease velocity from time to time, but agile processes like the sprint retrospective can help the scrum team ensure those setbacks are temporary.

In the beginning of a project, velocity will vary considerably from sprint to sprint. Velocity will become more consistent over time.

Scrum teams can also increase their velocity throughout agile projects, making projects shorter and less costly. In the next section, you will find ways to gain velocity in each consecutive sprint.

Increasing velocity

If a scrum team has a product backlog with 800 story points and an average velocity of 20 story points, the project will last 40 sprints — 80 weeks, with two-week sprints. But what if the scrum team could increase its velocity?

- ✔ Increasing the average velocity to 23 story points per sprint would mean 34.78 sprints. If you round that up to 35 sprints, the same project would last 70 weeks.

- ✔ An average velocity of 26 would take about 31 sprints, or 62 weeks.

- ✔ An average velocity of 31 would take about 26 sprints, or 52 weeks.

As you can see, increasing velocity can save a good deal of time and, consequently, money.

Velocity can naturally increase with each sprint, as the scrum team finds its rhythm of working together on the project. However, there are also opportunities to raise velocity on agile projects, past the common increases that come with time. Everyone on a scrum team plays a part in helping get higher velocity with every successive sprint.

- ✔ **Remove project impediments:** One way to increase velocity is to quickly remove project impediments, or roadblocks. Roadblocks are anything that keeps a development team member from working to full capacity. By definition, roadblocks can decrease velocity. Clearing roadblocks as soon as they arise increases velocity by helping the scrum team to be fully functional and productive. Find out more about removing project impediments in Chapter 9.

- ✔ **Avoid project roadblocks:** The best way to increase velocity is to strategically create ways to avoid roadblocks in the first place. By knowing — or learning about — the processes and the specific needs of groups your team will work with, you can head off roadblocks before they arise.

✔ **Eliminate distractions:** Another way to increase velocity is for the scrum master to protect the development team from distractions. By making sure people don't request non-sprint, goal-related work from the development team — even tasks that might take a small amount of time — the scrum master will be able to help keep the development team focused on the sprint.

✔ **Solicit input from the team:** Finally, everyone on the scrum team can provide ideas for increasing velocity in the sprint retrospective meeting. The development team knows its work the best, and may have ideas on how to improve output. The product owner may have insights into the requirements that can help the development team work faster. The scrum master will have seen any repetitive roadblocks and can discuss how to prevent the roadblocks in the first place.

Increasing velocity is very valuable, but remember that you may not see changes overnight. Scrum team velocity often has a pattern of slow increases, some big velocity jumps, a flat period, and then slow increases again as the scrum team identifies, experiments, and corrects constraints that are holding it back.

Consistency for useful velocity

Because velocity is a measure of work completed in terms of story points, it is an accurate indicator and predictor of project performance only when you use the following practices:

✔ **Consistent sprint lengths:** Each sprint should last the same amount of time throughout the life of the project. If sprint lengths are different, the amount of work the development team can complete in each sprint will be different, and velocity won't be relevant in predicting the remaining time on the project.

✔ **Consistent work hours:** Individual development team members should work the same number of hours in each sprint. If Sandy works 45 hours in one sprint, 23 in another, and 68 in yet another, then Sandy will naturally complete a different amount of work from sprint to sprint. However, if Sandy always works the same number hours in one sprint, then her velocity will be comparable between sprints.

✔ **Consistent development team members:** Different people work at different rates. Tom might work faster than Bob, so if Tom works on one sprint and Bob works on the next sprint, the velocity of Tom's sprint will not be a good prediction for Bob's sprint.

When sprint lengths, work hours, and team members remain consistent throughout a project, you can use velocity to truly know if development speed is increasing or decreasing and to accurately estimate the project timeline.

Preventing roadblocks

One development team I worked with needed feedback from its company's legal department but had not been able to get a response via e-mail or voicemail. One of the development team members stated this lack of response as a roadblock in a daily scrum meeting. After the scrum meeting was over, the scrum master walked over to the legal department and found the right person to work with. After talking to that person, the scrum master found out that her e-mail was constantly flooded with requests, and her voicemail was not much better.

The scrum master then suggested a process for future legal requests: Moving forward, the development team members could walk over to the legal department with requests and get feedback right there, in person, immediately. The new process took only a few minutes, but saved days on turnaround from the legal department, effectively preventing similar roadblocks in the future. Finding ways to proactively prevent roadblocks helps increase the scrum team's velocity.

Performance does not scale linearly with available time. For example, if you have two-week sprints with 20 story points per sprint, going to three-week sprints does not guarantee 30 story points. The new sprint length will generate an unknown change in velocity.

Once you know how to accurately measure and increase velocity, you have a powerful tool for managing time and cost on a project. In the next section, I talk about how to manage a timeline in an ever-changing agile environment.

Managing scope changes from a time perspective

Agile project teams welcome changing requirements, which means project scope reflects the real priorities of the business. It is "requirements Darwinism" at its purest — development teams complete requirements of highest priority first; those requirements that sound like good ideas in theory but never win the "either this requirement or that requirement" contest that fixed sprint lengths force are left out.

New requirements may have no effect at all on a project's timeline; you just have to prioritize. Working with the project stakeholders, the product owner can determine to develop only the requirements that will fit into a certain window of time or budget. The priority ranking of items in the product backlog determines which requirements are important enough to develop. The scrum team can guarantee completing higher-priority requirements. The lower-priority requirements might be part of another project, or may never be created at all.

In Chapter 12, I discuss how to manage scope changes with the product backlog. When you add a new requirement to an agile project, you prioritize that requirement against other user stories in your product backlog and add the new user story into the appropriate spot in the product backlog. This may move other user stories down in priority. If you keep your product backlog and its estimates up-to-date as new requirements arise, you will always have a good idea of the project timeline, even with constantly changing scope.

On the other hand, the product owner and the project stakeholders may determine that all the requirements in the product backlog, including new requirements, are useful enough to include in the project. In this case, you extend the project end date to accommodate the additional scope, increase velocity, or divide the project scope among multiple scrum teams that will work simultaneously on different product features.

Project teams often make schedule decisions about lower-priority requirements toward the end of a project. The reasons for these just-in-time decisions are because marketplace demands for specific scope items change, and also because velocity tends to increase as the development team gets into a rhythm. Changes in velocity increase your predictions about how many user stories the development team can complete in a given amount of time. On agile projects, you wait until the last responsible moment — when you know the most about the question at hand — to make decisions.

The next section shows you how to work with more than one scrum team on a project.

Managing time by using multiple teams

For larger projects, multiple scrum teams working in parallel will be able to complete a project in a shorter time frame.

You may want to create a project with multiple scrum teams if

- ✔ Your project is very large and will require more than five to nine development team members to complete.

- ✔ Your project has a specific end date that you must meet, and the scrum team's velocity will not be sufficient to complete the most valuable user stories by that end date.

The ideal size for a development team on an agile project is seven people, plus or minus two people. Groups of more than nine people start to build silos, and the number of communication channels makes self-management more difficult. When your product development requires more than nine development team members, it may be time to consider using multiple scrum teams.

Breaking up work with multiple teams

If you have multiple scrum teams on a project, break the work into themes, or logical groups of product features, for each team.

Before rushing into that, though, you need to consider the overall scope of the themes and the relationship between them. The work needs to be sufficiently separate to allow the teams to operate independently.

You also need to add an integration team to the project. An integration team's sole purpose is to take the working product functionality that the development teams create and get those features to work together.

Multiple team structure

Figure 13-1 shows a diagram created by Ken Schwaber, one of the signatories on the Agile Manifesto, for his book *The Enterprise and Scrum* (Microsoft Press, 2011). The diagram shows how a project with multiple scrum teams might look.

Each of these scrum teams has its own scrum master, product owner, and cross-functional development team members. Synchronize the sprints among the teams; the sprints should be the same length and should start and end at the same time for each team. The delivered sprint functionality from the task-level teams becomes product backlog to-do items for the associated activity-level team to integrate and make work together; the delivered sprint functionality from the activity-level teams becomes product backlog to-do items for the associated function-level team to integrate and make work together; the delivered sprint functionality from the function-level teams becomes product backlog to-do items for the associated product-level team to integrate and make work together.

Multiple teams require an additional layer of management. This may require

- ✔ **Additional daily scrum:** Called the *scrum of scrums,* this daily scrum occurs just after the individual team scrums, where representatives from each development team share information with each other and with the next level integration scrum master and product owner.
- ✔ **Joint sprint retrospectives:** In this retrospective, teams share their experiences, challenges, and best practices with the other teams.

What's great about working with multiple scrum teams is that it accelerates the project timeline. The challenge with working with multiple scrum teams is that it introduces additional overhead to manage the more complex inter-team coordinating.

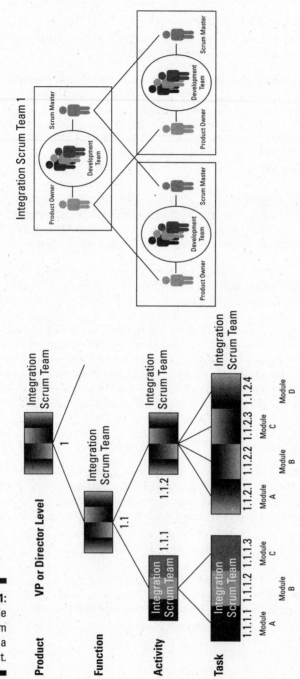

Figure 13-1:
Multiple
scrum
teams on a
project.

Using agile artifacts for time management

The product roadmap, release plan, product backlog, and sprint backlog all play a part in time management. Table 13-2 shows how each artifact contributes to time management.

Table 13-2	Agile Artifacts and Time Management Roles
Artifact	*Role in Time Management*
Product roadmap: The product roadmap is a prioritized, holistic view of the high-level requirements that support the product's vision. Find more about the product roadmap in Chapter 7.	The product roadmap is a strategic look at the overall project priorities. While the product roadmap likely will not have specific dates, it will have general date ranges for groups of functionality and will allow an initial framing for bringing the product to market.
Product backlog: The product backlog is a complete list of all currently known product require-ments. Find more about the product backlog in Chapters 7 and 8.	The user stories in your product backlog will have estimated story points. Once you know your development team's velocity, you can use the total number of story points in the product backlog to determine a realistic project end date.
Release plan: The release plan contains a release schedule for a minimum set of requirements. Find more about the release plan in Chapter 8.	The release plan will have a target release date for a specific goal that is supported by a minimal set of marketable functionalities. Scrum teams only plan and work on one release at a time.
Sprint backlog: The sprint backlog contains the requirements and tasks for the current sprint. Find more about the sprint backlog in Chapter 8.	During your sprint planning meeting, you estimate individual tasks in the backlog in hours. At the end of each sprint, you take the total completed story points from the sprint back-log to calculate your development team's velocity for that sprint.

In the next sections, you dive into cost management for agile projects. Cost management is directly related to time management. You compare traditional approaches to cost management to those within agile projects. You find out how to estimate costs on an agile project and how to use velocity to forecast your long-term budget.

What's Different About Cost in Agile

Cost is a project's financial budget. When you work on an agile project, you focus on value, you exploit the power of change, and you aim for simplicity. Agile Principles 1, 2, and 10 state the following:

1. Our highest priority is to satisfy the customer through early and continuous delivery of valuable software.

2. Welcome changing requirements, even late in development. Agile processes harness change for the customer's competitive advantage.

10. Simplicity — the art of maximizing the amount of work not done — is essential.

Because of this emphasis on value, change, and simplicity, agile projects have a very different approach to budget and cost management than traditional projects. Table 13-3 highlights some of the differences.

Table 13-3	Historical Versus Agile Cost Management
Cost Management with Traditional Approaches	*Cost Management with Agile Approaches*
Cost, like time, is based on fixed scope.	Project schedule, not scope, has the biggest impact on cost. You can start with a fixed cost and fixed amount of time, and complete requirements that fit into your budget and schedule.
Organizations estimate project costs and fund projects before the project starts.	Product owners often secure project funding after the product roadmap stage is complete. Some organizations even fund agile projects one release at a time; product owners will secure funding after completing release planning for each release.
New requirements mean higher costs. Because project managers estimate costs based on what they know at the project start, which is very little, cost overruns are common.	Project teams can replace lower-priority requirements with new, equivalently-sized high-priority requirements with no impact on time or cost.

Cost Management with Traditional Approaches	Cost Management with Agile Approaches
Scope bloat (see Chapter 12) wastes large amounts of money on features that people simply do not use.	Because agile development teams complete requirements by priority, they concentrate on creating only the product features that users really need, whether those features are added on day one or day 100 of the project.
Projects cannot generate revenue until the project is complete.	Project teams can release working, revenue-generating functionality early, creating a self-funding project.

When costs increase, project sponsors sometimes find themselves in a kind of hostage situation. The historical project management model does not call for any complete product functionality until the very end of a project. Since traditional approaches to development are all-or-nothing proposals, if costs increase and stakeholders don't pay more for the product, they will not get *any* finished requirements. The incomplete product becomes a kidnapped hostage; pay more, or get nothing.

In the following sections, you find out about cost approaches within agile projects, how to estimate costs for an agile project, how to control your budget, and how to lower costs.

How to Manage Cost in Agile

On agile projects, cost is mostly a direct expression of project time. Because scrum teams consist of full-time, dedicated team members, they have a set team cost — generally expressed as an hourly or fixed rate per person — that should be the same for each sprint. Consistent sprint lengths, work hours, and team members enable you to accurately use velocity to predict development speed. Once you use velocity to determine how many sprints your project will take — that is, how long your project will be — you can know how much your scrum team will cost for the whole project.

Project cost also includes the cost for resources like hardware, software, licenses, and any other supplies you might need to complete your project.

In this section, you find out how to create an initial budget and how to use the scrum team's velocity to determine long-range costs.

Creating an initial budget

To create your project budget, you need to know the cost for your scrum team, per sprint, and the cost for any additional resources you need to complete the project.

Typically, you calculate the cost for your scrum team using an hourly rate for each team member. Multiply each team member's hourly rate by his or her available hours per week by the number of weeks in your sprints to calculate your scrum team's per-sprint cost. Table 13-4 shows a sample budget for a scrum team — the development team, the scrum master, and the product owner — for a two-week sprint.

Table 13-4   Sample Scrum Team Budget for a Two-Week Sprint

Team Member	Hourly Rate	Weekly Hours	Weekly Cost	Sprint Cost (2 Weeks)
Don	$80	40	$3,200	$6,400
Peggy	$70	40	$2,800	$5,600
Bob	$70	40	$2,800	$5,600
Mike	$65	40	$2,600	$5,200
Joan	$85	40	$3,400	$6,800
Tommy	$75	40	$3,000	$6,000
Pete	$55	40	$2,200	$4,400
Total		280	$20,000	$40,000

The cost for additional resources will vary by project. Take the following into account when determining your project costs:

✔ Hardware costs

✔ Software, including license costs

✔ Hosting costs

✔ Training costs

✔ Miscellaneous team expenses, such as additional office supplies, team lunches, travel costs, and the price of any tools you may need

These costs may be one-time costs, rather than per-sprint costs. I suggest separating these costs within your budget; as you see in the next section, you need your cost for each sprint to determine the cost for the project.

Creating a self-funding project

A big benefit of agile projects is the capability to have a self-funding project. Scrum teams deliver working functionality at the end of each sprint and make that functionality available to the marketplace at the end of each release cycle. If your product is an income-generating product, you could use revenue from early releases to help fund the rest of your project.

For example, an e-commerce website might generate $15,000 a month in sales after the first release, $40,000 a month after the second release, and so on. Tables 13-5 and 13-6 compare income on a sample traditional project to the income from a self-funding agile project.

In Table 13-5, the project created $100,000 in income after six months of development. Now compare the income in Table 13-5 to the income generated in Table 13-6.

Table 13-5	Income from a Traditional Project with a Final Release After Six Months	
Month	*Income Generated*	*Total Project Income*
January	$0	$0
February	$0	$0
March	$0	$0
April	$0	$0
May	$0	$0
June	$100,000	$100,000

Table 13-6	Income from a Project with Monthly Releases and a Final Release after Six Months	
Month/Release	*Income Generated*	*Total Project Income*
January	$15,000	$15,000
February	$25,000	$40,000
March	$40,000	$80,000
April	$70,000	$150,000
May	$80,000	$230,000
June	$100,000	$330,000

In Table 13-6, the project generated income with the very first release. By the end of six months, the project had generated $330,000 — $230,000 more than the project in Table 13-5.

Using velocity to determine long-range costs

The "Using velocity to estimate the project timeline" section earlier in this chapter shows how to determine how much time a project will take, using the scrum team's velocity and the remaining story points in the product backlog. You can use the same information to determine the cost for the project or for your current release.

Once you know the scrum team's velocity, you can calculate the cost for the remainder of the project.

In the velocity example from earlier in this chapter, where your scrum team velocity averages 20 story points per sprint, your product backlog contains 800 story points, and your sprints are two weeks long, your project will take 40 sprints, or 80 weeks, to complete.

To determine the remaining cost for your project, multiply the cost per sprint by the number of sprints the scrum team needs to complete the product backlog.

If your scrum team cost is $40,000 per sprint, and you have 40 sprints left, your remaining cost for your project will be $1,600,000.

In the next sections, you find out different ways to lower your project costs.

Lowering cost by increasing velocity

In the time management section of this chapter, I talk about increasing the scrum team's velocity. Using the examples from the earlier section, and the $40,000 per two-week sprint from Table 13-4, increasing velocity could reduce your costs, as follows:

✔ If the scrum team increases its average velocity from 20 to 23 story points per sprint

  • You will have 35 remaining sprints, and

  • Your project will cost a little more than $1.4 million, saving you more than $200,000.

✔ If the scrum team increases its velocity to 26 story points

  • You will have 31 remaining sprints, and

  • Your project will cost $1,230,770.

✔ If the scrum team increases its velocity to 31 story points

• You will have 26 remaining sprints, and

• Your project will cost $1,032,258.

As you can see, removing impediments to increase the scrum team's velocity can provide real savings on project costs. See how to help the scrum team become more productive in the "Increasing velocity" section in this chapter.

Lowering cost by reducing time

You can also lower your project costs by not completing lower-priority requirements, thus lowering the number of sprints you need. On agile projects, because completed functionality is delivered with each sprint, the project stakeholders can make a business decision to end a project when the cost of future development is higher than the value of that future development.

Project stakeholders can then use the remaining budget from the old project to start a new, more valuable project. The practice of moving the budget from one project to another is called *capital redeployment*.

While you may have variable costs throughout your project, as long as your scrum team members stay the same, and those costs stay the same, your sprint costs for your scrum team will be stable. For example, if the scrum team in Table 13-4 stays the same for your entire project, your sprint cost will always be $40,000 per sprint. Scrum team costs are very often the greatest overall percentage of a project's budget.

To determine a project's end based on cost, you need to know

✔ The value (V) of the remaining requirements in the product backlog

✔ The actual cost (AC) of the work it will take to complete the requirements in the product backlog

✔ The opportunity cost (OC), or the value of having the scrum team work on a new project

When V < AC + OC, the project can stop. The cost you will sink into the project will be more than the value you will receive from the project.

Consider this example: A company is running an agile project and

✔ The remaining features in the product backlog will generate $100,000 in income (V = $100,000).

✔ It will take three sprints with a cost of $40,000 per sprint to create those features, with a total of $120,000 (AC = $200,000).

- ✔ The scrum team could be working on a new project that would generate $150,000 after three sprints, minus the scrum team's cost (OC = $150,000).

- ✔ The project value, $100,000, is less than the actual costs plus opportunity costs, or $350,000. This would be a good time to end the project.

The opportunity for capital redeployment sometimes arises in emergencies, when an organization needs members of the scrum team to pause a project for critical unplanned work. Project sponsors sometimes evaluate a project's remaining value and cost before restarting a paused project.

Pausing a project causes demobilization effort and costs.

Project sponsors may also compare the product backlog value to remaining development costs throughout the project, so they know just the right time to end the project and receive the most value.

Determining other costs

Similar to time management, once you know the scrum team's velocity, you can determine the cost of anything within the project. For example:

- ✔ You can calculate the cost for an individual release if you have an idea of the number of story points that will go into that release. At the release, your story point estimates will be more high-level than at the sprint, so your costs may change, depending upon how you determine your release date.

- ✔ You can calculate the cost for a specific group of user stories, like all high-priority stories, or all stories relating to a particular theme, by using the number of story points in that group of user stories.

Using agile artifacts for cost management

You can use the product roadmap, release plan, product backlog, and sprint backlog for cost management. Table 13-2 shows how each artifact helps you measure and evaluate project costs.

Time and cost forecasts based on actual development team performance are more accurate than forecasts based on hope.

Chapter 14

Managing Team Dynamics and Communication

Team dynamics and communication are significant parts of project management. In this chapter, you find out about traditional and agile approaches to project teams and communication. You will see how a high value on individuals and interactions makes agile project teams great teams to work on. You find out how face-to-face communication helps make agile projects successful.

What's Different About Team Dynamics in Agile

What makes a project team on an agile project unique? The core reason scrum teams are different from traditional teams are their team dynamics. The Agile Manifesto (refer to Chapter 2) sets the framework for how agile project team members work together: The very first item of value in the manifesto is *individuals and interactions* over processes and tools.

The following Agile Principles, also from Chapter 2, support valuing people on the project team and how they work together:

4. Business people and developers must work together daily throughout the project.

5. Build projects around motivated individuals. Give them the environment and support they need, and trust them to get the job done.

8. Agile processes promote sustainable development. The sponsors, developers, and users should be able to maintain a constant pace indefinitely.

11. The best architectures, requirements, and designs emerge from self-organizing teams.

12. At regular intervals, the team reflects on how to become more effective, then tunes and adjusts its behavior accordingly.

The Agile Principles apply to many different project management areas. You see some of these principles repeated in different chapters of this book.

On agile projects, the development team contains the people who do the physical work of creating the product. The scrum team contains the development team, plus the product owner and the scrum master. The project team is the scrum team and your project stakeholder. Everyone on the scrum team has responsibilities related to self-management.

Table 14-1 shows some differences between team management on traditional projects and on agile projects.

I've never liked the term "resources" when used for "people." Referring to people and equipment with the same term is the start of thinking of team members as interchangeable objects that can be swapped in and out. Resources are things, utilitarian and expendable. The people on your project team are human beings, with emotions, ideas, and priorities inside and outside of the project. People can learn and create and grow throughout the project. Respecting your fellow project team members by calling them "people" instead of "resources" is a subtle but powerful way to reinforce the fact that people are at the core of agile ideologies.

The following sections discuss how working with a dedicated, cross-functional, self-organizing, size-limited team benefits agile projects. You find out more about servant leadership and creating a good environment for a scrum team. In short, you find out how team dynamics help agile projects succeed.

How to Manage Team Dynamics in Agile

Time and again, when I talk with product owners, scrum masters, and development team members, I hear the same thing: People like working on agile projects. Agile team dynamics enable people to do great work in the best way they know how. People on scrum teams have opportunities to learn, to teach, to lead, and to really be part of a cohesive, self-managing team.

The following sections show you how to work as part of a scrum team and why agile approaches to teamwork make agile projects successful.

Table 14-1	Historical Versus Agile Team Dynamics
Team Management with Traditional Approaches	**Team Dynamics with Agile Approaches**
Project teams rely on *command and control* — a top-down approach to project management, where the project manager is responsible for assigning tasks to team members and attempting to control what the team does.	Scrum teams are self-managing, self-organizing, and benefit from *servant leadership.* Instead of top-down management, a servant-leader coaches, removes obstacles, and prevents distractions to help the scrum team thrive.
Companies evaluate individual employee performance.	Agile organizations evaluate scrum team performance; every member of the scrum team receives the same review. Scrum teams, like any sports team, succeed or fail as a whole team.
Team members often find themselves working on more than one project at a time, switching their attention back and forth.	Development teams are dedicated to one project at a time, and reap the benefits of focus.
Development team members have distinct roles, like "programmer" or "tester."	Development teams work *cross*-functionally, doing different jobs within the team to ensure they complete priority requirements quickly.
Development teams have no specific size limits.	Development teams are intentionally limited in size. Ideally, development teams have seven, plus or minus two people.
People are commonly referred to as "resources," a shortened term for "human resources."	People are called "people" or "team members." On an agile project, you probably will not hear the term "resource" used to refer to people.

Becoming self-managing and self-organizing

On agile projects, scrum teams are directly accountable for creating deliverables. Scrum teams manage themselves, organizing their own work and tasks. No one person tells the scrum team what to do. This doesn't mean that agile projects have no leadership. Each member of the scrum team has the opportunity to lead, based on his or her skills, ideas, and initiative.

On agile projects, the development team contains the people who are doing the physical work of creating the product. The scrum team contains the development team, plus the product owner and the scrum master. The project team is the scrum team and your project stakeholders. Both the development team and the overall scrum team have responsibilities related to self-management.

The idea of self-management and self-organization is a mature way of thinking about work. Self-management assumes that people are professional, motivated, and dedicated enough to commit to a job and see it through. At the core of self-management is the idea that the people who are doing a job from day-to-day know the most about that job and are best qualified to determine how to complete it. Working with a self-managing scrum team requires trust and respect within the team and within the team's organization as a whole.

Nonetheless, let's be clear: Accountability is at the core of agile projects. The difference is that in an agile project, teams are held accountable for tangible results that you can see and demonstrate. Traditionally, companies held teams accountable for compliance to the organization's step-by-step process — stripping them of the ability or incentive to be innovative. Self-management, however, returns innovation and creativity to development teams.

For a scrum team to be self-managing, you need an environment of trust. Everyone on the scrum team must trust one another to do his or her best for the scrum team and the project. The scrum team's company or organization must also trust the scrum team to be competent, to make decisions, and to manage itself. In order to create and maintain an environment of trust, each member of the scrum team must commit, individually and as a team, to the project and to one another.

Self-managing development teams create better product architectures, requirements, and design for a simple reason: ownership. When you give people the freedom and responsibility to solve problems, they are more mentally engaged in their work.

Scrum team members play roles in all areas of project management. Table 14-2 shows how scrum teams and development teams manage scope, procurement, time, cost, team dynamics, communication, quality, and risk.

All in all, people on agile projects tend to find a great deal of job satisfaction. Self-management speaks to a deeply rooted human desire to control our own destiny, and allows people this control on a daily basis.

The next section discusses another reason that people on agile projects are happy: the servant-leader.

Table 14-2   **Project Management and Self-Managing Teams**

Area of Project Management	How Development Teams Self-Manage	How Product Owners Self-Manage	How Scrum Masters Self-Manage
Scope	May suggest features based on technical affinity.	Use the product vision, the release goal, and each sprint goal to determine if and where scope items belong.	Remove impediments that limit the amount of scope the development team can create.
	Work directly with the product owner to clarify requirements.	Use product backlog prioritization to determine which requirements are developed.	Through coaching, help development teams become more productive with each successive sprint.
	Identify how much work they can commit to completing in a sprint.		
	Identify the tasks to complete scope in the sprint backlog.		
	Determine the best way to create specific features.		
Procurement	Identify the tools they need to create the product.	Secure necessary funding for tools and equipment for development teams.	Help procure tools and equipment that accelerate development team velocity.
	Work with the product owner to get those tools.		
Time	Provide effort estimates for product features.	Ensure that the development team correctly understands product features so that development teams can correctly estimate the effort to create those features.	Facilitate estimation poker games.
	Identify what features they can create in a given time frame — the sprint.		Help development teams increase velocity, which affects time.
	Often provide time estimates for tasks in each sprint.	Use velocity — development speed — to forecast long-term timelines.	Protect team from organizational time-wasters and distractions.
	Choose their own schedules and manage their own time.		

(continued)

Table 14-2 (continued)

Area of Project Management	How Development Teams Self-Manage	How Product Owners Self-Manage	How Scrum Masters Self-Manage
Cost	Provide effort estimates for product features.	Ultimately responsible for the budget and return on investment on an agile project. Use velocity to forecast long-term costs, based on timelines.	Facilitate estimation poker games. Help development teams increase velocity, which affects cost.
Team dynamics	Prevent bottlenecks by working cross-functionally, and are willing to take on different types of tasks. Continuously learn and teach one another. Commit, both individually and as part of the scrum team, to their projects and to one another. Strive to build consensus when making important decisions.	Commit to their projects and are integrated members of the scrum team.	Facilitate scrum team collocation. Help remove impediments to scrum team self-management. Commit to their projects and are integrated members of the scrum team. Strive to build consensus within the scrum team when making important decisions. Facilitate relationships between the scrum team and stakeholders.
Communication	Report on progress, upcoming tasks, and identify roadblocks in their daily scrum meetings. Keep the sprint backlog up-to-date daily, providing accurate, immediate information about a project's status. Present working functionality to project stakeholders at the sprint review meetings at the end of each sprint.	Communicate information about the product and the business needs to development teams on an ongoing basis. Communicate information about the project progress to product stakeholders. Help present working functionality to stakeholders at the sprint review meetings at the end of each sprint.	Encourage face-to-face communication between all scrum team members. Foster close cooperation between the scrum team and other departments within the company or organization.

Area of Project Management	How Development Teams Self-Manage	How Product Owners Self-Manage	How Scrum Masters Self-Manage
Quality	Commit to providing technical excellence and good design.	Add acceptance criteria to requirements.	Help facilitate the sprint retrospective.
	Test their work throughout the day and comprehensively test all development each day.	Ensure that the development team correctly understands and interprets requirements.	Help ensure face-to-face communication between scrum team members, which in turn helps ensure quality work.
	Inspect their work and adapt for improvements at sprint retrospective meetings at the end of each sprint.	Provide development teams with feedback about the product from the organization and from the marketplace.	Help create a sustainable development environment so that the development team can perform at its best.
		Accept features as Done during each sprint.	
Risk	Identify and develop the risk mitigation approach for each sprint.	Look at overall project risks as well as risks to their ROI commitment.	Help prevent roadblocks and distractions.
	Alert the scrum master to roadblocks and distractions.		Help remove roadblocks and identified risks.
	Use information from each sprint retrospective to reduce risk in future sprints.		Facilitate development team conversations about possible risks.
	Embrace cross-functionality to reduce risk if one member unexpectedly leaves the team.		
	Commit to delivering shippable functionality at the end of each sprint, reducing risk in the overall project.		

Supporting the team: The servant-leader

The scrum master serves as a servant-leader, someone who leads by removing obstacles, preventing distractions, and helping the rest of the scrum team do its job to the best of its ability. Leaders on agile projects help find solutions rather than assign tasks. Scrum masters coach, trust, and challenge the scrum team to manage itself.

Other members of the scrum team can also take on servant leadership roles. While the scrum master helps get rid of distractions and roadblocks, the product owner and members of the development team can also help where needed. The product owner can lead by proactively providing important details about the product needs and quickly providing answers to questions from the development team. Development team members can teach and mentor one another as they become more cross-functional. Each person on a scrum team may act as a servant-leader at some point in the project.

Larry Spears identified ten characteristics of a servant-leader in his paper, "The Understanding and Practice of Servant-Leadership" (Servant Leadership Roundtable, School of Leadership Studies, Regent University, August 2005). Here are those characteristics, along with my additions for how each characteristic can benefit the team dynamics on an agile project.

- **Listening:** Listening closely to other members of the scrum team will help the people on the scrum team identify areas to help one another. A servant-leader may need to listen to what people are saying, as well as what people are *not* saying, in order to remove obstacles.

- **Empathy:** A servant-leader tries to understand and empathize with people on the scrum team, and to help them understand one another.

- **Healing:** On an agile project, healing can mean undoing the damage of non-people-centric processes. These are processes that treat people like equipment and other replaceable parts. Many traditional project management approaches can be described as being non-people-centric.

- **Awareness:** On an agile project, the people on the scrum team may need to be aware of activities on many levels in order to best serve the scrum team.

- **Persuasion:** Servant-leaders rely on an ability to convince, rather than on top-down authority. Strong persuasion skills, along with organizational clout, will help a scrum master advocate for the scrum team to the company or organization. A servant-leader can also pass along persuasion skills to the rest of the scrum team, helping maintain harmony and build consensus.

- **Conceptualization:** Each member of a scrum team can use conceptualization skills on an agile project. The changing nature of agile projects encourages the scrum team to envision ideas beyond those at hand. A servant-leader will help nurture the scrum team's creativity, both for the development of the product and for team dynamics.

✔ **Foresight:** Scrum teams gain foresight with each sprint retrospective. By inspecting their work, processes, and team dynamics on a regular basis, the scrum team can continuously adapt and understand how to make better decisions for future sprints.

✔ **Stewardship:** A servant-leader is the steward of the scrum team's needs. Stewardship is about trust. Members of the scrum team trust one another to look out for the needs of the team and the project as a whole.

✔ **Commitment to the growth of people:** Growth is essential to a scrum team's ability to be cross-functional. A servant-leader will encourage and enable a scrum team to learn and grow.

✔ **Building community:** A scrum team is its own community. A servant-leader will help build and maintain positive team dynamics within that community.

Servant leadership works because it positively focuses on individuals and interactions, a key tenet of agile project management. Much like self-management, servant leadership requires trust and respect.

The concept of servant leadership is not specific to agile projects. If you have studied management techniques, you may recognize the works of Robert K. Greenleaf, who started the modern movement for servant-leadership — and coined the term "servant-leader" — in an essay in 1970. Greenleaf founded the Center for Applied Ethics, now known as the Greenleaf Center for Servant Leadership, which promotes the concept of servant leadership worldwide.

The next two sections largely relate to team factors for agile project success: the dedicated team and the cross-functional team.

Working with a dedicated team

Having a dedicated scrum team provides several important benefits to projects.

✔ **Keeping people focused on one project at a time helps prevent distractions.** Dedication to one project increases productivity by reducing *task-switching* — moving back and forth between different tasks without really completing any of them.

✔ **When people work on dedicated scrum teams, they know what they will be working on every day.** An interesting reality of behavioral science is that when people know what they will be working on in the immediate future, their minds engage those issues consciously at work, and unconsciously outside of the work environment. Stability of tasks engages your mind for much longer each day, enabling better solutions and higher quality products.

✔ **Dedicated scrum teams have fewer distractions — and fewer distractions mean fewer mistakes.** When a person doesn't have to meet the demands of more than one project, that person has the time and clarity to ensure his or her work is the best it can be. Chapter 15 discusses ways to increase product quality in detail.

✔ **Dedicated scrum team members are able to innovate more on projects.** When people immerse themselves in a product without distractions, they are able to come up with creative solutions for product functionality.

✔ **People on dedicated scrum teams are more likely to be happy in their jobs.** By being able to concentrate on one project, a scrum team member's job is easier. Many, if not most, people enjoy producing quality work, being productive, and being creative. Dedicated scrum teams lead to higher satisfaction.

✔ **When you have a dedicated scrum team working the same amount of time each week, you can accurately calculate *velocity* — the team's development speed.** In Chapter 13, I talk about determining a scrum team's velocity at the end of each sprint and using velocity to determine long-term timelines and costs. Because velocity relies on comparing output from one sprint to the next, using velocity to forecast time and cost works best if the scrum team's work hours are constant. If you are unable to have a dedicated scrum team, at least try to have team members allocated to your project for the same amount of time each week.

The idea of the productive multitasker is a myth. In the past 25 years, and especially in the last decade, a number of studies have concluded that task-switching reduces productivity, impairs decision-making skills, and results in more errors.

In order to have a dedicated scrum team, you need strong commitment from your organization. Many companies ask employees to work on multiple projects at one time, under the mistaken assumption that the company will save money by hiring fewer people. When companies start to embrace agile, they learn that the least expensive approach is to reduce defects and raise development productivity through focus.

Each member of the scrum team can help ensure dedication:

✔ If you are a scrum master, as the expert on agile approaches, you can educate the company on why a dedicated scrum team means increased productivity, quality, and innovation. A good scrum master should also have the organizational clout to keep the company from poaching people from the scrum team for other projects.

✔ If you are a member of the development team, if anyone requests that you do work outside the project, you can push back and involve the scrum master, if necessary. A request for outside work, regardless of how benign, is a potential roadblock.

✔ If you are a product owner, make sure that the company knows that a dedicated scrum team is a good fiscal decision. You are responsible for project return on investment, so be willing to fight for your project's success.

Another characteristic of scrum teams is that they are cross-functional.

Working with a cross-functional team

Cross-functional development teams are also very important on agile projects. The development team on an agile software project doesn't just include programmers; it could include all the people who will have a job on the project. For example, a development team on a software project might include programmers, business analysts, database experts, quality assurance people, usability experts, and graphic designers. While each person has specialties, being cross-functional means that everyone on the team is willing to pitch in on different parts of the project, as much as possible.

On an agile development team, you continuously ask yourself two questions: "What can I contribute today?" and "How can I expand my contribution in the future?" Everyone on the development team will use his or her current skills and specialties in each sprint. Cross-functionality gives development team members the opportunity to learn new skills by working on areas outside of their expertise. Cross-functionality also allows people to share their knowledge with their fellow development team members. You don't need to be a jack-of-all-trades to work on an agile development team, but you should be willing to learn new skills and help with all kinds of tasks.

Even though task-switching decreases productivity, cross-functionality works because you are not changing the actual context of what you are working on; you are looking at the same problem from a different perspective. Working on different aspects of the same problem actually increases knowledge depth and your ability to do a better job.

The biggest benefit of a cross-functional development team is the elimination of single points of failure. If you have worked on a project before, how many times have you experienced delays because a critical member of the team is on vacation, out sick, or, worse, because that person leaves the company permanently? Vacations, illness, and turnover are facts of life, but with a cross-functional development team, other team members can jump in and continue work with minimal disruption. Even if a specialist leaves the project team unexpectedly and abruptly, other development team members will know enough about the work to help quickly train a new person.

Development team members go on vacation and catch the flu. Don't sabotage your project by having only one person know a skill or functional area.

Cross-functionality takes strong commitment from the development team, both as individual members and as a group. The old phrase, "There is no 'i' in 'team'" is especially true on agile projects. Working on an agile development team is about skills, rather than titles.

Development teams without titles are more merit-based, since team seniority and status is based on current knowledge, skills, and contribution.

Letting go of the idea that you are a "senior quality assurance tester" or a "junior developer" can require a new way of thinking about yourself. Embracing the concept of being part of a cross-functional development team may take some work, but it can be rewarding as you learn new skills and develop a rhythm of teamwork.

When developers also test, they create code that is test-friendly.

Having a cross-functional development team also requires commitment and support from your organization. Some companies eliminate titles, or keep them intentionally vague (you might see something like "application development"), in order to encourage teamwork. Other techniques for creating a strong cross-functional development team from an organizational standpoint include offering training, recognizing scrum teams as a whole, and being willing to make changes if a particular person does not fit in with a team environment. When hiring, your company can actively look for people who will work well in a highly collaborative environment, who want to learn new tasks, and who are willing to work on all areas of a project.

Even though task-switching decreases productivity, cross-functionality works because you are not changing the actual context of what you are working on; you are looking at the same problem from a different perspective. Working on different aspects of the same problem actually increases knowledge depth and your ability to do a better job.

Both the physical environment and the cultural environment of an organization are important keys to success with agile projects. The next section shows you how.

Establishing an agile environment

As I explain in other chapters, a collocated scrum team is ideal. The Internet has brought people together globally like nothing else in history could, but nothing — not the best combination of e-mails, instant messages, videoconferencing, phone calls, and online collaboration tools — can replace the simplicity and effectiveness of a face-to-face conversation. Figure 14-1 illustrates the difference between an e-mail and a conversation in person.

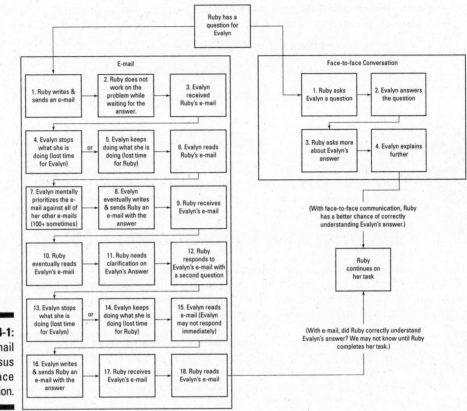

Figure 14-1:
E-mail
versus
face-to-face
conversation.

The idea of scrum team members working in the same physical location and being able to talk in person, instantly, is important to team dynamics. You find more details on communication later in this chapter. Also, Chapter 5 provides details on how to set up the physical environment for a scrum team.

Having a cultural environment conducive to scrum team growth is another success factor for agile projects. Everyone on a scrum team should be able to

- ✔ Feel safe.
- ✔ Speak his or her mind in a positive way.
- ✔ Challenge the status quo.
- ✔ Be open about challenges without being penalized.
- ✔ Request resources that will make a difference to the project.
- ✔ Make mistakes and learn from them.

✔ Suggest change and have other scrum team members seriously consider those changes.

✔ Respect fellow scrum team members.

✔ Be respected by other members of the scrum team.

Trust, openness, and respect are fundamental to team dynamics on an agile project.

Some of the best product and process improvements come from novices asking "silly" questions.

Another facet of agile team dynamics is the concept of the size-limited team.

Limiting development team size

An interesting psychological aspect of team dynamics on an agile project is the number of people on a development team. Development teams usually have between five and nine people. An ideal size is seven people; if you add or remove two people, you can still see benefits.

Keeping a development team at between five and nine people provides a team with enough diverse skills to take a requirement from paper to production. Communication and collaboration is easier between small groups of people. Development team members can easily interact with one another and make decisions by consensus.

When you have development teams with more than nine people, the people on those teams tend to break into sub-groups and build silos. This is normal social human behavior, but subgroups can be disruptive to a development team striving to be self-managing. It is also more difficult to communicate with larger development teams; there are more communication channels and more opportunities to lose or misconstrue a message. With more than nine people on a development team, you often need an extra person just to help manage communication.

Development teams with fewer than five people, on the other hand, tend to naturally gravitate to an agile approach. However, development teams that are too small may find working cross-functionally difficult because there may not be enough people with varying skills on the project.

If your product development requires more than nine development team members, consider breaking the work up between multiple scrum teams. Creating teams of people with similar personalities, skills and work styles can improve productivity. Find details on how to work with multiple scrum teams in Chapter 13.

Managing projects with dislocated teams

As I say throughout the book, a collocated scrum team is ideal for agile projects. However, sometimes it isn't possible for a scrum team to work together in one place. *Dislocated teams,* teams with people who work in different locations, exist for many different reasons and in different forms.

In some companies, the people with the right skills for a project may work in different offices, and the company may not want the cost of bringing those people together for the project duration. Some organizations work jointly with other organizations on projects, but may not wish or be able to share office space. Some people may telecommute, especially contractors, who could live long distances from the company they work with, and may never visit that company's office. Some companies work with offshore groups and create projects with people from a few different countries.

The good news is that you can still have an agile project with a dislocated scrum team or teams. As a matter of fact, if I had to work with a dislocated team, I would consider using only an agile approach because an agile approach allows me to see working functionality much sooner and limits my risk of the inevitable misunderstandings a dislocated team will experience.

In *A Scrum Handbook* (Scrum Institute Training Press), Jeff Sutherland describes three models of distributed scrum teams:

- **Isolated scrums:** With isolated scrums, scrum teams are in separate geographic locations. The teams work separately and may not all work with an agile methodology. Product development with isolated scrums has only code-level integration; that is, the different teams don't communicate or work together, but expect the code to work when it is time to integrate each module.

- **Distributed scrum of scrums:** With a distributed scrum of scrums model, scrum teams are in different locations. To coordinate work, scrum teams hold a scrum of scrums — a daily meeting of multiple scrum masters.

- **Integrated scrums:** Integrated scrum teams are cross-functional with members in different locations. Scrum of scrums still occurs.

Table 14-3, from Ambysoft's Agile Adoption Rate Survey Results in 2008, shows a comparison of success rates for projects with collocated scrum teams against those with geographically disperse scrum teams.

Table 14-3   Success of Collocated and Dislocated Scrum Teams

Team Location	Success Percentage
Collocated scrum team	83%
Dislocated but physically reachable	72%
Distributed across geographies	60%

Agile Adoption Rate Survey Results (Scott W. Ambler, Ambysoft, Copyright© 2008)

How do you have a successful agile project with a dislocated scrum team? I have three words: communicate, communicate, and communicate. Because daily in-person conversations are not possible, agile projects with dislocated scrum teams require unique efforts by everyone working on the project. Here are some tips for non-collocated scrum team members to successfully communicate:

✔ **Use videoconferencing technology to simulate face-to-face conversations.** A large percentage of interpersonal communication is visual, involving facial cues, hand gestures, even shoulder shrugs. Videoconferencing enables people to see one another and benefit from nonverbal communication as well as a discussion.

✔ **If possible, arrange for the scrum team members to meet in-person in a central location at least once at the beginning of the project, if not multiple times throughout the project.** The shared experience of meeting in-person, even once or twice, can help build teamwork among dislocated team members.

✔ **Use an online collaboration tool.** Some tools simulate white boards and user story cards, track conversations, and enable multiple people to update wikis with the latest information on a given topic.

✔ **Include scrum team members' pictures on online collaboration tools, or even in e-mail address signature lines.** Humans respond to faces more than written words alone. A simple picture can help humanize instant messages and e-mails.

✔ **Be cognizant of time zone differences.** Put multiple clocks, showing different time zones, on the wall so you do not accidentally call someone's cellphone at 3 a.m. and wake that person up — or wonder why he or she isn't answering.

✔ **Be flexible because of time zone differences as well.** You may need to take video calls or phone calls at odd hours from time to time to help keep project work moving. For drastic time zone differences, consider trading off on times you are available. One week, Team A can be available in the early morning. The next, Team B can be available later in the evening. That way, no one always has an inconvenience.

✔ **If you have any doubt about a conversation or an e-mail, ask for clarification.** It always helps to double-check when you are unsure of what someone meant. Follow up with a call, an instant message, or an e-mail to avoid mistakes from miscommunication.

✔ **Be aware of language and cultural differences between scrum team members, especially when working with groups in multiple countries.** Understanding colloquialisms and pronunciation differences can increase the quality of your communication across borders. It helps to know about local holidays, too. I've been blindsided more than once by closed offices outside of my region.

✔ **Make an extra attempt to discuss non-work topics sometimes.** Discussing non-work topics helps you grow closer to scrum team members, regardless of location.

With dedication, awareness, and strong communication, distributed agile projects can succeed.

The unique approaches to team dynamics on agile projects are part of what make agile projects successful. Communication is closely related to team dynamics, and the communication methods on agile projects also have big differences from traditional projects, as you see in the following section.

What's Different About Communication in Agile

Communication, in project management terms, is the formal and informal ways the people on the project team convey information to each other. As with traditional projects, good communication is a necessity for agile projects.

However, the Agile Principles set a different tone for agile projects, emphasizing simplicity, directness, and face-to-face conversations. The following Agile Principles relate to communication:

4. Business people and developers must work together daily throughout the project.

6. The most efficient and effective method of conveying information to and within a development team is face-to-face conversation.

7. Working software is the primary measure of progress.

10. Simplicity — the art of maximizing the amount of work not done — is essential.

12. At regular intervals, the team reflects on how to become more effective, then tunes and adjusts its behavior accordingly.

The Agile Manifesto also addresses communication, valuing working software over comprehensive documentation. While documentation has value, working software has more importance on an agile project.

Table 14-4 shows some differences between communication on traditional projects and on agile projects.

The question of how much documentation is required is not a volume question but an appropriateness question. Why do you need a specific document? How can you create it in the simplest way possible? You can use poster-sized sticky sheets to put on the wall and make information digestible. This can also work best for visually conveying artifacts like the vision statement, the definition of done, the impediments log, and important architectural decisions. Pictures truly are worth a thousand words.

The following sections show how to take advantage of the agile framework's emphasis on in-person communication, focus on simplicity, and value of working software as a communication medium.

Table 14-4	Historical Versus Agile Communication
Communication Management with Traditional Approaches	**Communication Management with Agile Approaches**
Team members might make no special effort for in-person conversations.	Agile project management approaches value face-to-face communication as the best way to convey information.
Traditional approaches place high value on documentation. Teams may create a large number of complex documents and status reports based on process, rather than considering actual need.	Agile documents, or *artifacts*, are intentionally simple and provide information that is barely sufficient. Agile artifacts only contain essential information and can often convey project status at a glance.
	Project teams use the *show, don't tell* concept, showing working software to communicate progress on a regular basis in the sprint review.
Team members may be required to attend a large number of meetings, whether or not those meetings are useful or necessary.	Meetings on agile projects are, by design, as quick as possible and will include only people who will truly add to the meeting and benefit from the meeting. Agile meetings provide all the benefits of face-to-face communication without wasting time. The structure of agile meetings is to enhance, not reduce, productivity.

How to Manage Communication in Agile

To manage communication on agile projects, you need to understand how different agile communication methods work and how to use them together. You also need to know why status on an agile project is different and how to report project progress to stakeholders. The following sections show you how.

Understanding agile communication methods

There are many ways to communicate on an agile project, through artifacts, meetings, and informally.

Face-to-face conversations are the heart and soul of agile projects. When scrum team members talk with one another about the project throughout every day, communication is easy. Over time, scrum team members understand each other's personality, communication style, and thought processes, and will be able to communicate quickly and effectively.

Figure 14-2, from Alistair Cockburn's presentation *Software Development as a Cooperative Game* (Copyright Humans and Technology, Inc.), shows the effectiveness of face-to-face communication versus other types of communication.

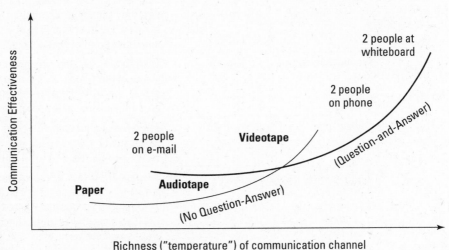

Figure 14-2: Comparison of communication types.

In previous chapters, I describe a number of artifacts and meetings that fit with agile projects. All the agile artifacts and meetings play a role in communication. Agile meetings provide a format for communicating in a face-to-face environment. Meetings on agile projects have a specific purpose and a specific amount of time in order to allow the development team the time to work, rather than spend time in meetings. Agile artifacts provide a format for written communication that is structured, but not cumbersome or unnecessary.

Table 14-5 provides a view of the different communication channels on an agile project.

Table 14-5	Agile Project Communication Channels	
Channel	*Type*	*Role in Communication*
Project planning, release planning, and sprint planning	Meetings	Planning meetings communicate the details of the project, the release, and the sprint to the scrum team. Learn more about planning meetings in Chapters 7 and 8.
Product vision statement	Artifact	The product vision statement communicates the end goal of the project to the project team and the organization. Find out more about the product vision in Chapter 7.
Product roadmap	Artifact	The product roadmap communicates a long-term view of the features that support the product vision and are likely to be part of the project. Find out more about the product roadmap in Chapter 7.
Product backlog	Artifact	The product backlog communicates the scope of the project as a whole to the project team. Find out more about the product backlog in Chapters 7 and 8.
Release plan	Artifact	The release plan communicates the goals for a specific release. Find out more about the release plan in Chapter 8.
Sprint backlog	Artifact	When updated daily, the sprint backlog provides immediate sprint and project status to anyone who needs that information. The burndown chart on the sprint backlog provides a quick visual of the sprint status. Find out more about the sprint backlog in Chapters 8 and 9.

Channel	Type	Role in Communication
Task board	Artifact	Using a task board visually radiates out status of the current sprint or release to anyone who walks by the scrum team's work area. Find out more about the task board in Chapter 9.
Daily scrum	Meeting	The daily scrum provides the scrum team with a verbal, face-to-face opportunity to coordinate the priorities of the day and identify any challenges. Find out more about daily scrum meetings in Chapter 9.
Face-to-face conversations	Informal	Face-to-face conversations are the most important mode of communication on an agile project.
Sprint review	Meeting	The sprint review is the embodiment of the show, don't tell philosophy. Displaying working software to the entire project team conveys project progress in a more meaningful way than a report ever could. Find out more about sprint reviews in Chapter 10.
Sprint retrospective	Meeting	The sprint retrospective allows the scrum team to communicate with one another specifically for improvement. Find out more about sprint retrospectives in Chapter 10.
Meeting notes	Informal	Meeting notes are an optional, informal communication method on an agile project. Meeting notes can capture action items from a meeting to ensure people on the scrum team remember them for later. Notes from a sprint review can record new features for the product backlog. Notes from a sprint retrospective can remind the scrum team of commitments for improvement.
Collaborative solutions	Informal	White boards, sticky notes, and electronic collaboration tools all help the scrum team communicate. Ensure that these tools augment, rather than replace, face-to-face conversations.

Artifacts, meetings, and more informal communication channels are all tools. Keep in mind that even the best tools need people to use those tools correctly to be effective. Agile projects are about people and interactions; tools are secondary to success.

The next section addresses a specific area of agile project communication: status reporting.

Status and progress reporting

All projects have stakeholders, people outside of the immediate scrum team who have a vested interest in the project. At least one of the stakeholders is the person responsible for paying for your project. It is important for stakeholders, especially those responsible for budgets, to know how the project is progressing. This section shows how to communicate your project's status.

Status on an agile project is a measure of the features that the scrum team has completed. Using the definition of done from Chapter 2, a feature is complete if the scrum team has developed, tested, integrated, and documented that feature, per the agreement between the product owner and the development team.

If you have worked on a traditional software project, how many times have you been in a status meeting and reported that the project was, say, 64 percent complete? If your stakeholders had replied, "Great! We would like that 64 percent now; we ran out of funds," you and the stakeholders alike would be at a loss, because you did not mean that 64 percent of your features were ready to use. You meant that each one of the product features was only 64 percent in progress, you had no working functionality, and you still had a lot of work to do before anyone could use the product.

On an agile project, working software that meets the definition of done is the primary measure of progress. You can confidently say that project features are complete. Since scope changes constantly on agile projects, you would not express status as a percentage. Instead, you can think of your completed requirements in terms of story points — just add up the number of story points the scrum team has completed to date — or simply as the number of features that are done.

Track progress of your sprint and of the project on a daily basis. Your primary tools for communicating status and progress are the daily scrum, task board, sprint backlog, product backlog, burndown charts, and the sprint review.

The sprint review is where you demonstrate working software to your project stakeholders. Resist creating slides or handouts; the key to the sprint review is showing your stakeholders progress as a demonstration, rather than simply telling them what you completed. Show, don't tell.

Strongly encourage anyone who may have an interest in your project to come to your sprint reviews. When people see the working product in action, especially on a regular basis, they get a much better sense of the work you completed.

Companies and organizations that are new to agile may expect to see traditional status reports, in addition to agile artifacts. These organizations may also want members of the scrum team to attend regular status meetings, outside of the daily scrums and other agile meetings. This is called *double work agile,* because you are doing twice as much work as necessary. Double work agile is one of the top pitfalls for agile projects. Scrum teams will burn out quickly if they try to meet the demands of two drastically different project approaches. You can avoid double work agile by educating your company about why the agile artifacts and events are a better replacement for the old documents and meetings. Insist on doing things the right way in order to conduct a successful agile project.

The sprint backlog has a report of the daily status of your current sprint. The sprint backlog contains the sprint's user stories and those user stories' related tasks and estimates. The sprint backlog also often has a burndown chart that visually shows the status of the work the development team has completed.

If you are a project manager now, or if you study project management in the future, you may come across the concept of *Earned Value Management,* or EVM, as a way of measuring project progress and performance. Some agile practitioners are trying to use an agile-like version of EVM. I don't like EVM for agile projects. EVM assumes that your project has a fixed scope, which is antithetical to agile methodologies. Instead of trying to change agile approaches to fit into old models, use the tools here — they work.

The burndown chart quickly shows, rather than tells, status. When you look at a sprint burndown chart, you can instantly see if the sprint is going well, or if it might be in trouble. In Chapter 9, I show you an image of sample burndown charts for different sprint scenarios; here it is again in Figure 14-3.

If you update your sprint backlog every day, you will always have an up-to-date status for your project stakeholders. You can also show them the product backlog so that they know which features the scrum team has completed to date, which features will be part of future sprints, and the priority of the features.

The product backlog will change as you add and reprioritize features. Make sure that people who review the product backlog, especially for status purposes, understand this concept.

A task board is a great way to quickly show your project team the status of a sprint, release, or even of the entire project. Task boards have sticky notes with user story titles in at least four columns: To Do, In Progress, Accept, and Done. If you display your task board in the scrum team's work area, then anyone who walks by can see a high-level status of which product features are done and which features are in progress. The scrum team always knows where the product stands, because the scrum team sees the task board every day.

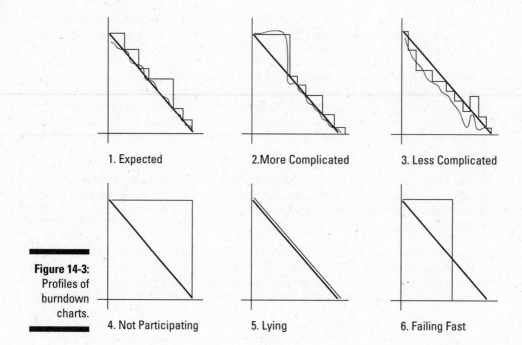

1. Expected   2. More Complicated   3. Less Complicated

4. Not Participating   5. Lying   6. Failing Fast

Figure 14-3:
Profiles of
burndown
charts.

Chapter 15

Managing Quality and Risk

. . . .

In This Chapter

▶ Learning how agile project management quality approaches reduce project risk

▶ Reading about ways to proactively ensure quality development

▶ Seeing how to take advantage of automated testing for better productivity

▶ Understanding how agile project approaches reduce risk

. . . .

*Q*uality and risk are closely related parts of project management. In this chapter, you find out how to deliver quality products using agile project management methods. You understand how to take advantage of agile approaches to manage risk on your projects. You see how quality has historically affected project risk, and how quality management on agile projects fundamentally reduces project risk.

What's Different About Quality in Agile

Quality refers to whether a product works, and whether it fulfills the project stakeholders' needs. Quality is an inherent part of agile project management. All of the 12 Agile Principles that I list in Chapter 2 promote quality either directly or indirectly. Those principles are

1. Our highest priority is to satisfy the customer through early and continuous delivery of valuable software.

2. Welcome changing requirements, even late in development. Agile processes harness change for the customer's competitive advantage.

3. Deliver working software frequently, from a couple of weeks to a couple of months, with a preference to the shorter timescale.

4. Business people and developers must work together daily throughout the project.

5. Build projects around motivated individuals. Give them the environment and support they need, and trust them to get the job done.

6. The most efficient and effective method of conveying information to and within a development team is face-to-face conversation.

7. Working software is the primary measure of progress.

8. Agile processes promote sustainable development. The sponsors, developers, and users should be able to maintain a constant pace indefinitely.

9. Continuous attention to technical excellence and good design enhances agility.

10. Simplicity — the art of maximizing the amount of work not done — is essential.

11. The best architectures, requirements, and designs emerge from self-organizing teams.

12. At regular intervals, the team reflects on how to become more effective, then tunes and adjusts its behavior accordingly.

Through these principles, the agile framework places a large emphasis on creating an environment where scrum teams are able to create valuable, working products. Agile approaches encourage quality both in the sense of products working correctly and meeting the needs of project stakeholders.

Table 15-1 shows some differences between quality management on traditional projects and on agile projects.

Table 15-1	Historical Versus Agile Quality
Quality Management with Traditional Approaches	**Quality Dynamics with Agile Approaches**
Testing is the last phase of a project before product deployment. Some features are tested months after they were created.	Testing is a daily part of each sprint and is included in each requirement's definition of done. You use automated testing, allowing quick and robust testing every day.
Quality is often a reactive practice, with focus mostly on product testing and issue resolution.	You address quality both reactively, through testing, and proactively, encouraging practices to set the stage for quality work. Examples of proactive quality approaches include face-to-face communication, pair programming, and established coding standards.
Problems are riskier when found at the end of a project. Sunk costs are high by the time teams reach testing.	You can create and test riskier features in early sprints, when sunk costs are still low.
Problems, sometimes called *bugs*, are hard to find at the end of a project, and fixes for problems at the end of a project are costly.	Problems are easy to find when you test a smaller amount of work. Fixes are easier when you fix something you just created, rather than something you created months earlier.
Sometimes, in order to meet a deadline or save money, teams cut the testing phase short.	Testing is assured on agile projects, because it is part of every sprint.

Bugs. Bugs? Bugs!

Why do we call computer problems "bugs"? The very first computers were large, glass-encased machines that took up entire rooms. In 1945, one of these behemoth computers, the Mark II Aiken Relay Calculator at Harvard University, had problems with one of its circuits. Engineers traced the issue to a moth — a literal bug — in the machine. After that, the team's running joke was that any issue with the computer had to be a bug. The term stuck, and people still use "bug" today to describe hardware problems, software problems, and sometimes even problems outside of the computer science realm. The engineers at Harvard even taped the moth to a logbook. That first bug is now on display at the Smithsonian National Museum of American History.

At the start of this chapter, I state that quality and risk are closely related. The agile approaches in Table 15-1 greatly reduce the risk and unnecessary cost that usually accompany quality management.

Another difference about quality on agile projects is the multiple quality feedback loops throughout a project. In Figure 15-1, you see the different types of product feedback a scrum team receives in the course of a project. The development team incorporates this feedback into the product, increasing product quality on a regular basis.

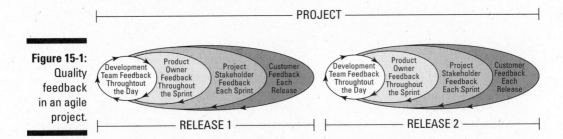

Figure 15-1: Quality feedback in an agile project.

In Chapter 14, I tell you that development teams on agile projects can include everyone who works on a product. Development teams on agile projects typically include people who are experts in creating and executing tests and ensuring quality. Development team members are cross-functional; that is, every team member may do different jobs at different times within the projects. Cross-functionality extends to quality activities like preventing issues, testing, and fixing bugs.

In the next section, you see how to use agile project management techniques to increase quality.

How to Manage Quality in Agile

Agile development teams have the primary responsibility for quality on agile projects. The responsibility for quality is an extension of the responsibilities and freedoms that come with self-management. When the development team is free to determine its development methods, the development team is also responsible for ensuring that those methods result in quality work.

Organizations often refer to quality management as a whole as quality assurance, or QA. You may see QA departments, QA testers, QA managers, QA analysts, and all other flavors of QA-prefixed titles to refer to people who are responsible for quality activities. QA is also sometimes used as shorthand for testing, as in "we performed QA on the product" or "now we are in the QA phase."

The other members of the scrum team — the scrum master and the product owner — also play parts in quality management. Product owners provide clarification on requirements and also accept those requirements as being done throughout each sprint. Scrum masters help ensure development teams have a work environment where the people on development teams can work to the best of their abilities.

Luckily, agile project management approaches have several ways to help scrum teams create quality products. In this section, you see how testing in sprints increases the likelihood of finding bugs and reduces the cost of fixing bugs. You gain an understanding of the many ways agile project management proactively encourages quality product development. You see how the inspecting and adapting on a regular basis addresses quality. Finally, you find out how automated testing is essential to delivering valuable products continuously throughout an agile project.

Quality and the sprint

Quality management is a daily part of agile projects. Scrum teams run agile projects in sprints, short development cycles that last one to four weeks. Each cycle includes activities from the different phases of a traditional project: requirements, design, development, testing, and integration for deployment. Find out more about working in sprints in Chapters 8, 9, and 10.

Here's a quick riddle: Is it easier to find a quarter on a table or in a stadium? Obviously, the answer is a table. Just as obvious is that it is easier to find a defect in 100 lines of code than in 100,000 lines of code. Iterative development makes quality product development easier.

Scrum teams test throughout each sprint. Figure 15-2 shows how testing fits into sprints on an agile project. Notice that testing begins in the first sprint, right after programmers start creating the first requirement in the project.

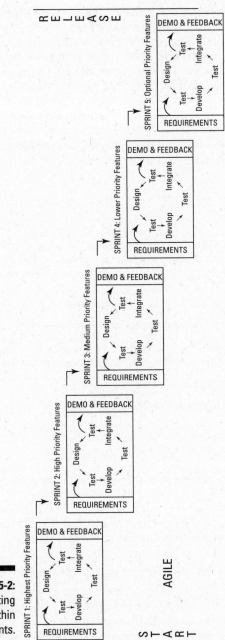

Figure 15-2:
Testing
within
sprints.

When development teams test throughout each sprint, they are able to find and fix bugs very quickly. With agile project management, development teams create product requirements, immediately test those requirements, and fix any problems immediately. Instead of trying to remember how to fix something they created weeks or months ago, development teams are, at the most, fixing the requirement they worked on one or two days earlier.

Testing almost every day on an agile project is a great way to ensure product quality. Another way to ensure product quality is to create a better product from the start. The next section shows you different ways that agile project management helps you avoid errors and create an excellent product.

Proactive quality

An important and often-neglected aspect of quality is the idea of preventing problems. Agile approaches have a number of practices that allow and encourage scrum teams to proactively create quality products. These practices include

- An emphasis on technical excellence and good design
- Incorporation of quality-specific development techniques into product creation
- Daily communication between the development team and the product owner
- Acceptance criteria built into user stories
- Face-to-face communication and collocation
- Sustainable development
- Regular inspection and adaption of work and behavior

The following sections provide a detailed look at each of these proactive quality practices.

Quality means both that a product works correctly and that the product does what the project stakeholders need it to do.

Continuous attention to technical excellence and good design

A focus on technical excellence and good design are part of the 12 Agile Principles, because technical excellence and good design lead to valuable products. How do development teams provide great technical solutions and designs?

One way that development teams provide technical excellence is through the concept of self-management. Self-management provides development teams with the freedom to innovate technically. Traditional organizations may have mandatory technical standards that may or may not make sense for a given project. Self-organizing development teams have the freedom to decide if a standard will actually provide value in creating a product, or if a different approach will work better. Innovation can lead to good design, technical excellence, and product quality.

Self-management also provides development teams with a sense of product ownership. When people on development teams feel a deep responsibility for the product they are creating, they often strive to find the best solutions and execute those solutions in the best way possible.

Nothing is more sophisticated than a simple solution.

Organizational commitment also plays a role in technical excellence. Some companies and organizations, regardless of their project management approaches, have a commitment to excellence. Think about the products that you use every day and associate with quality; chances are those products come from companies that value good technical solutions. If you are working on an agile project for a company that believes in and rewards technical excellence, enacting this Agile Principle will be easy.

Other companies may undervalue technical excellence; agile project teams at these companies may struggle when trying to justify training or tools that will help create better products. Some companies do not make the connection between good technology, good products, and profitability. Scrum masters and product owners may need to educate their companies on why good technology and design are important and may need to lobby to get development teams what they need to create a great product.

Don't confuse technical excellence with using new technologies for the sake of using something new or trendy. Your technology solutions should efficiently support the product needs, not just add to a resume or a company skills profile.

By incorporating technical excellence and good design into your everyday work, you create a quality product that you are proud of.

Quality development techniques

Agile methodologies have generated a number of development techniques that focus on quality. This section provides a high-level view of a few agile development approaches that help ensure quality from a proactive standpoint.

Many agile quality management techniques were initially created with software development in mind. You can adapt some of these techniques when creating other types of products, like hardware products or even building construction. If you are going to work on a non-software project, read about the development methods in this section with adaptability in mind.

- **Test-driven development (TDD):** A development method that begins with a developer creating a test for the requirement he or she wants to create. The developer then runs the test, which should fail at first because the requirement does not yet exist. The developer develops until the test passes, then refactors the code — takes as much code out as possible, while still having the test pass. With TDD, you know that a requirement works correctly, because you test while you create the requirement, and you develop the requirement until the test passes. TDD evolved from the extreme programming (XP) methodology. For more information on XP methodology, see Chapter 4.

- **Pair programming:** Another extreme programming practice. With pair programming, developers work in groups of two. Both developers sit at the same computer and work as a team to create one product requirement. The developers pass the keyboard and mouse back and forth to collaborate. Because the developers are literally looking over one another's shoulder, they can catch errors quickly. Pair programming increases quality by providing instant error checks and balances.

- **Peer reviews:** Sometimes called *peer code reviews,* they involve members of the development team reviewing one another's code. Like pair programming, peer reviews have a collaborative nature; when developers review each other's finished products, the developers work together to provide solutions for any issues they find. Peer reviews increase quality by allowing development experts to look for structural problems within product code.

- **Collective code ownership:** Another extreme programming practice. It means that everyone on the development team can create, change, or fix any part of the code on the project. Collective code ownership can speed up development, encourage innovation, and with multiple pairs of eyes on the code, help development team members quickly find bugs.

- **Continuous integration:** The practice of creating integrated code builds one or more times each day. Continuous integration allows members of the development team to check how the user story the development team is creating works with the rest of the product. Continuous integration helps ensure quality by allowing the development team to check for conflicts on a regular basis. Continuous integration is essential to automated testing on agile projects; you need to create a code build at the end of the day before running automated tests overnight. Find out more about automated testing later in this chapter.

On an agile project, the development team decides which tools and techniques will work best for the project, the product, and the individual development team.

Many agile software development techniques help ensure quality, and there is a lot of discussion and information about these techniques within the community of people who use agile project management approaches. I encourage you to learn more about these approaches if you are going to work on an agile project, especially if you are a developer. Whole books are dedicated to some of these techniques, such as test-driven development. The information I provide here is at the tip of the iceberg.

The product owner and development team

Another aspect of agile project management that encourages quality is the close relationship between the development team and the product owner. The product owner is the voice of business needs for the product. In this role, the product owner works with the development team every day to ensure that the product meets those business needs.

During planning stages, the product owner's job is to help the development team understand each requirement correctly. During the sprint, the product owner answers questions that the development team has about requirements. During the sprint, the product owner is also responsible for reviewing requirements and accepting them as done. When the product owner accepts requirements, he or she ensures that the development team correctly interpreted the business need for each requirement, and that the requirement performs the task that it needs to perform.

Sometimes a development team's work will start to stray from the original product goals set out in the product vision statement. A product owner who reviews requirements daily catches misinterpretations early. The product owner can then set the development team back on the right path, avoiding a lot of wasted time and effort.

The product vision statement communicates how your product supports the company's or organization's strategies. The vision statement articulates the product's goals. Chapter 7 explains how to create a product vision statement.

User stories and acceptance criteria

Another proactive quality measure on agile projects is the acceptance criteria you build into each user story. In Chapter 7, I explain that a user story is one format for describing product requirements. User stories play a special role in quality by providing the steps to take to know that a requirement works correctly and meets business needs. Figure 15-3 shows a user story and its acceptance criteria.

Even if you don't describe your requirements in a user story format, consider adding validation steps to each of your requirements. Acceptance criteria don't just help the product owner review requirements; they help the development team understand how to create the product in the first place.

Face-to-face communication

Have you ever had a conversation with someone and known, just by looking at that person's face, that he or she didn't understand you? In Chapter 14, I explain that face-to-face conversations are the quickest, most effective form of communication. This is because humans convey information with more than just words; our facial expressions, gestures, body language, and even where we are looking contribute to communicating and understanding one another.

Face-to-face communication helps ensure quality on agile projects because it leads to better interpretation of requirements, of roadblocks, and of discussions between scrum team members. Regular face-to-face communication requires a collocated scrum team.

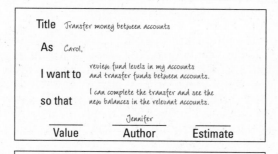

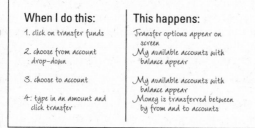

Figure 15-3: A user story and acceptance criteria.

Sustainable development

Chances are, at some point in your life, you have found yourself working or studying long hours for an extended period of time. You may have even pulled an all-nighter or two, getting no sleep at all for a night. How did you feel during this time? Did you make good decisions? Did you make any silly mistakes?

Unfortunately, many teams on traditional projects find themselves working long, crazy hours, especially toward the end of a project, when a deadline is looming and it seems like the only way to finish is to spend weeks working extra-long days. Those long days often mean more problems later, as team members start making mistakes — some silly, some more serious — and eventually burn out.

On agile projects, scrum teams help ensure that they do quality work by creating an environment where members of the development team sustain a constant working pace throughout the project. Working in sprints helps sustain a constant working pace; when the development team chooses the work it can accomplish in each sprint, it shouldn't have to rush at the end.

The development team can determine what sustainable means for itself, whether that means working a regular 40-hour workweek, a schedule with more or fewer days or hours, or working outside of a standard nine-to-five time frame.

If your fellow scrum team members start coming to work with their shirts on inside out, you might want to double-check that you are maintaining a sustainable development environment.

Keeping the development team happy, rested, and able to have a life outside of work can lead to fewer mistakes, more creativity and innovation, and better overall products.

Being proactive about quality saves you a lot of headaches in the long run. It is much easier and more enjoyable to work on a product with fewer bugs to fix. The next section discusses an agile approach that addresses quality from both a proactive and a reactive standpoint: inspect and adapt.

Quality through regular inspecting and adapting

The agile tenet of inspect and adapt is a key to creating quality products. Throughout an agile project, you look at both your product and your process (inspect) and make changes as necessary (adapt). Chapter 7 has more information about this tenet.

In the sprint review and sprint retrospective meetings, agile project teams regularly step back and review their work and methods and determine how to make adjustments for a better project. I provide details on the sprint review and sprint retrospective in Chapter 10. Following is a quick overview of how these meetings help ensure quality on agile projects.

In a sprint review, agile project teams review requirements completed at the end of each sprint. Sprint reviews address quality by letting project stakeholders see working requirements and provide feedback on those requirements throughout the course of the project. If a requirement doesn't meet stakeholder expectations, the stakeholders tell the scrum team immediately. The scrum team can then adjust the product in a future sprint. The scrum team can also apply its revised understanding of how the product needs to work on other product requirements.

In a sprint retrospective, scrum teams meet to discuss what worked and what might need adjusting at the end of each sprint. Sprint retrospectives help ensure quality by allowing the team to discuss and immediately fix problems. Sprint retrospectives also allow the team to come together and formally discuss changes to the product, project, or work environment that might increase quality.

The sprint review and sprint retrospective aren't the only opportunities for inspecting and adapting for quality on an agile project. Agile approaches encourage reviewing work and adjusting behavior and methods throughout each workday. Daily inspecting and adapting everything you do on the project help ensure quality.

Another way to manage and help assure quality on an agile project is to use automated testing tools. The next section explains why automated testing is important to agile projects and how to incorporate automated testing into your project.

Automated testing

Automated testing is the use of software to test your product. Automated testing is critical to agile projects. If you want to quickly create requirements that meet the definition of done — coded, tested, integrated, and documented — you need a way to quickly test those requirements. Automated testing means quick and robust testing on a daily basis.

Throughout this book, I explain how agile project teams embrace low-tech solutions. Why, then, is there a section in this book about automated testing, a rather high-tech quality management technique? The answer to this question is efficiency. Automated testing is like the spell-check feature in word-processing programs. As a matter of fact, spell-checking is a form of automated testing. Spell-checking is a much quicker and often more accurate way to catch misspellings in a document than manual proofreading. In the same way, automated testing is a much quicker and often more accurate — thus, more efficient — method of finding software bugs than manual testing.

To develop a product using automated testing, development teams develop and test using the following steps:

1. **Develop code and automated tests in support of user stories during the day.**

2. **Create an integrated code build at the end of each day.**

3. **Schedule the automated testing software to test the newest build overnight.**

4. **Check the automated test results first thing each morning.**

5. **Fix any bugs immediately.**

Comprehensive code testing while you are sleeping is cool.

Automated testing allows development teams to take advantage of non-working time for productivity; it allows development teams to have rapid create-test-fix cycles. Also, automated testing software can often test requirements quicker and with more accuracy and consistency than a person testing those requirements.

Today's market has a lot of automated testing tools. Some automated testing tools are open-source and free, other automated testing tools are available for purchase. The development team needs to review automated testing options and choose the tool that will work best.

Automated testing changes the work for people in quality roles on the development team. Traditionally, a large part of a quality management person's work involved manually testing products. The tester on a traditional project would use the product and look for problems. With automated testing, however, quality activities largely involve creating tests to run on automated testing software. Automated testing tools augment, rather than replace, people's skills, knowledge, and work.

It is still a good idea to have humans periodically check that the requirements you are developing work correctly, especially when you first start using an automated testing tool. Any automated tool can have hiccups from time to time. By manually double-checking (sometimes called smoke-testing) small parts of automated tests, you help avoid getting to the end of a sprint and finding out that your product doesn't work like it should.

You can automate almost any type of software test. If you are new to software development, you may not know that there are many different types of software testing. A small sample includes

- ✔ **Unit testing:** Tests individual units, or the smallest parts, of product code.

- ✔ **Regression testing:** Tests an entire product start to finish, including requirements you have tested previously.

- ✔ **User acceptance testing:** Product stakeholders or even some of the product's end users review a product and accept it as complete.

- ✔ **Functional testing:** Tests to make sure the product works according to acceptance criteria from the user story.

- ✔ **Integration testing:** Tests to make sure the product works with other products, as necessary.

> ✔ **Performance testing:** Tests how fast a product runs on a given system under different scenarios.
>
> ✔ **Smoke testing:** Tests on small but critical parts of code or of a system to help determine if the system as a whole is likely to work.
>
> ✔ **Static testing:** Focuses on checking code standards, rather than working software.

Automated testing works for these tests and the many other types of software tests out there.

As you may understand by now, quality is an integral part of agile projects. Quality is just one factor, however, that differentiates risk on agile projects from traditional projects. In the next sections, you see how risk on traditional projects compares to risk on agile projects.

What's Different About Risk in Agile

Risk refers to the factors that contribute to a project's success or failure. On agile projects, risk management doesn't have to involve formal risk documentation and meetings. Instead, risk management is part of the agile framework. Consider the following Agile Principles:

1. Our highest priority is to satisfy the customer through early and continuous delivery of valuable software.

2. Welcome changing requirements, even late in development. Agile processes harness change for the customer's competitive advantage.

3. Deliver working software frequently, from a couple of weeks to a couple of months, with a preference to the shorter timescale.

4. Business people and developers must work together daily throughout the project.

7. Working software is the primary measure of progress.

The preceding principles and the practices that demonstrate those principles drastically change many risks that frequently lead to project challenges and failure. According to the Standish Group's *2011 Chaos Report*, agile projects are three times more likely to succeed than traditional projects. Table 15-2 shows some of the differences between risk on traditional projects and on agile projects.

Table 15-2	Historical Versus Agile Risk
Risk Management with Traditional Approaches	*Risk Dynamics with Agile Approaches*
Large numbers of projects fail or are challenged.	Risk of catastrophic failure — spending large amounts of money with nothing to show — is almost eliminated.
The bigger, longer, and more complex the project, the more risky it is. Risk is highest at the end of a project.	You gain product value immediately, rather than sinking costs into a project for months or even years with the growing chance of failure.
Conducting all the testing at the end of a project means that finding serious problems can put the entire project at risk.	You test at the same time you develop. If a technical approach, a requirement, or even an entire product is not feasible, the development team discovers this in a short time, and you have more time to course correct. If correction is not possible, stakeholders spend less money on a failed project.
Projects are unable to accommodate new requirements mid-project without increased time and cost because there is extensive sunk cost in even the lowest-priority requirements.	You welcome change for the benefit of the product. Agile projects accommodate new high-priority requirements without increasing time or cost by removing a low-priority requirement of equal time and cost.
Traditional projects require time and cost estimates at the project start, when teams know the least about the project. Estimates are often inaccurate, creating a gap between expected and actual project schedules and budgets.	You can estimate project time and cost using the scrum team's actual performance, or velocity. You refine estimates throughout the project, because the longer you work on a project, the more you learn about the project, the requirements, and the scrum team.
When stakeholders do not have a unified goal, they can end up confusing the project team with conflicting information about what the product should achieve.	You have a single product owner, who is responsible for creating a vision for the product and represents the stakeholders to the project team.
Unresponsive or absent stakeholders can cause project delays and result in products that do not achieve the right goals.	The product owner is responsible for providing information about the product immediately. You also have a scrum master, who helps remove impediments on a daily basis.

Risk on agile projects declines as the project progresses. Figure 15-4 shows a comparison of risk and time between waterfall projects and agile projects.

All projects have some risk, regardless of your project approach. However, with agile project management, the days of catastrophic project failure — spending large amounts of time and money with no return on investment (ROI) — are over. The elimination of large-scale failure is the biggest difference between risk on traditional projects and on agile projects. In the next section, you see why.

How to Manage Risk in Agile

In this section, you examine key structures of agile projects that reduce risk over the life of the project. You find out how to use agile tools and events to find risks at the right time in a project and how to prioritize and mitigate those risks.

Reducing risk inherently

Agile approaches, when implemented correctly, inherently reduce risk in product development. Developing in sprints ensures a short time between project investment and proof that the product works. Sprints also provide the potential for a project to generate revenue early on. The sprint review, the sprint retrospective, and the product owner's involvement during each sprint provide constant product feedback to the development team. Ongoing feedback helps prevent deviations between product expectations and the completed product.

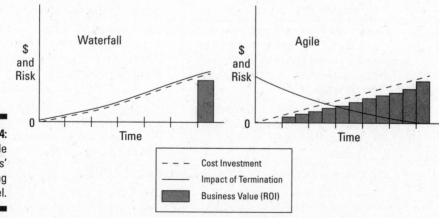

Figure 15-4:
Agile projects' declining risk model.

Three especially important factors in risk reduction on agile projects are the definition of done, self-funding projects, and the idea of failing fast. You find out more about each of these factors in the next sections.

Risk and the definition of done

In Chapter 10, I discuss when a requirement is done. To consider a requirement complete and ready to demonstrate at the end of a sprint, that requirement must meet the scrum team's definition of done. The product owner and the development team agree upon the details of the definition; definitions of done usually include

- **Developed:** The development team must fully create the working product requirement.

- **Tested:** The development team must have tested that the product works correctly and is bug-free.

- **Integrated:** The development team must have ensured that the requirement works in conjunction with the whole product and any related systems.

- **Documented:** The development team must have created notes about how it created the product.

Figure 15-5 shows a sample definition of done, with details.

Definition of Done

Sprint	Release	Risks Accepted
QA Environment	Staging Environment	Load Testing
Unit Tested	Performance Tested	
Functional Tested	Security Tested	
Integration Tested	Enterprise System Integrated	
User Acceptance Tested	Focus Group Tested	
Regression Tested	User Documentation	
XDocs	Training Documentation	

Figure 15-5: Sample definition of done.

The product owner and the development team may also create a list of acceptable risks. For example, they may agree that end-to-end regression testing or performance testing are overkill for the sprint definition of done. Acceptable risks allow the development team to concentrate on the most important activities.

The definition of done drastically changes the risk factor for agile projects. By creating a product that meets the definition of done in every sprint, you end each sprint with a working build and a usable product. Even if outside factors cause a project to end early, project stakeholders will always see some value and have a working product to use now and build upon later.

Self-funding projects

Agile projects can mitigate financial risk in a unique way that traditional projects cannot: the self-funding project. Chapter 13 includes examples of self-funding projects. If your product is an income-generating product, you could use that income to help fund the rest of your project.

In Chapter 13, I show you two different project ROI models. Here they are again, in Tables 15-3 and 15-4. The projects in both tables are to create identical products.

Table 15-3	Income from a Traditional Project with a Final Release after Six Months	
Month	**Income Generated**	**Total Project Income**
January	$0	$0
February	$0	$0
March	$0	$0
April	$0	$0
May	$0	$0
June	$100,000	$100,000

In Table 15-3, the project created $100,000 in income after six months of development. Now compare the ROI in Table 15-3 to the ROI in Table 15-4.

Table 15-4	Income from an Agile Project with Monthly Releases and a Final Release After Six Months	
Month/Release	**Income Generated**	**Total Project Income**
January	$15,000	$15,000
February	$25,000	$40,000
March	$40,000	$80,000
April	$70,000	$150,000
May	$80,000	$230,000
June	$100,000	$330,000

In Table 15-4, the project generated income with the very first release. By the end of six months, the project had generated $330,000 — $230,000 more than the project in Table 15-3.

The ability to generate income in a short amount of time has a number of benefits for companies and project teams. Self-funding agile projects make good financial sense for almost any organization, but they can be especially useful to organizations that may not have the funds to create a product up front. For groups short on cash, self-funding can enable projects that would otherwise not be feasible.

Self-funding projects also help mitigate the risk that a project would be cancelled due to lack of funds. A company emergency may dictate diverting a traditional project's budget elsewhere, delaying or cancelling the project. However, a project that generates additional revenue with every release has a good chance of continuing during a crisis.

Finally, self-funding projects help sell stakeholders on a project in the first place; it's hard to argue with a project that provides continuous value and pays for at least part of the project costs from the start.

Failing fast

All product development efforts carry some risk of failure. Testing within sprints introduces the idea of *failing fast:* Instead of sinking costs into a long effort for requirements, design, and development, and then finding problems that will prevent the project from moving forward, development teams on agile projects can identify critical problems within a few sprints. This quantitative risk mitigation can save organizations large amounts of money.

Tables 15-5 and 15-6 illustrate the difference in sunk costs for a failed waterfall project and a failed agile project. The projects in both tables are for identical products with identical costs.

Table 15-5	Cost of Failure on a Waterfall Project		
Month	*Phase and Issues*	*Sunk Project Cost*	*Total Sunk Project Cost*
January	Requirements Phase	$80,000	$80,000
February	Requirements Phase	$80,000	$160,000
March	Design Phase	$80,000	$240,000
April	Design Phase	$80,000	$320,000
May	Design Phase	$80,000	$400,000
June	Development Phase	$80,000	$480,000

(continued)

Table 15-5 *(continued)*

Month	Phase and Issues	Sunk Project Cost	Total Sunk Project Cost
July	Development Phase	$80,000	$560,000
August	Development Phase	$80,000	$640,000
September	Development Phase	$80,000	$720,000
October	QA Phase: Large-scale problem uncovered during testing.	$80,000	$800,000
November	QA Phase: Development team attempted to resolve problem to continue development.	$80,000	$880,000
December	Project cancelled; product not viable.	0	$880,000

In Table 15-5, the project stakeholders spent six months and close to a million dollars to find out that a product idea would not work. Compare the sunk cost in Table 15-5 to that in Table 15-6.

Table 15-6   **Cost of Failure on an Agile Project**

Month	Sprint and Issues	Sunk Project Cost	Total Sunk Project Cost
January	Sprint 1: No issues.	$80,000	$80,000
	Sprint 2: No issues.		
February	Sprint 3: Large-scale problem uncovered during testing resulted in failed sprint; sprint still failed.	$80,000	$160,000
	Sprint 4: Development team attempted to resolve problem to continue development; sprint ultimately failed.		
Final	Project cancelled; product not viable.	0	$160,000

By testing early, the development team from Table 15-6 determined that the product would not work by the end of February, spending one-third of the money spent in the project in Table 15-5.

Because of the definition of done, even failed projects produce something tangible that an organization may leverage or improve upon. For example, the failed project in Table 15-5 would have provided working product features in the first two sprints.

The concept of failing fast can apply beyond technical problems with a product. You can also use development within sprints and fast failure to see if a product will work in the marketplace, and to cancel the project early if it looks like customers won't buy or use the product. By releasing small parts of the product and testing the product with potential customers early in the project, you get a good idea of whether your product is commercially viable, and save large amounts of money if you find that people will not buy the product. You also discover important changes you might make to the product to better meet customer needs.

Finally, failing fast does not necessarily mean project cancellation. If you find catastrophic issues when sunk costs are low, you may have the time and budget to determine a completely different approach to create a product.

The definition of done, self-funding projects, and the idea of failing fast, along with the foundation of the Agile Principles, all help lower risk on agile projects. In the next section, you see how to actively use agile project management tools to manage risk.

Identifying, prioritizing, and responding to risks

While the structure of agile projects inherently reduces many traditional risks, development teams still should be aware of the problems that can arise during a project. Scrum teams are self-managing; in the same way that they are responsible for quality, scrum teams are responsible for trying to identify risks and ways to prevent those risks from materializing.

On agile projects, you prioritize the highest-value and highest-risk requirements first.

Instead of spending hours or days documenting all of a project's potential risks, the likelihood of those risks happening, the severity of those risks, and ways to mitigate those risks, scrum teams use existing agile artifacts and meetings to manage risk. Scrum teams also wait until the last responsible minute to address risk, when they know the most about the project and problems that are more likely to arise. Table 15-7 shows how scrum teams can use the different agile project management tools to manage risk at the right time.

Table 15-7	Agile Project Risk Management Tools
Artifact or Meeting	**Role in Risk Management**
Product vision	The product vision statement helps unify the project team's definition of product goals, mitigating the risk of misunderstandings about what the product will need to accomplish. While creating the product vision, the project team might think of risks on a very high level, in conjunction with the marketplace, customers, and organizational strategy. Find out more about the product vision in Chapter 7.
Product roadmap	The product roadmap provides a visual overview of the project's requirements and priorities. This visual overview allows the project team to quickly identify gaps in requirements and incorrectly prioritized requirements. Find out more about the product roadmap in Chapter 7.
Product backlog	The product backlog is a tool for accommodating change within the project. Being able to add changes to the product backlog and reprioritize requirements regularly helps turn the traditional risk associated with scope changes into a way to create a better product. Keeping the requirements and the priorities on the product backlog current helps ensure the development team can work on the most important requirements at the right time. Find out more about the product backlog in Chapters 7 and 8.
Release planning	During release planning, the scrum team discusses risks to the release and how to mitigate those risks. Risk discussions in the release planning meeting should be high-level and relate to the release as a whole. Save risks to individual requirements for the sprint planning meetings. Find out more about release planning in Chapter 8.
Sprint planning	During each sprint planning meeting, the scrum team discusses risks to the specific requirements and tasks in the sprint and how to mitigate those risks. Risk discussions during sprint planning can be done in depth, but should only relate to the current sprint. Find out more about sprint planning in Chapter 8.
Sprint backlog	The burndown chart on the sprint backlog provides a quick view of the sprint status. This quick view helps the scrum team manage risks to the sprint just as they arise and minimize impact by addressing problems immediately. Find out more about sprint backlogs and how burndown charts show project status in Chapter 9.

Artifact or Meeting	Role in Risk Management
Daily scrum	During each daily scrum, development team members discuss roadblocks. Roadblocks, or impediments, are sometimes risks. Talking about roadblocks every day gives the development team and the scrum master the chance to mitigate those risks immediately. Find out more about the daily scrum in Chapter 9.
Task board	The task board provides an unavoidable view of the sprint status, allowing the scrum team to catch risks to the sprint and manage them right away. Find out more about task boards in Chapter 9.
Sprint review	During the sprint review, the scrum team regularly ensures that the product meets stakeholders' expectations. The sprint review also provides opportunities for stakeholders to discuss changes to the product to accommodate changing business needs. Both features of the sprint review help manage the risk of getting to the end of a project with the wrong product. Find out more about sprint reviews in Chapter 10.
Sprint retrospective	During the sprint retrospective, the scrum team discusses issues with the past sprint and identifies which of those issues may be risks in future sprints. The development team needs to determine ways to prevent those risks from becoming problems again. Find out more about sprint retrospectives in Chapter 10.

The documents and meetings discussed in this section are all great ways to help manage risk on an agile project. Agile projects also provide one more important way to identify, prevent, and respond to risks: regular face-to-face communication between project team members. Collocated development team members benefit from ad-hoc conversations about risks to their immediate work.

Part V
Ensuring Agile Success

"Sorry, Cedric the King cut my budget for additional fools. He said the project already had enough fools on it."

In this part . . .

When you start to embrace agility, you want to ensure that your projects are successful and deliver value quickly. To realize the benefits of agile project management, you'll need to build a strong foundation with your team and your organization.

In the chapters in this part, I show you ways to secure organizational commitment to change. I talk about how to find the right team members and establish the right environment for agile project management. I also discuss the importance of training and why a safety net of professional support can help you avoid disasters. Finally, I cover the key steps in a successful transition to agile project management.

Chapter 16

Building a Foundation

To successfully move from traditional project management processes to agile processes, you need to start with a good foundation. You need commitment, both from your organization and from people as individuals, and you need to find a good project team for your first agile project. You must create an environment conducive to good agile practices. You want to find the right training for your project team, and you need to be able to support your organization's agile approach so that it can grow beyond your first project.

In this chapter, I show you how to build a strong agile foundation within your organization.

Commitment of the Organization and of Individuals

Commitment to agile project management means making an active, conscious effort to work with new methods and to abandon old habits. Commitment at both an individual level and at an organizational level is critical to agile transition success.

Without organizational support, even the most enthusiastic agile project team may find itself being forced back into old project management processes. Without the commitment of individual project team members, a company that embraces agile approaches may encounter too much resistance, or even sabotage, to be able to become an agile organization.

The following sections provide details on how organizations and people can support an agile transition.

Organizational commitment

Organizational commitment plays a large role in agile transition. When a company and the groups within that company support the changes that come with agile methodologies, the transition can be easier for the project team members.

Organizations can commit to an agile transition by doing the following:

- Engaging an experienced agile expert to create a realistic transition plan and to guide the company through that plan
- Investing in employee training, starting with the members of the company's first agile project team
- Allowing scrum teams to abandon waterfall processes, meetings, and documents in favor of streamlined agile approaches
- Providing all of the scrum team members necessary for each agile project: the development team, the product owner, and the scrum master
- Providing dedicated scrum team members for agile projects
- Encouraging development teams to become cross-functional
- Providing automated testing tools
- Logistically supporting scrum team collocation
- Allowing scrum teams to manage themselves
- Giving the agile project team the time and freedom to go through a healthy trial and error process
- Encouraging agile project teams and celebrating successes

Organizational support is also important beyond the agile transition. Companies can ensure that agile processes continue to work by hiring with agile project teams in mind and by providing agile training to new employees. Organizations can also engage the ongoing support of an agile mentor, who can guide project teams as they encounter new and challenging situations.

Organizations, of course, are made up of individuals. Organizational commitment and individual commitment go hand in hand.

Individual commitment

Individual commitment has an equal role to organizational commitment in agile transitions. When each person on a project team works at adopting agile practices, the changes become easier for everyone on the project team.

People can individually commit to an agile transition by using these methods:

- Attending training and conferences and being willing to learn about agile methods
- Being open to change, willing to try new processes, and making an effort to adapt new habits
- Resisting the temptation to fall back on old processes
- Acting as a peer coach for project team members who are less experienced in agile techniques
- Allowing themselves to make mistakes and learn from those mistakes
- Reflecting on each sprint honestly in the sprint retrospective and committing to improvement efforts
- Actively becoming cross-functional development team members
- Letting go of ego and working as a part of a team
- Taking responsibility for successes and failures as a team
- Taking the initiative to be self-managing
- Being active and present throughout each agile project

Like organizational commitment, individual commitment is important beyond the agile transition period. The people on the first agile project team will become change agents throughout the company, teaching other project teams to work with agile methods.

How to get commitment

Commitment to agile methods may not be instant. You'll need to help people in your organization overcome the natural impulse to resist change.

A good early step in an agile transition is to find an *agile champion,* a senior-level manager or executive who can help ensure organizational change. The fundamental process changes that accompany agile transitions require support from the people who make and enforce business decisions. A good agile champion will be able to rally the organization and its people around process changes.

Another important way to get commitment is to identify problems with the organization's current projects and provide potential solutions with agile approaches. Agile project management can address many problems, including issues with product quality, customer satisfaction, team morale, regular budget and schedule overruns, and overall project failure.

Finally, highlight some of agile project management's overall benefits. Some of the real and tangible benefits that drive shifts from traditional methods of project management to agile methods include the following:

- **Profit benefits:** Agile approaches allow project teams to deliver products to market quicker than with traditional approaches. Agile organizations can realize higher return on investment.

- **Defect reduction:** Quality is a key part of agile approaches. Proactive quality measures, continuous integration and testing, and continuous improvement all contribute to higher-quality products.

- **Improved morale:** Agile practices such as sustainable development and self-managing development teams can mean happier employees, improved efficiency, and less company turnover.

- **Happier customers:** Agile projects often have higher customer satisfaction because agile project teams produce working products quickly, can respond to change, and collaborate with customers as partners.

You can find more benefits of agile project management in Chapter 18.

Will it be possible to make the transition?

You've established all kinds of justifications to move to an agile method, and your case looks good. But will your organization be able to make the transition? Here are some key questions to consider:

- **What are the organizational roadblocks?** Is there a value-delivery culture or a risk-management culture? Does your organization support coaching and mentorship alongside management? Is there support for training? How does the organization define success? Is there an open culture that will embrace high visibility of project progress?

- **How are you doing business today?** How are projects planned at the macro level? Is the organization fixated on fixed scope? How engaged are business representatives? Do you outsource development?

- **How do your teams work today, and what will need to shift under agile methods?** How ingrained is waterfall? Is there a strong command and control mentality in the team? Can good ideas come from anywhere? Is there trust in the team? Are people shared across teams? What do you need to ask for to secure a shift? Can you get people, tools, space, and commitment to pilot the change?

✔ **What are the regulatory challenges?** Are there processes and procedures that relate to regulatory requirements? Are these requirements imposed upon you from externally or internally adopted regulations and standards? Will you need to create additional documentation to satisfy regulatory requirements? Are you likely to be audited for compliance, and what would be the cost of noncompliance?

As you review your analysis of the roadblocks and challenges, you may uncover the following concerns:

✔ **Agile approaches reveal that the organization needs to change.** As you compare agile practices and results with waterfall, you'll reveal that performance has not been all it could have been. You need to tackle this head on. Your organization has been operating within a framework of how projects were expected to be run. Your organization has done its best to produce a result, often in the face of extreme challenges. For all parties involved, you have to acknowledge their efforts and introduce the potential of agile processes to allow them to produce yet greater results.

✔ **Project management leaders can see agile processes as a threat.** Current project management leaders earned their position through hard work, long hours of study, certification, and years of leadership. They may view some of that value slipping away in a transition to agile processes. Present the agile methodology as an extension of project managers' capabilities and career, not as devaluing anything they've worked hard to secure.

✔ **Moving from leadership to service model can be challenging.** When you move to an agile methodology, leaders are now in service. Command and control gives way to facilitation. This is a big shift for the project team. You have to consider how to demonstrate the shift as a positive result for everyone. You can read more about servant leadership in Chapter 14.

Keep in mind that some resistance will arise, and is natural, as change can't happen without opposition. Be ready for resistance, but don't let it thwart your overall plan.

What is the best timing for moving to agile?

Organizationally, you can start your initiative to move to an agile approach at any time. You might consider a few optimal times:

✔ **When you need to prove that agile project management is necessary:** Use the end of a large project, when you can see clearly what did not work (for example, during a sunset review). You'll be able to demonstrate clearly the issues with waterfall, and you'll gain a springboard for piloting your first agile project.

✔ **When your consideration is doing accurate budgeting:** Run your first agile project in the quarter before the start of the annual budget year (namely one quarter before the end of the current budget cycle). You'll get metrics from your first project that will allow you to be more informed when planning next year's budget.

✔ **When you are starting a new project:** Moving to agile processes when you have a new project lets you start fresh without the baggage of old approaches.

✔ **When you have new leadership:** Management changes are great opportunities for setting new expectations with agile approaches.

✔ **When you are trying to reach a new market or industry:** Agile techniques allow you to deliver quick innovation to help your organization create products for new types of customers.

These are all great times to start using agile processes. The best time to move to agile project management is . . . today!

Choosing the Right Project Team Members

Choosing the right people to work with, especially in early stages, is important to agile project success. Here are things to think about when picking people for the different roles in your organization's first agile project.

The development team

On agile projects, the self-managing development team is central to the success of the project. The development team determines how to go about the work of creating the product. Good development team members should be able to do the following:

✔ Be, in one word, versatile.

✔ Be willing to work cross-functionally.

✔ Plan a sprint and self-manage around that plan.

✔ Understand the product requirements and provide effort estimates.

✔ Provide technical advice to the product owner so that he or she can understand the complexity of the requirements and make appropriate decisions.

✔ Respond to circumstances and adjust processes, standards, and tools to optimize performance.

When choosing a development team for the pilot project, you want to select people who are open to change, enjoy a challenge, like to be in the forefront of new development, and are willing to do whatever it will take to ensure success, including learning and using new skills outside their current skill set.

The scrum master

The scrum master on a company's first agile project may need to be more sensitive to potential development team distractions than on later projects. A good scrum master should

✔ Have, in one word, clout.

✔ Have enough organizational influence to remove outside distractions that prevent the project team from successfully using agile methods.

✔ Be knowledgeable enough about agile project management to be able to help the project team uphold agile processes throughout a project.

✔ Have the communication and facilitation skills to guide the development team in reaching consensus.

✔ Be trusting enough to step back and allow the development team to organize and manage itself.

When determining the scrum master for a company's first agile project, you want to select someone who is willing to be a servant-leader. At the same time, the scrum master will need to have a strong enough temperament to help thwart distractions and uphold agile processes in the face of organizational and individual resistance.

The product owner

Product owners often come from the business side of an organization. During a first agile project, the product owner may need to acclimate to working on the project daily with the development team. A good product owner should

✔ Be, in one word, decisive.

✔ Be an expert about customer requirements and business needs.

✔ Have the decisiveness and business authority to prioritize and reprioritize product requirements.

✔ Be organized enough to manage ongoing changes to the product backlog.

✔ Be committed to working with the rest of the scrum team and to being available throughout a project.

✔ Have the ability to obtain project funding and other resources.

When choosing a product owner for a first agile project, pick someone who can provide product expertise and commitment to the project.

The agile champion

At the beginning of an agile transition, the agile champion will be a key person in helping ensure the project team can succeed. A good agile champion should be able to do all these tasks:

✔ Be, in one word, passionate.

✔ Make decisions about company processes.

✔ Get the organization excited about what's possible with agile processes.

✔ Support the project team as it goes through the steps to establish agile processes.

✔ Acquire the project team members necessary for success, both for the first project and in the long term.

✔ Be an escalation point to remove unnecessary distractions and non-agile processes.

When choosing an agile champion, look for someone who has authority in the organization — whose voice is respected and who has led change initiatives successfully in the past.

The agile mentor

An agile mentor, sometimes called an agile coach, is a big help to an organization's first agile project. A good agile mentor should

✔ Be, in one word, experienced.

✔ Be an expert at agile processes, especially in the agile processes your organization chooses.

✔ Be familiar with projects of different sizes, large and small.

✔ Be able to provide useful advice and support without taking over a project.

✔ Be able to help guide the project team through its first sprint at the beginning of the project and be available to answer questions as needed throughout the project.

✔ Be able to work with and relate to the development team members, the scrum master, and the product owner.

✔ Be a person from outside a department or organization. Internal agile mentors often come from a company's project management group or center of excellence.

If the agile mentor comes from inside the organization, he or she should be able to put aside political considerations when making suggestions and providing advice.

A number of organizations offer agile strategy, planning, and mentorship, including my company, Platinum Edge.

The project stakeholders

On an organization's first agile project, good project stakeholders should

✔ Be, in one word, involved.

✔ Be able to defer to the product owner for final product decisions.

✔ Be willing and able to attend sprint reviews and provide product feedback.

✔ Have an understanding of agile processes. Sending project stakeholders to the same training as the rest of the project team will help them be more comfortable with new processes.

✔ Be willing to receive project information in agile formats, such as product backlogs and sprint backlogs.

✔ Be available to provide details from time to time when the product owner and development team have questions.

✔ Be able to work collaboratively with the product owner and the rest of the project team.

The project stakeholders for a first agile project should be trustworthy, cooperative, active contributors to a project.

Creating an Environment That Works for Agile

When you're laying the foundation for moving to an agile methodology, you want to create an environment where agile projects can be successful and project teams can thrive. This means a good physical environment, like the one I describe in Chapter 5, as well as a good organizational environment. To create a good agile project environment, you want to have the following:

- **Good use of agile processes:** This may seem obvious, but start your project by using agile practices from the beginning. Use the Roadmap to Value from Figure 16-1 and follow the processes faithfully. Start with the basics; build on them only when the project and your knowledge progresses. Progress doesn't mean perfection; get started and learn.
- **Transparency:** Be open about project status and about upcoming process changes. People on the project team and throughout the organization should be privy to project details.
- **Inspection:** Use the regular opportunities that agile processes provide to see firsthand how the project is going.
- **Adaptation:** Follow up on inspection by making necessary changes for improvement throughout the project.
- **A dedicated scrum team:** Ideally, the development team, scrum master, and product owner will be fully allocated to the agile project.
- **A collocated scrum team:** For best results, the development team, scrum master, and product owner should sit together, in the same area of the same office.
- **A well-trained project team:** When the members of the project team have worked together to learn about agile processes, they know what they're supposed to do.

Luckily, many opportunities for training in agile processes are available. You can find formal certification programs as well as agile courses and workshops. Available agile certifications include the following:

- The Project Management Institute Agile Certified Practitioner (PMI-ACP) accreditation
- From the Scrum Alliance:
  - Certified Scrum Master (CSM)
  - Certified Product Owner (CSPO)
  - Certified Scrum Developer (CSD)
  - Certified Scrum Professional (CSP)
- Numerous university certificate programs

With a good environment, you have a good chance at success.

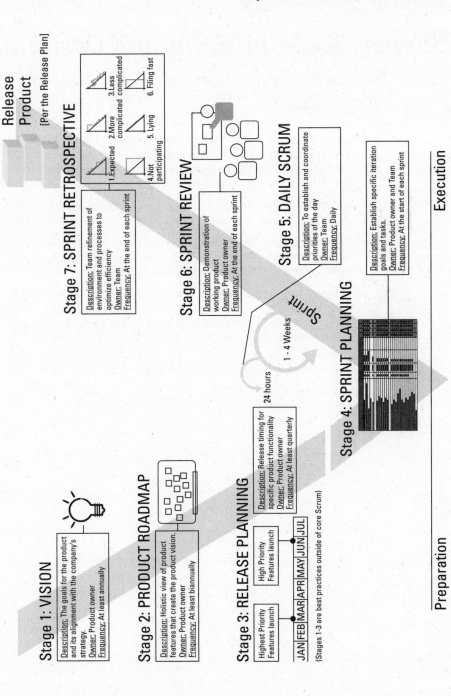

Figure 16-1:
The Agile
Roadmap to
Value.

Release
Product
[Per the Release Plan]

Stage 7: SPRINT RETROSPECTIVE

<u>Description:</u> Team refinement of
environment and processes to
optimize efficiency
<u>Owner:</u> Team
<u>Frequency:</u> At the end of each sprint

1.Expected   2.More   3.Less
              complicated   complicated

4.Not   5. Lying   6. Filing fast
participating

Stage 6: SPRINT REVIEW

<u>Description:</u> Demonstration of
working product
<u>Owner:</u> Product owner
<u>Frequency:</u> At the end of each sprint

Stage 5: DAILY SCRUM

<u>Description:</u> To establish and coordinate
priorities of the day
<u>Owner:</u> Team
<u>Frequency:</u> Daily

<u>Description:</u> Establish specific iteration
goals and tasks.
<u>Owner:</u> Product owner and Team
<u>Frequency:</u> At the start of each sprint

Execution

24 hours

Sprint

1 - 4 Weeks

Stage 4: SPRINT PLANNING

Stage 2: PRODUCT ROADMAP

<u>Description:</u> Holistic view of product
features that create the product vision.
<u>Owner:</u> Product owner
<u>Frequency:</u> At least biannually

Stage 3: RELEASE PLANNING

<u>Description:</u> Release timing for
specific product functionality
<u>Owner:</u> Product owner
<u>Frequency:</u> At least quarterly

High Priority
Features launch

Highest Priority
Features launch

JAN|FEB|MAR|APR|MAY|JUN|JUL

(Stages 1-3 are best practices outside of core Scrum)

Stage 1: VISION

<u>Description:</u> The goals for the product
and its alignment with the company's
strategy.
<u>Owner:</u> Product owner
<u>Frequency:</u> At least annually

Preparation

Support Agile Initially and Over Time

When you first launch into agile processes, you have much to take care of. Give your agile transition every chance for success by paying attention to key success factors:

- ✔ **Choose a good pilot.** Select a project that's important enough to get everyone's support. At the same time, set expectations: Although the project will produce measurable savings, the results will be modest while the project team is learning the methods and will improve over time.

- ✔ **Get an agile mentor.** Use a mentor to increase your chances of setting up a good agile environment and maximizing your chances of great performance.

- ✔ **Communicate — a lot.** Keep talking about agile processes around the organization at every level. Use your champion to encourage progress through the pilot and toward more extensive use of agile.

- ✔ **Prepare to move forward.** Keep thinking ahead. Consider how you'll take the lessons from the pilot to new projects and teams. Also think about how you'll scale from a single project to many projects, including those with multiple teams.

Chapter 17

Being a Change Agent

In This Chapter

▶ Following steps for adopting agile in your company

▶ Avoiding common problems in adopting agile

▶ Asking the right questions to prevent issues along the way

*I*f you're contemplating the idea of introducing agile project management to your company or organization, this chapter can help get you started. In this chapter, you find key steps to implementing agile project management techniques. I also cover common pitfalls to avoid in your agile transition.

Making Agile Work in Your Organization

Throughout this book, I highlight the fact that agile processes are very different from traditional project management. Moving an organization from waterfall to agile is a significant change. Through my experience guiding companies through this type of change, I've identified the following important steps to take in order to successfully become an agile organization.

Step 1: Conduct an implementation strategy

An *implementation strategy* is a plan that outlines how your organization will transition to agile project management. Ask yourself the questions in the following list as you build your implementation strategy:

✔ **Current processes:** How does your organization run projects today? What does it do well? What are its problems?

✔ **Future processes:** How can your company benefit from agile approaches? What agile methodology or methodologies will you use? What key changes will your organization need to make? What will your transformed company look like from a team and process perspective?

✔ **Step-by-step plan:** How will you move from existing processes to agile processes? What will change immediately? In six months? In a year or longer? This plan should be a roadmap of successive steps getting the company to a sustainable state of agile maturity.

✔ **Benefits:** What advantages will the agile transition provide for the people and groups in your organization and the organization as a whole? Agile techniques are a win for most people; identify how they will benefit.

✔ **Potential challenges:** What will be the most difficult changes? What departments or people will have the most trouble with agile approaches? Whose fiefdom is being disrupted? What are your potential roadblocks? How will you overcome these challenges?

✔ **Success factors:** What organizational factors will help you while switching to agile processes? How will the company commit to a new approach? Which people or departments will be agile champions?

A good implementation strategy will guide your company through its move to agile practices. A strategy can provide supporters with a clear plan to rally around and support, and it can set realistic expectations for your organization's agile transition.

Step 2: Establish a transformation team

Identify a team within your company that can be responsible for the agile transformation at the organization level. This team is made up of company executives who will systematically improve processes, reporting requirements and performance measurements across the organization.

The transformation team will create changes within sprints, just like the development team creates product features within sprints. The transformation team will focus on the highest-priority agile changes in each sprint and will demonstrate its implementation, when possible, during a sprint review.

Step 3: Build awareness and excitement

When you know how you'll transition to agile, you need to communicate the coming changes to people within your organization. Agile approaches have many benefits; be sure to let everyone in your company know about those benefits and get them excited about the coming changes. Here are some ways to build awareness:

✔ **Educate people.** People in your organization may not know much — or anything — about agile project management. Educate people about agile approaches and the change that will accompany the new approaches. You can create an agile wiki, hold lunchtime learning sessions, and even have "hot-seat" discussions to address concerns with the transition.

✔ **Use a variety of communication tools.** Take advantage of communication channels such as newsletters, blogs, intranets, e-mail, and face-to-face workshops to get word out about the change coming to your organization.

✔ **Highlight the benefits.** Make sure people in your company know how an agile approach will help the organization create high-value products, lead to customer satisfaction, and increase employee morale. Chapter 18 has a great list of the benefits of agile project management for this step.

✔ **Share the implementation plan.** Make your transition plan available to anyone who is interested in reading it. Offer to walk people through it and answer questions. I often print the transition roadmap on posters and distribute it throughout the organization.

✔ **Involve the initial scrum team.** As early as you can, let the people who may work on your company's first agile project know about the upcoming changes. Involve the initial scrum team members in planning the transition to help them become enthusiastic agile practitioners.

✔ **Be open.** Drive the conversation about new processes. Try to stay ahead of the company rumor mill by speaking openly, answering questions, and quelling myths about agile project management. Structured communications like the "hot-seat" sessions I mention earlier are a great example of open communication.

Building awareness will help you generate support for the upcoming changes. It can also help alleviate some of the fear that naturally comes with change. Communication will be an important tool to help you successfully implement agile processes.

Step 4: Identify a pilot project

Starting your transition to agile with just one pilot project is a great idea. Having one initial project allows you to figure out how to work with agile methods with little disruption to your organization's overall business. Concentrating on one project to start also lets you work out some of the kinks that inevitably follow change. Figure 17-1 shows the types of projects that benefit most from the agile approach.

When selecting your first agile project, look for an endeavor that has these qualities:

✔ **Appropriately important:** Make sure the project you choose is important enough to merit interest within your company. However, avoid the most important project coming up; you want room to make and learn from mistakes. See the note on the blame game in the later section "Avoiding Pitfalls."

✔ **Sufficiently visible:** Your pilot project should be visible to your organization's key influencers, but don't make it the most high-profile item on their agenda. You will need the freedom to adjust to new processes; critical projects may not allow for that freedom.

✔ **Clear and containable:** Look for a product with clear requirements and a business group that can commit to defining and prioritizing those requirements. Try to pick a project that has a distinct end point, rather than one that can expand indefinitely.

✔ **Not too large:** Select a project that you can complete with no more than two scrum teams working simultaneously to prevent too many moving parts at once.

✔ **Tangibly measurable:** Pick a project that you know can show measurable value within sprints.

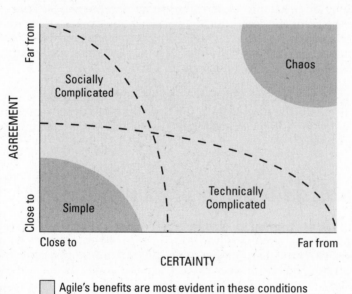

Figure 17-1:
Projects that can benefit from agile techniques.

Agile's benefits are most evident in these conditions

People need time to adjust to organizational changes of any type, not just agile transitions. Studies have found that with large changes, companies and teams will see dips in performance before they see improvements. *Satir's Curve,* shown in Figure 17-2, illustrates the process of teams' excitement, chaos, and finally adjustment to new processes.

After you've successfully run one agile project, you'll have a foundation for future successes.

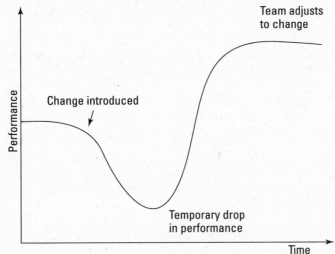

Figure 17-2:
Satir's
Curve.

Step 5: Identify success metrics

For your first agile project, identify a quantifiable way to recognize project success. Using metrics will give you a way to instantly demonstrate success to project stakeholders and your organization. Metrics provide specific goals and talking points for sprint retrospectives and help set clear expectations for the project team.

Here are some good areas to measure for your first project:

✔ How often did the scrum team meet sprint goals? Did the rate of sprint goal success rise throughout the project?

✔ Did the number of defects in each sprint decrease throughout the project?

- How much time lapsed between finding and fixing defects?

- How soon was the scrum team able to release a valuable product to the marketplace? How often did the scrum team provide valuable updates?

- If the product generated income, when did the first dollar come in? What was the overall return on investment?

- How did the agile project time to market and return on investment compare with that of past projects using the company's old methodologies?

- Is the customer happy? Are stakeholders happy? Did customer and/or stakeholder satisfaction increase throughout the project?

- Did scrum team member satisfaction increase throughout the project?

- What other types of metrics does your organization value? Can your project demonstrate any specific company goals?

Metrics related to people and performance work best when related to teams, rather than to individuals. Scrum teams manage themselves as a team, succeed as a team, fail as a team — and should be evaluated as a team.

Keeping track of project success measurements can do more than help you improve throughout the project. Metrics can provide clear proof of success when you move past your first project and start to scale agile practices throughout your organization.

Chapter 19 describes metrics for success in detail.

Step 6: Train sufficiently

Training is a critical step when adopting agile methods. The combination of face-to-face communication with an agile project management expert and the ability to work through exercises using agile processes is the best way to help the project team to absorb and retain the skills needed to successfully run an agile project.

Training works best when the members of the project team can train and learn together. As an agile trainer and mentor, I've had the opportunity to overhear conversations between project team members that start, "Remember when Mark showed us how to . . . ? That worked when we did it in class. Let's try that and see what happens." If the development team, product owner, scrum master, and project stakeholders can attend the same class, they can apply lessons to their work as a team.

Step 7: Develop a product strategy

When you've chosen your pilot project, don't fall into the trap of using a plan from an old methodology. Instead, use agile processes from the project start.

To begin, the product owner will create the product vision statement to define the product and its overall goals. To create a product vision, follow the plan from Chapter 7.

Step 8: Develop the product roadmap, the product backlog, and estimates

When you have a vision statement defining the product strategy, you can start determining product features. The product owner will work with the business stakeholders and the rest of the scrum team to create the product roadmap, the product backlog, and the first release plan.

With an agile project, although you'll have a long-range view of the product through the product roadmap, you don't need to define the entire product or project scope up front in order to get started. Don't worry about gathering exhaustive requirements at the beginning of your project; just add the features the project team currently knows. You can always add more requirements later.

The development team will estimate the effort to create the requirements in the product backlog. You can find out how to create the product roadmap, the product backlog, the release plan, and estimates in Chapters 7 and 8.

Step 9: Running your first sprint

When you have a clear agile implementation strategy, an excited and trained project team, a pilot project with a product backlog, and clear measures for success, congratulations! You're ready to run your first sprint.

After you establish overall goals through the product's vision statement, product roadmap, and initial release goal, your product backlog needs only enough user story level requirements (see Chapter 8) for one sprint for the scrum team to start development.

As the scrum team plans its first sprint, it should try not to bite off too many requirements. Keep in mind that you're just starting to learn about a new process and a new product. New scrum teams often take on a smaller amount of work than they think they can complete in their first sprints. Here's a typical progression:

- ✔ **In sprint 1,** scrum teams take on 25 percent of the work they think they can complete during sprint planning.

- ✔ **In sprint 2,** scrum teams take on 50 percent of the work they think they can complete during sprint planning.

- ✔ **In sprint 3,** scrum teams take on 75 percent of the work they think they can complete during sprint planning.

- ✔ **In sprint 4 and beyond,** scrum teams take on 100 percent of the work they think they can complete during sprint planning.

By sprint 4, the scrum team will be more comfortable with new processes, will know more about the product, and will be able to estimate tasks with more accuracy.

You cannot plan away uncertainty. Don't fall victim to analysis paralysis; set a direction and go!

Throughout the first sprint, be sure to consciously stick with agile practices. Think about the following during your first sprint:

- ✔ Have your scrum meeting every day, even if you feel like you didn't make any progress. Remember to state roadblocks, too!

- ✔ The development team may need to remember to manage itself and not look to the product owner, the scrum master, or anywhere besides the sprint backlog for task assignments.

- ✔ The scrum master may have to remember to protect the development team from outside work and distractions, especially while other members of the organization get used to having a dedicated agile project team around.

- ✔ The product owner may have to become accustomed to working directly with the development team, being available for questions, and reviewing and accepting completed requirements immediately.

In the first sprint, expect the road to be a little bumpy. That's okay; agile processes are about learning and adapting.

In Chapter 8, you can see how the scrum team can plan the sprint. Chapter 9 provides the day-to-day details on running the sprint.

Step 10: Make mistakes, gather feedback, and improve

At the end of your first sprint, you'll gather feedback and improve with two very important meetings: the sprint review and the sprint retrospective.

In your first sprint review, it'll be important for the product owner to set expectations about the format of the meeting, along with the sprint goal and completed product functionality. The sprint review is about product demonstration — fancy presentations and handouts are unnecessary overhead. Project stakeholders may initially be taken aback by a bare-bones approach. However, those stakeholders will soon be impressed as they find a working product replacing the fluff of slides and lists. Show, rather than tell.

The first sprint retrospective may require setting some expectations as well. It will help to conduct the meeting with a preset format, like the one in Chapter 10, both to spark conversation and avoid a free-for-all complaining session.

In your first sprint retrospective, pay extra attention to the following:

- ✔ Keep in mind how well you met the sprint goal, not how many user stories you completed.

- ✔ Go over how well you completed requirements to meet the definition of done: created, tested, integrated, and documented.

- ✔ Discuss how you met your project success metrics.

- ✔ Talk about how well you stuck with agile processes.

- ✔ Remember to celebrate successes, even small gains, as well as examine problems and solutions.

- ✔ Remember that the scrum team should manage the meeting as a team, gain consensus on action items, and leave the meeting with a plan.

You can find more details about both sprint reviews and sprint retrospectives in Chapter 10.

Step 11: Mature

Inspecting and adapting enables scrum teams to grow as a team and to mature with each sprint.

Agile practitioners sometimes compare the process of maturing with the martial arts learning technique of *Shu Ha Ri*. Shu Ha Ri is a Japanese term that can translate to mean "maintain, detach, transcend." The term describes three stages in which people learn new skills:

- **In the *Shu* stage,** students follow a new skill as they were taught, without deviation, in order to commit that skill to memory and make it automatic.

  New scrum teams can benefit from making a habit of closely following agile processes, until those processes become familiar. During the Shu stage, scrum teams may work closely with an agile coach or mentor to follow processes correctly.

- **In the *Ha* stage,** students start to improvise as they understand more about how their new skill works. Sometimes the improvisations will work, and sometimes they won't; the students will learn more about the skill from these successes and failures.

  As scrum teams understand more about how agile approaches work, they may try variations on processes for their own project.

  During the Ha stage, the sprint retrospective will be a valuable tool for scrum teams to talk about how their improvisations worked or did not work. In this stage, scrum team members may still learn from an agile mentor, but they may also learn from one another, from other agile professionals, and from starting to teach agile skills to others.

- **In the *Ri* stage,** the skill comes naturally to the former student, who will know what works and what doesn't. The former student can now innovate with confidence.

  With practice, scrum teams will get to the point where agile processes are easy and comfortable, like riding a bicycle or driving a car. In the Ri stage, scrum teams can customize processes, knowing what works in the spirit of the Agile Manifesto and Principles.

At first, maturing as a scrum team can take a concentrated effort and commitment to using agile processes and upholding agile values. Eventually, however, the scrum team can be humming along, improving from sprint to sprint, and inspiring others throughout the organization.

With time, as scrum teams and project stakeholders mature, entire companies can mature into successful agile organizations.

Step 12: Scale virally

Completing a successful project is an important step in moving an organization to agile project management. With metrics that prove the success of your project and the value of agile methodologies, you can garner commitment from your company to support new agile projects.

To scale agile project management across an organization, start with the following:

- **Seed new teams.** An agile project team that has reached maturity — the people who worked on the first agile project — should now have the expertise and enthusiasm to become agile ambassadors within the organization. These people can join new agile project teams and help those teams learn and grow.

- **Redefine metrics.** Identify measurements for success, across the organization, with each new scrum team and with each new project.

- **Scale methodically.** It can be exciting to produce great results, but companywide improvements can require wide process changes. Don't move faster than the organization can handle.

- **Identify new challenges.** Your first agile project may have uncovered roadblocks that you didn't consider in your original implementation plan. Update your strategy as needed.

- **Continue learning.** As you roll out new processes, make sure that new team members have the proper training, mentorship, and resources to effectively run agile projects.

The preceding steps work for successful agile project management transitions. Use these steps and return to them as you scale, and you can make agile practices thrive in your organization.

Avoiding Pitfalls

Project teams can make a number of common but serious mistakes when implementing agile practices. Table 17-1 provides an overview of some typical problems and ways for scrum teams to turn them around.

Table 17-1   Common Agile Transition Problems and Solutions

Problem	Description	Potential Solution
Faux agile: Cargo cult agile and double work agile	Sometimes organizations will say that they are "doing agile." They may go through some of the practices used on agile projects, but they haven't embraced the principles of agile and are ultimately creating waterfall deliverables and products. This is sometimes called *cargo cult agile* and is a sure path to avoiding the benefits of agile techniques. Trying to complete agile processes in addition to waterfall processes, documents, and meetings is another faux agile approach. *Double work agile* results in quick project team burnout. If you're doing twice the work, you aren't adhering to Agile Principles.	Insist on following one process — an agile process. Garner support from management to avoid non-agile principles and practices.
Lack of training	Investment in a hands-on training class will provide a quicker, better learning environment than even the best book, blog, or white paper. Lack of training often indicates an overall lack of organizational commitment to agile practices. Keep in mind that training can help scrum teams avoid many of the mistakes on this list.	Build training into your implementation strategy. Giving teams the right foundation of skills is critical to success and necessary at the start of your agile transition.

Problem	Description	Potential Solution
Ineffective product owner	No role is more different than traditional roles than that of the product owner. Agile project teams need a product owner who is an expert on business needs and priorities and can work well with the rest of the scrum team on a daily basis. An absent or indecisive product owner will quickly sink an agile project.	Start the project with a person who has the time, expertise, and temperament to be a good product owner. Ensure the product owner has proper training. The scrum master can help coach the product owner and may try to clear roadblocks preventing the product owner from being effective. If removing impediments doesn't work, the scrum team should insist on replacing the ineffective product owner with a product owner — or at least an agent — who can make product decisions and help the scrum team be successful.
Lack of automated testing	Without automated testing, it may be impossible to fully complete and test work within a sprint. Manual testing is a waste of time that fast-moving scrum teams don't have.	You can find many low-cost, open-source testing tools on the market today. Look into the right tools and make a commitment as a development team to using those tools.
Lack of transition support	Making the transition successfully is difficult and far from guaranteed. It pays to do it right the first time with people who know what they are doing.	When you decide to move to agile project management, enlist the help of an agile mentor — either internally from your organization or externally from a consulting firm — who can support your transition. Process is easy, but people are hard. It pays to invest in professional transition support with an experienced partner who understands behavioral science and organizational change.

(continued)

Table 17-1 *(continued)*

Problem	Description	Potential Solution
Inappropriate physical environment	When scrum teams are not collocated, they lose the advantage of face-to-face communication. Being in the same building isn't enough; scrum teams need to sit together in the same area.	If your scrum team is in the same building but not sitting in the same area, move the team together. Consider creating a room or annex for the scrum team. Try to keep the scrum team area away from distracters, such as the guy who can talk forever or the manager who needs just one small favor. Before starting a project with a dislocated scrum team, do what you can to enlist local talent. If you must work with a dislocated scrum team, take a look at Chapter 14 to see how to manage dislocated teams.
Poor team selection	Scrum team members who don't support agile processes, who don't work well with others, or who don't have capacity for self-management will sabotage a new agile project from within.	When creating a scrum team, consider how well potential team members will enact the Agile Principles. The keys are versatility and a willingness to learn.
Discipline slips	Remember that agile projects still need requirements, design, development, testing, and releases. Doing that work in sprints requires discipline.	You need more, not less, discipline to deliver working products in a short iteration. Progress needs to be consistent and constant. The daily scrum helps ensure progress is occurring throughout the sprint. Use the sprint retrospective as an opportunity to reset approaches to discipline.

Problem	Description	Potential Solution
Lack of support for learning	Scrum teams succeed as teams and fail as teams; calling out one person's mistakes (known as the *blame game*) destroys the learning environment and destroys innovation.	The scrum team can make a commitment at the project start to leaving room for learning and to accepting success and failures as a group.
Diluting until dead	Watering down agile processes with old waterfall habits erodes the benefits of agile processes until those benefits no longer exist.	When making process changes, stop and consider whether those changes support the Agile Manifesto and the Agile Principles. Resist changes that don't work with the manifesto and principles. Remember to maximize work not done.

As you may notice, many of these pitfalls are related to lack of organizational support, lack of training, and falling back on old project management practices. If your company supports positive changes, if the project team is trained, and if the scrum team makes an active commitment to upholding agile values, you'll have a successful agile transition.

Questions to Prevent Problems

The following list of questions helps you see warning signs and provide ideas on what to do if problematic circumstances arise:

✔ **Are you doing "scrum, but . . ."?**

ScrumBut is a known condition when organizations partially adopt agile practices. Some agile purists say that ScrumBut is unacceptable; other agile practitioners allow room for gradual growth into a new methodology. Having said that, beware of old practices that thwart the Agile Principles, such as finishing sprints with incomplete code.

✔ **Are you still documenting and reporting in the old way?**

If you're still burning hours on hefty documentation and reporting, it's a sign that the organization has not accepted agile approaches for conveying project status. Help managers understand how to use existing agile reporting artifacts and quit doing double work!

✔ **A team completing 50 story points in a sprint is better than another team doing 10, right?**

No. Keep in mind that story points are relative and consistent within one scrum team, not across multiple scrum teams. You can see more about story points in Chapter 8.

✔ **When will the stakeholders sign off on all the specifications?**

If you're waiting for sign-offs on comprehensive requirements to start developing, you're not following agile practices. You can start development as soon as you have enough requirements for one sprint.

✔ **Are we using offshore to reduce costs?**

Ideally, scrum teams are collocated. The ability for instant face-to-face communication saves more time and money and prevents more costly mistakes than the initial hourly savings you may see with some offshore teams.

If you do work with offshore teams, invest in good collaboration tools like individual video cameras and virtual team rooms.

✔ **Are development team members asking for more time in a sprint to finish tasks?**

The development team may not be working cross-functionally or swarming on priority requirements. Development team members can help one another finish tasks, even if those tasks are outside of a person's core expertise.

This question can also indicate outside pressures to underestimate tasks and fit more work into a sprint than the development team can handle.

✔ **Are development team members asking what they should do next?**

If the team members are waiting for direction from the scrum master or product owner, they aren't self-organizing. The development team should be telling the scrum master and the product owner what they're doing next, not the other way round.

✔ **Are team members waiting until the end of the sprint to do testing?**

Agile development teams should test every day in a sprint. All development team members are testers.

✔ **Are the stakeholders showing up for sprint reviews?**

If the only people at sprint reviews are the scrum team members, it's time to remind stakeholders how agile processes work. Let stakeholders know that they're missing their chance to review working product functionality and see first hand how the project is progressing.

✔ **Is the scrum team complaining about being bossed around by the scrum master?**

Command and control techniques are the antithesis of self-management and are in direct conflict with the Agile Principles. Scrum teams are teams of peers — the only boss is the team. Have a discussion with the agile mentor and act quickly to reset the scrum master's expectations of his or her role.

✔ **Is the scrum team putting in a lot of overtime?**

If the end of each sprint becomes a rush to complete tasks, you aren't practicing sustainable development. Look for root causes, such as pressure to underestimate. The scrum master may need to coach the development team and shield them from product owner pressure if this is the case. Reduce the story points for each sprint until the development team can get a handle on the work.

✔ **What retrospective?**

If scrum team members start avoiding or cancelling sprint retrospectives, you're on the slide back to waterfall. Remember the importance of inspecting and adapting and be sure to look at why people are missing the retrospective in the first place. Even if the scrum team has great velocity, development speed can always be better, so keep the retrospective, and keep improving.

Part VI
The Part of Tens

The 5th Wave   By Rich Tennant

"We've failed to meet our October 31 launch date for TREAT this year, but we're developing a new more agile version that should be available by the first or second quarter of next year."

In this part . . .

I share some handy tips and resources to help you better use and understand agile approaches and help you connect with a wide community of agile practitioners.

In the three chapters in this part, I show you ten important benefits of agile project management that highlight why agile approaches work. I also walk you through ten useful metrics you can use as tools to inspect and adapt your projects. Finally, I provide ten great resources where you can find more about agile project management and get support as you progress from agile start-up to agile maturity.

Chapter 18

Ten Key Benefits of Agile Project Management

In This Chapter

▶ Ensuring that projects are rewarding

▶ Making reporting easy

▶ Improving results

▶ Reducing risk

*H*ere are ten important benefits that agile project management provides to organizations, project teams, and products.

REMEMBER To take advantage of agile project management benefits, you need to trust in agile practices, learn more about different agile methodologies, and use the agile approach that's best for your project team.

Better Product Quality

Projects exist to build great products. Agile methods have excellent safeguards to make sure that quality is as high as possible. Agile project teams help ensure quality by doing the following:

✔ Taking a proactive approach to quality to prevent product problems

✔ Embracing technological excellence, good design, and sustainable development

✔ Defining and elaborating on requirements just in time so that knowledge of product features is as relevant as possible

✔ Building acceptance criteria into user stories so that the development team better understands them and the product owner can accurately validate them

✔ Incorporating continuous integration and daily testing into the development process, allowing the development team to address issues while they're fresh

✔ Taking advantage of automated testing tools in order to develop during the day, test overnight, and fix bugs in the morning

✔ Conducting sprint retrospectives, allowing the scrum team to continuously improve processes and work

✔ Completing work using the definition of done: developed, tested, integrated, and documented

You can find more information about project quality in Chapter 15.

Higher Customer Satisfaction

Agile project teams are committed to producing products that satisfy customers. Agile approaches for happier project sponsors include the following:

✔ Collaborating with customers as partners and keeping customers involved and engaged throughout projects.

✔ Having a product owner who is an expert on product requirements and customer needs. (Check out Chapters 6 and 9 to find out more information about the product owner role.)

✔ Keeping the product backlog updated and prioritized in order to respond quickly to change. (You can find out about the product backlog in Chapter 8 and its role in responding to change in Chapter 12.)

✔ Demonstrating working functionality to customers in every sprint review. (Chapter 10 shows you how to conduct a sprint review.)

✔ Delivering products to market quicker and more often with every release.

✔ Possessing the potential for self-funding projects. (Chapter 13 tells you about self-funding projects.)

Higher Team Morale

Working with happy people who enjoy their jobs can be satisfying and rewarding. Agile project management improves the morale of scrum teams in these ways:

✔ Being part of a self-managing team allows people to be creative, innovative, and acknowledged for their expertise.

✔ Focusing on sustainable work practices ensures people don't burn out from stress or overwork.

✔ Encouraging a servant-leader approach assists scrum teams in self-management and actively avoiding command-and-control methods.

✔ Having a scrum master, who serves the scrum team, removes impediments and shields the development team from external interferences.

✔ Providing an environment of support and trust increases people's overall motivation and morale.

✔ Having face-to-face conversations helps reduce the frustration of miscommunication.

✔ Working cross-functionally allows development team members to learn new skills and to grow by teaching others.

You can find out more about team dynamics in Chapter 14.

Increased Collaboration and Ownership

When development teams take responsibility for projects and products, they can produce great results. Agile development teams collaborate and take ownership of product quality and project performance by doing the following:

✔ Having the development team, the product owner, and the scrum master work closely together on a daily basis

✔ Conducting sprint planning meetings, allowing the development team to organize its work

✔ Having daily scrum meetings led by the development team, where development team members organize around work completed, future work, and roadblocks

✔ Conducting sprint reviews, where the development team can demonstrate and discuss the product directly with stakeholders

✔ Conducting sprint retrospectives, allowing development team members to review past work and recommend better practices with every sprint

✔ Working in a collocated environment, allowing for instant communication and collaboration among development team members

✔ Making decisions by consensus, using techniques such as estimating poker and the fist of five

You can find out how development teams estimate effort for requirements, decompose requirements, and gain team consensus in Chapter 7. You can discover more about sprint planning and daily scrum meetings in Chapter 9. For more information about sprint retrospectives, check out Chapter 10.

Customized Team Structures

Self-management puts decisions that would normally be made by a manager or the organization into scrum team members' hands. Because of the limited size of development teams — which consist of five to nine people — agile projects can have multiple scrum teams on one project. Self-management and size-limiting mean that agile projects can provide unique opportunities to customize team structures and work environments. Here are a few examples:

- ✔ Development teams may organize their team structure around people with specific work styles and personalities. Organization around work styles provides these benefits:

  - • Allows team members to work the way they want to work

  - • Encourages team members to expand their skills in order to fit into teams they like

  - • Helps increase team performance because people who do good work like to work together and naturally gravitate toward one another

- ✔ Development teams may also organize themselves into groups with specific skills or to work on specific types of product features.

- ✔ Scrum teams can make decisions tailored to provide balance between team members' professional and personal lives.

- ✔ Ultimately, scrum teams can make their own rules about who they work with and how they work.

The idea of team customization allows agile workplaces to have more diversity. Organizations with traditional management styles tend to have monolithic teams where everyone follows the same rules. Agile work environments are much like the old salad bowl analogy. Just like salads can have ingredients with wildly different tastes that fit in to make a delicious dish, agile projects can have people on teams with very diverse strengths that fit in to make great products.

More Relevant Metrics

The metrics that agile project teams use to estimate time and cost, measure project performance, and make project decisions are often more relevant and more accurate than metrics on traditional projects. On agile projects, you provide metrics by

- ✔ Determining project timelines and budgets based on each development team's actual performance and capabilities

- ✔ Having the development team that will be doing the work, and no one else, provide effort estimates for project requirements

- ✔ Using relative estimates, rather than hours or days, to tailor estimated effort to an individual development team's knowledge and capabilities

- ✔ Refining estimated effort, time, and cost on a regular basis, as the development team learns more about the project

- ✔ Updating the sprint burndown chart every day to provide accurate metrics about how the development team is performing within each sprint

- ✔ Comparing the cost of future development with the value of that future development, which helps project teams determine when to end a project and redeploy capital to a new project

You might notice that velocity is missing from this list. *Velocity* (a measure of development speed, as detailed in Chapter 13) is a tool you can use to determine timelines and costs, but it works only when tailored to an individual team. The velocity of Team A has no bearing on the velocity of Team B. Also, velocity is great for measurement and trending, but it doesn't work as a control mechanism. Trying to make a development team meet a certain velocity number only disrupts team performance and thwarts self-management.

If you're interested in finding out more about relative estimating, be sure to check out Chapter 7. You can find out about tools for determining timelines and budgets, along with information about capital redeployment in Chapter 13. Chapter 19 shows you ten key metrics for agile project management.

Improved Performance Visibility

On agile projects, every member of the project team has the opportunity to know how the project is going at any given time. Agile projects can provide a high level of performance visibility by

✔ Placing a high value on open, honest communication among the scrum team, stakeholders, customers, and anyone else within an organization who wants to know about a project.

✔ Providing daily measurements of sprint performance with sprint backlog updates. Sprint backlogs can be available for anyone in an organization to review.

✔ Providing daily insight into the development team's immediate progress and roadblocks through the daily scrum meeting. Although only the development team may speak at the daily scrum meeting, any member of the project team may attend.

✔ Physically displaying progress by using task boards and posting sprint burndown charts in the development team's work area every day.

✔ Demonstrating accomplishments in sprint reviews. Anyone within an organization may attend a sprint review.

Improved project visibility can lead to greater project control and predictability, as described in the following sections.

Increased Project Control

Agile project teams have numerous opportunities to control project performance and make corrections as needed because of the following:

✔ Adjusting priorities throughout the project allows the organization to have fixed-time and fixed-price projects while accommodating change.

✔ Embracing change allows the project team to react to outside factors like market demand.

✔ Daily scrum meetings allow the scrum team to quickly address issues as they arise.

✔ Daily updates to sprint backlogs mean sprint burndown charts accurately reflect sprint performance, giving the scrum team the opportunity to make changes the moment it sees problems.

✔ Face-to-face conversations remove roadblocks to communication and issue resolution.

✔ Sprint reviews let project stakeholders see working products and provide input about the products before release.

✔ Sprint retrospectives enable the scrum team to make informed course adjustments at the end of every sprint to enhance product quality, increase development team performance, and refine project processes.

The many opportunities to inspect and adapt throughout agile projects allow all members of the project team — the development team, product owner, scrum master, and stakeholders — to exercise control and ultimately create better products.

Improved Project Predictability

Agile project management techniques help the project team accurately predict how things will go as the project progresses. Here are some practices, artifacts, and tools for improved predictability:

✔ Keeping sprint lengths and development team allocation the same throughout the project allows the project team to know the exact cost for each sprint.

✔ Using individual development team speed allows the project team to predict timelines and budgets for releases, the remaining product backlog, or any group of requirements.

✔ Using the information from daily scrum meetings, sprint burndown charts, and task boards allows the project team to predict performance for individual sprints.

You can find more information about sprint lengths in Chapter 8.

Reduced Risk

Agile project management techniques virtually eliminate the chance of absolute project failure — spending large amounts of time and money with no return on investment. Agile project teams run projects with lower risk by

✔ Developing in sprints, ensuring a short time between initial project investment and either failing fast or knowing that a product or an approach will work

✔ Always having a working product, starting with the very first sprint, so that no agile project fails completely

✔ Developing requirements to the definition of done in each sprint so that project sponsors have completed, usable features, regardless of what may happen with the project in the future

✔ Providing constant feedback on products and processes through

- Daily scrum meetings and constant development team communication

- Regular clarification about requirements and review and acceptance of features by the product owner

- Sprint reviews, with stakeholder and customer input about completed product features

- Sprint retrospectives, where the development team discusses process improvement

- Releases, where the end user can see and react to new features on a regular basis

✔ Generating revenue early with self-funding projects, allowing organizations to pay for a project with little up-front expense

You can find more information about managing risk in Chapter 15.

Chapter 19

Ten Key Metrics for Agile Project Management

*O*n an agile project, metrics can be powerful tools for planning, inspecting, adapting, and understanding progress over time. Rates of success or failure can let a scrum team know if it needs to make positive changes or keep up its good work. Time and cost numbers can highlight the benefits of agile projects and provide support for an organization's financial activities. Metrics that quantify people's satisfaction can help a scrum team identify areas for improvement with customers and with the team itself.

This chapter describes ten key metrics to help guide agile project teams.

Sprint Goal Success Rates

One way to measure agile project performance is with the rate of sprint success. The sprint may not need all the requirements and tasks in the sprint backlog to be complete. However, a successful sprint should have a working product feature that fulfills the sprint goals and meets the scrum team's definition of done: developed, tested, integrated, and documented.

Throughout the project, the scrum team can track how frequently it succeeds in reaching the sprint goals and use success rates to see whether the team is maturing or needs to correct its course. Sprint success rates are a useful launching point for inspection and adaptation.

You can find out more about setting sprint goals in Chapter 8.

Defects

Defects are a part of any project. However, testing and fixing bugs can be time-consuming and costly. Agile approaches help development teams proactively minimize defects.

Tracking defect metrics can let the development team know how well it's preventing issues and when to refine its processes. To track defects, it helps to look at the following numbers:

- **Build defects:** If the development team uses automated testing and continuous integration, it can track the number of bugs at the build level in each sprint.

  By understanding the number of build defects, the development team can know whether to adjust development processes and environmental factors.

- **User acceptance testing (UAT) defects:** The development team can track the number of bugs the product owner finds when accepting requirements in each sprint.

  By tracking UAT defects, the development team and the product owner can identify the need to refine processes for understanding requirements. The development team can also determine whether adjustments to automated testing tools are necessary.

- **Release defects:** The development team can track the number of bugs that make it past the release to the marketplace.

  By tracking release defects, the development team and the product owner can know whether changes to the UAT process, automated testing, or the development process are necessary. Large numbers of defects at the release level can be indicative of bigger problems within the scrum team.

The number of defects and whether defects are increasing, decreasing, or staying the same are good metrics to spark discussions on project processes and development techniques at sprint retrospectives.

You can find out more about proactive quality management and testing in Chapter 15.

Total Project Duration

Agile projects get done quicker than traditional projects. By starting development sooner and cutting out bloatware — unnecessary requirements — agile project teams can deliver products quicker.

Measure total project duration to help demonstrate efficiency.

Time to Market

Time to market is the amount of time an agile project takes to provide value by releasing working products and features to users. Organizations may perceive value in a couple of ways:

- ✔ When a product directly generates income, its value is the money it can make.

- ✔ When a product is for an organization's internal use, its value will be the employees' ability to use the product and will contain subjective factors based on what the product can do.

When measuring time to market, consider the following:

- ✔ Measure the time from the project start until you first show value.

- ✔ Some scrum teams deploy new product features for use at the end of each sprint. For scrum teams with a release with every sprint, the time to market is simply the sprint length, one to four weeks, measured in days.

- ✔ Other scrum teams plan releases after multiple sprints and deploy product features in groups. For scrum teams that use longer release times, the time to market is the number of days between each release.

Time to market helps organizations recognize and quantify the ongoing value of agile projects. Time to market is especially important for companies with revenue-generating products, because it aids in budgeting throughout the year. It's also very important if you have a self-funding project — a project that is being paid for by the actual income from the product.

You can find out more about product-income generation and self-funding projects in Chapter 13.

Total Project Cost

Cost on agile projects is directly related to duration. Since agile projects are faster than traditional projects, they can also cost less.

Organizations can use project cost metrics to plan budgets, determine return on investment, and know when to exercise capital redeployment. You find out about return on investment and capital redeployment in the following sections. For more information on cost management, check out Chapter 13.

Return on Investment

Return on investment (ROI) is income generated by the product, less project costs: money in versus money out. On agile projects, ROI is fundamentally different than it is on traditional projects. Agile projects have the potential to generate income with the very first release and can increase revenue with each new release.

To fully appreciate the difference between ROI on traditional and agile projects, compare the examples in Tables 19-1 and 19-2. The projects for both examples have the same project costs and take the same amount of time to complete. Both products have the potential to generate $100,000 in income every month when all the requirements are finished.

First, look at the ROI on a traditional project in Table 19-1.

Table 19-1   **ROI on a Traditional Project**

Month	Monthly Income	Monthly Costs	Monthly ROI	Total Income	Total Costs	Total ROI
January	$0	$80,000	–$80,000	$0	$80,000	–$80,000
February	$0	$80,000	–$80,000	$0	$160,000	–$160,000
March	$0	$80,000	–$80,000	$0	$240,000	–$240,000
April	$0	$80,000	–$80,000	$0	$320,000	–$320,000
May	$0	$80,000	–$80,000	$0	$400,000	–$400,000
June (project launch)	$100,000	$80,000	$20,000	$100,000	$480,000	–$380,000
July	$100,000	$0	$100,000	$200,000	$480,000	–$280,000
August	$100,000	$0	$100,000	$300,000	$480,000	–$180,000
September	$100,000	$0	$100,000	$400,000	$480,000	–$80,000
October (break-even)	$100,000	$0	$100,000	$500,000	$480,000	$20,000
November	$100,000	$0	$100,000	$600,000	$480,000	$120,000
December	$100,000	$0	$100,000	$700,000	$480,000	$220,000

Here are some key points of the traditional project in Table 19-1:

- ✔ The project first generated income in June, at the project launch.
- ✔ The project finally had a positive total ROI in October, ten months after the project started.
- ✔ By the end of one year, the project generated $700,000 in revenue.
- ✔ At the year's end, the project's total ROI was $220,000.

Now look at the ROI for an agile project in Table 19-2.

Pay special attention to these points of the agile project in Table 19-2:

- ✔ The project first generated income in January, shortly after the project start.
- ✔ The project had a positive total ROI in August — two months earlier than the traditional project.
- ✔ By the end of one year, the project generated $930,000 in revenue, 25 percent more than the traditional project.
- ✔ At the year's end, the total ROI was $450,000, a whopping 51 percent higher than the ROI on the traditional project.

Like time to market, ROI metrics are a great way for an organization to appreciate the ongoing value of an agile project. ROI metrics help justify projects from the start because companies can fund projects based on ROI potential. Organizations can track ROI for individual projects as well as for the organization as a whole.

Table 19-2

ROI on an Agile Project

Month	Monthly Income	Monthly Costs	Monthly ROI	Total Income	Total Costs	Total ROI
January	$15,000	$80,000	–$65,000	$15,000	$80,000	–$65,000
February	$25,000	$80,000	–$55,000	$40,000	$160,000	–$120,000
March	$40,000	$80,000	–$40,000	$80,000	$240,000	–$160,000
April	$70,000	$80,000	–$10,000	$150,000	$320,000	–$170,000
May	$80,000	$80,000	$0	$230,000	$400,000	–$170,000
June (project end)	$100,000	$80,000	$20,000	$330,000	$480,000	–$150,000
July	$100,000	$0	$100,000	$430,000	$480,000	–$50,000
August (break-even)	$100,000	$0	$100,000	$530,000	$480,000	$50,000
September	$100,000	$0	$100,000	$630,000	$480,000	$150,000
October	$100,000	$0	$100,000	$730,000	$480,000	$250,000
November	$100,000	$0	$100,000	$830,000	$480,000	$350,000
December	$100,000	$0	$100,000	$930,000	$480,000	$450,000

New Requests Within ROI Budgets

Agile projects' ability to quickly generate high ROI provides organizations with a unique way to fund additional product development. New product features may translate to higher product income.

For example, suppose that in the example project from Table 19-2, the project team were to identify a new feature that would take one month to complete and would boost the product income from $100,000 a month to $120,000 a month. Here's what the effect would be on ROI:

- ✓ The project would still have its first positive ROI in August, with an ROI of $20,000 instead of $50,000.

- ✓ By the end of the year, the project would have generated a total income of $1,080,000 — 14 percent more than if it generated $100,000 a month.

- ✓ By the end of the year, the total ROI would be $520,000 — 17 percent higher than the original project.

If a project is already generating income, it can make sense for an organization to roll that income back into new development and see higher revenue.

Capital Redeployment

On an agile project, when the cost of future development is higher than the value of that future development, it's time for the project to end.

The product owner prioritizes requirements, in part, by their ability to generate revenue. If only low-revenue requirements remain in the backlog, a project may end before the project team has used its entire budget. The organization may then use the remaining budget from the old project to start a new, more valuable project. The practice of moving a budget from one project to another is called *capital redeployment*.

To determine a project's end, you need the following metrics:

- ✓ The value (V) of the remaining requirements in the product backlog

- ✓ The actual cost (AC) for the work to complete the requirements in the product backlog

- ✓ The opportunity cost (OC), or the value of having the scrum team work on a new project

When V < AC + OC, the project can stop. The cost you will sink into the project will be more than the value you will receive from the project.

Capital redeployment allows an organization to spend efficiently on valuable product development and maximize the organization's overall ROI. You can find the details on capital redeployment in Chapter 13.

Satisfaction Surveys

On agile projects, a scrum team's highest priority is to satisfy the customer. At the same time, the scrum team strives to motivate individual team members and promote sustainable development practices.

A scrum team can benefit from digging deeper into customer and team member experiences. One way to get measurable information about how well a scrum team is fulfilling the Agile Principles is through satisfaction surveys:

- **Customer satisfaction surveys:** Measure the customer's experience with the project, the process, and the scrum team.

  The scrum team may want to use customer surveys multiple times during a project. The scrum team can use customer survey results to examine processes, continue positive practices, and adjust behavior as necessary.

- **Team satisfaction surveys:** Measure the scrum team members' experience with the organization, the work environment, processes, other project team members, and their work. Everyone on the scrum team can take team surveys.

  As with the customer survey, the scrum team may choose to give team surveys throughout a project. Scrum team members can use team survey results to regularly fine-tune and adjust personal and team behaviors. The scrum team can also use results to address organizational issues. Customer survey results over time can provide a quantitative look at how the scrum team is maturing as a team.

You can put together informal paper surveys, or use one of the many online survey tools. Some companies even have survey software available through their human resources department.

Team Member Turnover

Agile projects tend to have higher morale. One way of quantifying morale is by measuring turnover. You can look at the following metrics:

- **Scrum team turnover:** Low scrum team turnover can be one sign of a healthy team environment. High scrum team turnover can indicate problems with the project, the organization, the work, individual scrum team members, burnout, ineffective product owners forcing development team commitments, personality incompatibility, a scrum master who fails to remove impediments, or overall team dynamics.

- **Company turnover:** High company turnover, even if it doesn't include the scrum team, can affect morale and effectiveness. High company turnover can be a sign of problems within the organization. As a company adopts agile practices, it may see turnover decrease.

When the scrum team knows turnover metrics and understands the reasons behind those metrics, it may be able to take actions to maintain morale and improve the work environment.

Chapter 20

Ten Key Resources for Agile Project Management

In This Chapter

▶ Finding support for successful agile transitions

▶ Getting involved with core agile communities

▶ Accessing resources for popular agile approaches

Many organizations, websites, blogs, and companies exist to provide information about and support for agile project management. To help you get started, I've compiled a list of key resources you can use to support your journey to agile project management.

Agile Project Management For Dummies Online Cheat Sheet

www.dummies.com/cheatsheet/agileprojectmanagement

You can use my online Cheat Sheet as a companion to this book as you start implementing the 12 Agile Principles and models outlined in previous chapters. You'll find how-to guides, tools, templates and other helpful resources for your agile toolkit.

The Agile Alliance

www.agilealliance.org

The Agile Alliance is the original global agile community, with a mission to help advance the 12 Agile Principles and practices, regardless of methodology. The Agile Alliance site has an extensive resources section that includes articles, videos, presentations, and an index of independent agile community groups across the world.

The Scrum Alliance

http://scrumalliance.org

The Scrum Alliance is a nonprofit professional membership organization that promotes understanding and usage of scrum. The alliance achieves this goal by promoting scrum training and certification classes, hosting international scrum gatherings, and supporting scrum user groups. The Scrum Alliance site is rich in blog entries, white papers, case studies, and other tools for learning and working with scrum.

The Project Management Institute Agile Community

www.pmi.org/agile

The Project Management Institute (PMI) is the largest nonprofit project management membership association in the world. It has more than 500,000 members and a presence in more than 185 countries. PMI supports an agile community of practice and a certification, the PMI Agile Certified Practitioner (PMI-ACP).

The PMI website provides information and requirements for certification along with access to papers, books, and seminars about agile project management. PMI members can also access PMI's agile community website, with an extensive knowledge center including blog posts, forums, webinars, and information about local agile networking events.

Agile Leadership Network

http://agileleadershipnetwork.org

The Agile Leadership Network is a nonprofit community development organization that supports learning and networking for local agile leaders. The Agile Leadership Network supports project leadership through leadership summits focusing on the ideas and values outlined in its Declaration of Interdependence. The site has links to many events and resources, including to the Los Angeles Agile Project Leadership Network, which I founded and continue to chair.

Scrum Development Yahoo! Group

http://groups.yahoo.com/group/scrumdevelopment

Started in 2000, the Scrum Development Yahoo! Group continues to be one of the best scrum message boards on the Internet. It has thousands of members, including several signatories of the Agile Manifesto, and receives hundreds of posts monthly. The Scrum Development Yahoo! Group is one of my core sources for staying in tune with the global scrum community.

InfoQ

www.infoq.com/agile

InfoQ is an independent online community with a prominent agile section offering news, articles, video interviews, video presentations, and minibooks, all written by domain experts in agile techniques. The resources at InfoQ tend to be very high quality, and the content is both unique and relevant to the issues facing agile project teams.

Lean Essays

www.leanessays.com

Mary and Tom Poppendieck are thought leaders in the use of lean concepts within the software development space. Authors of several books about lean software development, the Poppendiecks maintain an active blog at www.lean essays.com that blends humor and empirical data into fun, informative articles that I've found to be useful when coaching struggling development teams.

What Is Extreme Programming?

http://xprogramming.com/what-is-extreme-programming

Ron Jeffries was one of the originators of the extreme programming (XP) development approach, along with Kent Beck and Ward Cunningham. Ron provides resources and services in support of XP's advancement on the http://xprogramming.com site. The "What Is Extreme Programming?" section of the site summarizes the core concepts of XP. Other articles and extreme programming resources are also available on Ron's website.

Platinum Edge

http://platinumedge.com

Since 2001, my team at Platinum Edge has been helping companies success-fully take their project management practices to a higher level. Visit our blog to get the latest insights on practices, tools, and innovative solutions emerging from the dynamic agile community.

We also provide the following services:

✔ Develop transition strategies and provide training and coaching for organizations moving to agile project management

✔ Provide public and customized agile training for budding agile experts, including

- Certified ScrumMaster classes (CSM)

- Certified Scrum Product Owner classes (CSPO)

- PMI-ACP preparation classes

Index

● *B* ●

● *C* ●

• *S* •